D0906319

The Death of the Shtetl

THE DEATH OF
THE SHTETL

Yehuda Bauer

Yale University Press
New Haven & London

Copyright © 2009 by Yale University.
All rights reserved.
This book may not be reproduced, in whole or in part, including
illustrations, in any form (beyond that copying permitted by
Sections 107 and 108 of the U.S. Copyright Law and except by
reviewers for the public press), without written permission from the publishers.

Set in Electra type by Tseng Information Systems, Inc.
Printed in the United States of America.

Library of Congress Cataloging-in-Publication Data
Bauer, Yehuda.
The death of the shtetl / Yehuda Bauer.
p. cm.
Includes bibliographical references and index.
ISBN 978-0-300-15209-8 (alk. paper)
1. Shtetls. 2. Jews—Europe, Eastern—History—20th century. 3. Jews—Europe,
Eastern—Social conditions—20th century. 4. Jews—Europe, Eastern—Politics
and government—20th century. 5. Europe, Eastern—Ethnic relations—History—
20th century. 6. World War, 1939–1945—Jews. 7. Holocaust, Jewish (1939–1945)—
Europe, Eastern. I. Title.
DS135.E83B374 2009
305.892′404709041—dc22
2009023581

A catalogue record for this book is available from the British Library.

This paper meets the requirements of ANSI/NISO z39.48-1992 (Permanence of Paper).

10 9 8 7 6 5 4 3 2 1

CONTENTS

PREFACE

This book was written as a contribution to the victims' side of Holocaust history. It addresses an under-researched aspect of the genocide of the Jewish people — namely, the death of Jewish communities in Poland before and during the Holocaust. In effect, it deals with about one-fifth of all the Holocaust victims and their communities. Because I believe that historians must analyze the factors and historical processes that may explain a given historical reality while also accepting history as, in the end, the story of real people in real situations, the methodology I employ here combines analysis with testimonies. To deal with only stories or only historical analysis is unsatisfactory in the extreme. Real history combines both. My approach does not accept the popular postmodernist view. Rather, I claim that real events that happened in real time can, with a great deal of effort, be reconstructed, at least in their main outlines; the events happened to real people, whose stories must be heard and analyzed.

I am grateful to all those who made this book possible — first and foremost, the archivists and librarians at Yad Vashem, the United States Holocaust Memorial Museum (USHMM), the Jewish Historical Institute in Warsaw, the Shoah Foundation Visual Archive, and the Fortunoff Archive at Yale University. My thanks go to my friend and colleague Israel Gutman; to David Bankier, Dan Michman, Yakov Lozowick, and Avner Shalev at Yad Vashem; to Saul Friedlander at UCLA; to Douglas Greenberg and Karen Jungblut at the Shoah Foundation, USC, who listened and gave advice; to Jack Kagan of London, who helped me with material; and to Paul Shapira at the USHMM. They all, whether they were aware of it or not, influenced my writing. I owe special thanks to Shlomit Shulchani, who translated Russian texts for me, and Havi Ben-Sasson, who found a crucial diary. Omer Bartov and Christopher Browning did parallel work on different aspects of the same general theme, and I was privileged to be able to share some of my thoughts with these good friends of mine and utilize some of their insights. (See especially Omer Bartov, "From the Holocaust in Galicia to Contemporary Genocide: Common Ground—Historical Differences," Mayerhoff Annual Lecture, U.S Holocaust Memorial Museum, Washington, DC, December 2002.) My late friend Raul Hilberg heard me out on what I was doing and, with his usual skeptical smile, said, "Okay, go ahead, and we shall see what you come up with." We rarely agreed on anything, but I always learned from his critical remarks, which I now sorely miss.

As always, my peace of mind was kept up by my family—my two daughters, Danit and Anat, their husbands and their wonderful children, my three stepsons and grandchild, and, above all and everything else, Elana, my wife, best friend, partner, first reader, and critic.

The Kresy and Prewar Poland
The kresy comprise northeastern Poland, Volhynia, and East Galicia.

The Kresy, 1939–1941
The area controlled by Germany (in stripes) includes western Poland. The kresy are
included in the area under Russian control (shaded dark gray).

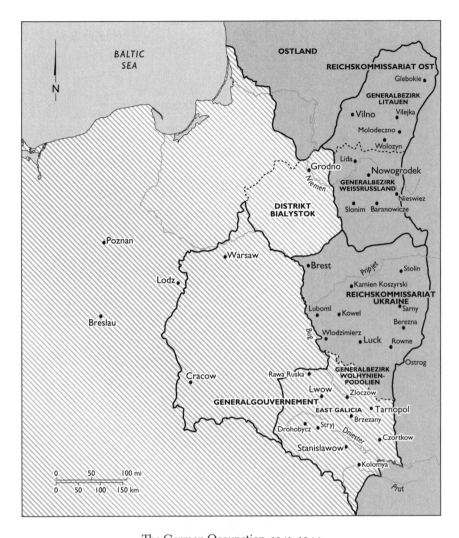

The German Occupation, 1941–1944
The kresy are now under separate German administrations. Part is in the
Ostland (shaded dark gray). East Galicia is in the Generalgouvernement.
The German Reich (striped area) includes the Bialystok district, but the
district also has a separate administration.

East Galicia, 1941–1944
East Galicia and Volhynia are both in western Ukraine.

Volhynia, 1941–1944
The Pripjet Marshes start in the north.

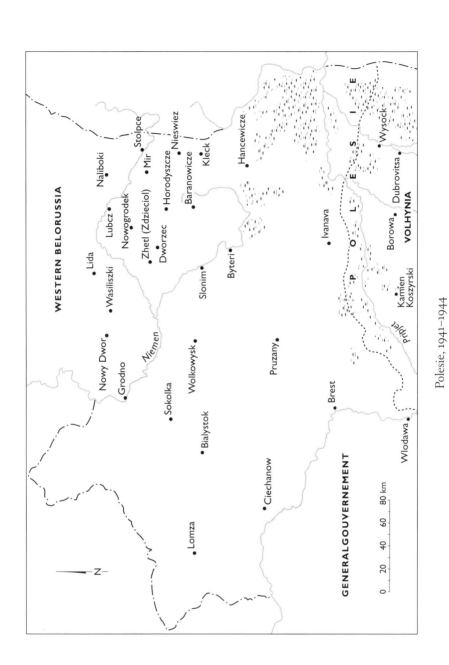

Polesie, 1941–1944

Polesie, between Vollhynia and western Belorussia, is home to the vast Pripjet Marshes.

Western Belorussia (Belarus), 1941–1944

One

---◆---

BACKGROUND

Of the approximately 3.3 million Jews who lived in prewar Poland, some 30–40 percent—the exact number cannot be determined—lived in small towns and communities. The large cities with their Jewish communities—Warsaw, Lodz, Cracow, Vilno (Vilnius), Bialystok, Czestochowa, and others—were largely concentrated in the central, northern, and western part of the country. In the eastern part, where the Poles were a minority and the majorities were mainly Ukrainian and Belorussian (except in the Bialystok district), there was one major city—Lwow (Lemberg, today Lviv; again excepting Bialystok)—and a number of medium-sized towns, including Brest-Litovsk (Polish: Brzesc nad Bugiem; Yiddish: Brisk deLita), Rowne (Ukrainian: Rivne; Yid.: Rowno or Rowna), Lutsk, Kovel, and a few others.[1] This eastern part of the country, known in Polish as the *kresy* (marches), contained about 1.3 million Jews, most of whom lived in the smaller towns, townships, and villages. The townships that had a large Jewish population were called *shtetlach* (Yid.: "small towns"; sing.: *shtetl*) by their Jewish inhabitants. We may conclude that well over a third of Polish Jewry lived in shtetlach all over Poland, as did probably at least 60 percent of the Jews of the kresy. In fact, some statistics purport to show that 60 percent of all Polish Jews lived in places where there were fewer than 10,000 Jews.[2]

There is a tremendous wealth of literature on, and there has been some historical investigation into, the history of the shtetlach in the nineteenth and early twentieth centuries. The emergence of Yiddish as a literary language in the nineteenth century made it possible for great writers to appear and describe the shtetlach in their fiction, poetry and drama. Mendele Moicher Sforim (Shalom Y. Abramowicz), Sholem Aleichem (Shalom N. Rabinowicz), Yehuda Leib Peretz, Sholem Asch, and others created colorful images of Jewish life in these places.

Their descriptions were not laudatory in any sense: they were harshly critical of the degrading poverty, the religious fanaticism, the authoritarian oligarchies that ruled over most, if not all, of these places, and the hopelessness of a people who were faced with antisemitic bureaucracies and, from the second half of the nineteenth century on, wanted nothing more than to escape by emigrating to the West. The writers described the internal social conflicts and the corruption, not only of the gentile rulers but also of the Jewish populations. Yet they also identified with these poor Jews, applauded their loyalty to each other and to family life, and admired their constancy in observing their religious customs. After World War I, this literary output dried up, although some fine writers, such as Isaac Bashevis Singer, continued to write about Polish Jews generally and about the shtetlach Jews. What was left was an image of the shtetl, the *heim* (home), that the millions of emigrants, largely to the United States, carried with them as they fled to the new land or lands of "unlimited opportunities." In the nineteen forties and after World War II, unrealistic, saccharine nostalgia took over remembrance of the shtetl, as manifested in the well-known musical *Fiddler on the Roof*, a distorted and bowdlerized version of a story by Sholem Aleichem (which actually deals with a village, not a shtetl). In this sickeningly sweet, made-up world of Eastern Jewry, all Jews were deeply religious, naïve, and clever, and the shtetl was a place where goodness and ethical uprightness ruled despite the difficult conditions.

Very little sociological or historical analysis of the shtetlach has been offered for the thirties or the Holocaust period.[3] Nor is the literature about the internal life of Polish Jews in the thirties abundant. Amazingly, until the early twenty-first century no attempt was made to tell the story of the changes that occurred in the shtetlach between the world wars, especially in the thirties; and, perhaps even more surprisingly, few attempts were made to find out what happened to the shtetlach during the Holocaust, beyond documenting their destruction. We know that the Jews were murdered—for that we do not need more research. We have a fairly detailed account of who murdered them, where, how, and when. We have a reasonably good analysis of the German-Nazi motivations and ideology and the economic and social policies pursued by the German occupiers, and we have some first attempts at describing the attitudes of the surrounding non-Jewish populations toward the Jews—although there is still a great deal to be done. But what we want to know, and do not know, is how the Jews lived before they were murdered, what their reactions were in the face of the sudden, unexpected, and, for them, inexplicable assault on their lives by a power whose policies they did not and could not understand.

For all of Poland there are few books, on a few shtetlach.[4] Some of these, such as those by Shimon Redlich (on Brzezany, in East Galicia), Daniel Mendelsohn and Anatol Reignier (on Bolechow, also in East Galicia), and Theo Richmond (on Konin, in western Poland), are attempts either to discover the roots of the writers or to deal with the experiences of survivors against the background of interethnic relationships. Redlich relies on testimonies of local people, largely Ukrainians, most of who claim, of course, to have helped Jews. Whether such testimonies are reliable is doubtful. Other books, such as those by Rose Lehman (on Jasliska) and Jack Kagan (on Nowogrodek) are serious attempts to deal with historical or sociological issues.[5] Richmond's book on Konin is most impressive, but he scarcely deals with the wartime experiences. However, it so happens that Esther Farbstein, in a volume that analyzes rabbinical responses in Poland during the Holocaust, deals, in some detail, with the rabbi of Sanniki, Yehoshua Moshe Aharonson, who was deported to the slave-labor camp of Konin and whose diary and memoirs she retrieved. Her brilliant description and analysis make clear how much more we could learn about Konin from other sources.[6] Jack Kagan's book is a valuable account of the fate of Jewish Nowogrodek, especially since he managed to get hold of a number of German and Soviet documents; Peter Duffy's parallel account, also of Nowogrodek, is a good example of investigative journalism; although he adds some important information, he appears to be looking for scoops. His account of dialogues between some of the figures in his story is not credible and detracts from the historical value of his book. Rose Lehmann's account of Jasliska is a very interesting anthropological and sociological analysis of prewar Polish-Jewish relations, and her insights into these are of great value. But her account of the internal communal life of the Jews in the village-township is almost nonexistent, and the story of the Holocaust there adds little to our knowledge.[7]

I have investigated a number of shtetlach, and much of what follows is based on that and my other ongoing research.[8]

One of the first problems that anyone encounters when dealing with this subject is that sociologists and historians did not define what they meant when they talked about the shtetl. To deal with the different aspects of the topic, a definition is essential, even an arbitrary one. I have tried my hand and offer this: a shtetl was a township with 1,000 to 15,000 Jews, who formed at least a third of the total population, and their life was regulated by the Jewish calendar and by customs derived from a traditional interpretation of the Jewish religion. The Jews living in a shtetl were ruled by an informal oligarchy; from among these rulers were elected those who bore communal responsibilities in the framework of the *kahal*, or *kehille* (Hebrew plur.: *kehillot*; Yid. plur.: *kehilles*), which in different forms had existed for hundreds of years as the organizational expression of Jewish communal life. In interwar Poland, in 1927, the government recognized the kehillot as religious communities only, although aspects of social welfare were included in their tasks. This was the result of both negotiations with the authorities and some inner-Jewish maneuvering. From 1927, then, the kahal leaders controlled the religious, the social, and to a limited extent the economic lives of the Jewish population, aided by a network of voluntary organizations.[9]

I put the lower limit of a shtetl's population at 1,000 Jews because a Jewish population smaller than that found it almost impossible to establish the wealth of voluntary organizations that made a shtetl's Jewish life what it was. Village Jews were therefore excluded from my examination, which does not mean that their story is any less valuable and important. Beyond the upper limit I propose, the intimacy of social life so characteristic of the shtetl was no longer possible. Thus, in an examination of the fate of the Jews in Brest-Litovsk (Yid.: Brisk), which I did for comparison's sake, it became clear that although the number of Jews in the ghetto there was about 14,000 in late 1941—the same, more or less, as in some larger shtetlach—Brest was different from the shtetlach around it.[10] It was a large town, and although the Jews had, prior to the war, made up about 44 percent of the population, numbering 21,440 out of about 48,000, the Jewish social organizations had a character that was less intimate and less compact than that of the organizations in smaller places.[11]

To deal with all the shtetlach in Poland was impossible—that task will take generations—so I concentrated on the kresy, the Eastern Marches of interwar Poland. In much of Polish literature the kresy are understood not to have included East Galicia (now western Ukraine), which had a majority of Ukrainians, although the capital, the only large city (Lwow), was predominantly Polish.[12] On the other hand, in some sources the kresy include the Bialystok region in the northeast, which was predominantly Polish (and is now part of the Polish Republic). For simplicity's sake, I include here all those areas that are now western Belarus and western Ukraine where Poles were a minority in the interwar period. The Eastern Marches thus include East Galicia and largely exclude Bialystok, as well as the city of Vilnius (now the capital of Lithuania, called Vilna or Vilno in Yiddish but called Wilno at the time; it was a predominantly Polish city). In many ways, the kresy were the center of traditional Jewish existence. Many of the great figures of Jewish as well as broader importance came from the kresy: Sigmund Freud's family; Chaim Weitzmann; the Soloveitchik rabbinical family in the United States; the historian Emmanuel Ringelblum; the Israeli novelist Shmuel Yossef Agnon (Czaczkes); the Nazi hunter Simon Wiesenthal; many Israeli politicians and cultural leaders, and so on.

But it was impossible to deal with all the shtetlach in the kresy either, so I chose to analyze a dozen shtetlach in some depth and deal with a large number of others in a more general and superficial way. Account had to be taken of the differences between different areas. The Ukrainian areas included Volhynia, which had a relatively small, though very important, minority of Poles, and East Galicia, where the Polish minority was larger and even formed a majority in Lwow. There were also small minorities of Czechs (in Volhynia) and Germans. The Belorussian areas in the north contained three prewar Polish provinces where there was a fairly large and deeply rooted minority Polish ethnic group, apart from Lithuanians, Tatars, and others.

The religious differences were considerable, too. The Poles were Roman Catholic, the Ukrainians were partly Greek Catholic and partly Greek or Russian Orthodox, the Belorussians were overwhelmingly Orthodox, and the Tatars were Muslim. In Volhynia there was also a very important, though small, minority of some 6,000–7,000 Baptists-Mennonites, who became very significant in the story of the Jews during the Holocaust. An even smaller minority, in the area called Polesie, which straddles the border between Ukraine and Belorussia, an area of forests and marshes, there were some villages of Old Believers (Staroveryi), members of a fundamentalist Orthodox sect that opposed the established Orthodox Church and were persecuted by the Tsarist regime. They and the Baptists laid special emphasis on the Old Testament and saw the Jews as God's Chosen People.

I have not dealt here with another geographic area where shtetlach existed before 1939: the former Pale of Settlement, east of the kresy—that is, prewar Soviet Belorussia and Soviet Ukraine.[13] Not only is the situation regarding source material much more problematic there than elsewhere, but the Soviet regime destroyed the Jewish communities as such, so masses of shtetl Jews migrated to towns and cities in search of industrial and other jobs. There were Jews, but no Jewish communities. This made the basis for Jewish reactions to the German murder campaign quite different from that obtaining in the Polish-controlled areas. The fact that Jewish communities sprang up under German rule because of German policies still has to be explored and explained. We would have to take into consideration the influence of communist ideology on the generations of Jews growing up under Soviet rule—an influence that was very marked and important and may have colored Jewish reactions to German oppression. Also, relations between Jews and non-Jews in the Soviet areas may have differed from those in areas farther west—another issue that awaits more research beyond the efforts already made.

In the end, I concentrated on the Polish kresy, focusing on three shtetlach in each region: Kosow (Kosiv) Huculski, Buczacz, and Zborow (Zboriv) in East

Galicia; Krzemieniec (Kremenets), Rokitna (Ukr.: Rokitnoye; Yid.: Rokitno), and Sarny in Volhynia; and Baranowicze (Baranavichi), Kurzeniec (Kurenets), and Nowogrodek (Navagrudok), and to some extent Dereczin in the Belorussian areas. A manuscript by Martha Goren on Czortkow, in East Galicia, which has not yet been published, enabled me to include that important shtetl and smaller places in its vicinity as well.[14]

The questions that I asked of the material I examined concerned, primarily, internal Jewish issues. For the prewar period of the thirties, mainly the late thirties, I asked questions about internal communal developments, including support for political parties and movements; economic and social changes in the wake of modernization, and the impact of the world economic crisis; the growth and impact of youth movements; attempts to emigrate from the kresy; and cultural and ideological developments.

In September 1939, Poland was divided between Germany and the Soviet Union, and the Soviets occupied the kresy. What was the impact on the Jewish communities of Sovietization? How many refugees from German-occupied Poland arrived in the kresy? What was their fate? Did they report to local Jews about what they had experienced under the Germans? Can we say anything of value about the arrests and the deportations of Jews to Siberia? What happened to the Jewish institutions under the Soviets? How did the Jews manage economically? What was the impact of communist ideology on the Jews, especially on the young generation? What was the attitude of the Soviet authorities to the Jews?

In June 1941 the Germans invaded the Soviet Union. Within a few weeks, practically all of western Belarus and western Ukraine were conquered by the invaders. Mass murders of Jews began. By the end of 1942 most Jews in those areas had been murdered, and only isolated groups exploited for labor purposes remained here and there. We know that the Jews were murdered. German and other historians have clarified most of the dates and the places of their murder, identified the German units and their local collaborators who participated in the murders, and named many of the commanders who directed the mass slaughter. More work on these aspects is being done, including the identification of the places where the Jews were tortured and shot.[15] This is important work, and it will surely continue for many more years. But that is not the main issue here. Rather, I would like to know what the Jewish reaction to the unexpected onslaught was before the Jews were murdered. I know that they died. I want to know how they lived.

My questions are: Did the Jewish communities maintain a measure of cohesion in these very cruel circumstances before they were annihilated? Or were they atomized and destroyed, ceasing to function even before the individuals composing them were murdered? What was the nature of the Jewish councils (*Judenräte*), and what options did they have—that is, how did they react/behave? Was there what I elsewhere called *Amidah* (Heb.: "standing up against"), that is, unarmed and armed reactions intended to keep the community and its components going and to stand up to the existential threat posed by the German regime?[16]

This question of Amidah is crucial, and necessitates further consideration. Research on the Holocaust in eastern Europe has emphasized the fate of the large communities. Detailed monographic investigations of cities such as Warsaw, Lodz, Bialystok, Vilno, Kovno (Kaunas), Cracow, Lwow, Riga, Czestochowa, and others have shown that in most of these concentrations of Jews attempts were made to counter the increasing brutality of German policies at first by unarmed action and finally by attempts, in some of these cities—for example, Warsaw, Vilno, Kovno, Cracow, and Czestochowa—to organize armed action against the murderers. The unarmed actions were very important. In Warsaw, for instance, there were more than a thousand so-called house committees, elected from among the occupants of apartments in a complex of buildings; these buildings, and the apartments in them, were usually situated around a central courtyard, and the committees tried to organize education for the youngest, or at least keep the children occupied. Cultural activities were organized for everyone, and the committees tried to protect the weakest against starvation by supplying some bread through self-taxation; they also tried to protect the inhabitants from the depredations of Jewish and non-Jewish policemen, who took away not only people but also their bedding and clothes for so-called disinfection, which often resulted in illness or death. Social work in the ghetto consisted, among other things, of aid to orphans and medical care. Sick bays and even hospitals were staffed by doctors and nurses who tried their best, with little or no medication, to keep people from dying from the illnesses induced by undernourishment and, worse, actual starvation. Many doctors, and especially many nurses, died because they contracted typhoid. Food was supplied, whenever possible, through soup kitchens—organized in part by the *Judenrat* (Jewish council) and in large part by social activists (in Warsaw by the American Jewish Joint Distribution Committee [JDC], in which the historian Emmanuel Ringelblum played a leading role)— which doubled as centers of underground political activities. In Vilno there was an emphasis on cultural activity to keep up morale. In Kovno, the Judenrat concentrated on helping children and providing social welfare. And so on.

In some cities, such as Lodz, conditions were so harsh that social welfare work became extremely difficult. But even in such places elements of what I call Amidah were evident. However, lest we fall into the trap of misplaced nostalgia, let me emphasize that almost everywhere there also was corruption, collaboration with the murderers, and a decline in societal and personal norms that affected considerable parts of the Jewish population. A large amount of detailed research exists on all this, and the questions become clearer, although the answers may be in dispute.

The problem faced by anyone who investigates the kresy is whether the developments in the larger towns and cities of western and central Poland parallel those in the eastern shtetlach. The answer is no, they do not, at least not much. Armed resistance was more prevalent in the kresy than elsewhere—and no wonder. Forests were nearby, which made it a viable option.

Generalized answers such as these overlook the vast differences between shtetlach. The approach to the problem has to be more systematic and more focused, I believe. We should compare the shtetlach with each other and with the cities to the west and north, in central and western Poland and in Lithuania and Latvia, and we must ask questions about possible manifestations of Amidah in detail: forms of Amidah may differ from one place to another. We have to ask about the education of children; about forced labor and the reaction to it; about the policies pursued by the Judenräte regarding labor, food smuggling, soup kitchens, social welfare, and the protection of individuals from the torture and humiliation administered by the Germans and their collaborators. We have to ask about the continuation or otherwise of religious life and about possible attempts to maintain some modicum of cultural activity. Finally, we have to ask about underground political activities and armed resistance in the shtetlach themselves. In parts of the kresy, escaping to the forests was an option, and escapees could try to survive there with the help of locals or try to join groups of anti-German partisans. We therefore have to deal with, on the one hand, the Soviet partisan movement and the relations between these anti-German fighters and the Jews who fled into the forests and, on the other hand, Jewish participation in the partisan movement.

This leads to another complex of questions: the relations between Jews and non-Jews. In the kresy, the non-Jews were, first and foremost, Ukrainians, Poles, and Belorussians. While, to my knowledge, no research exists on Jewish Amidah in the kresy or in the Polish shtetlach generally (Bessarabian, Lithuanian, and Latvian shtetlach were annihilated immediately upon the occupation of these areas by the Germans or Romanians in 1941), a growing number of important studies have been published on Jewish–non-Jewish relations and the Soviet partisan movement and its attitude toward the Jews. On these issues, I can therefore bring in arguments offered by other colleagues and perhaps add something from the results of my own work.

Sources for all of this are very problematic. For the prewar period, Polish sources offer some information, although the Polish authorities were interested not in the internal workings of Jewish societies but in their politics and their economic activities. Even there, the information is not always enlightening or even necessarily accurate—Polish officials in the late thirties were often antisemitic, and that bias colored their reports. Much of the shtetl material was destroyed or lost in the war, and only remnants survive. Occasionally municipal archives have preserved some of it.

The outlook is even bleaker for the Soviet period, 1939–1941. Whatever information was in Soviet sources has to a large extent already been worked out. But the Soviets, too, were not interested in inner Jewish life. They destroyed the communal institutions, forbade all social and political activity that did not directly serve the regime, and concentrated on opposition to the regime, relying largely on denunciations. Beyond that, the development of the local economy and its integration into the Soviet system were primary concerns. Only a handful of Jewish documents are available that tell us something about Jewish reactions to the Soviet rule and the rest of the issues addressed here.

There is plenty of German material on the destruction of the Jews during the German occupation.[17] But the Germans had no interest in internal Jewish matters and very rarely reported on them. The same can be said of the scattered sources on the Polish underground in the kresy. Reports on Soviet partisan detachments after the initial consolidation of the partisan movement and the establishment of a central command of the Soviet partisans in May 1942 do mention Jews, however, and sometimes the reports relate to the problems that Jews encountered within the movement. The active participation of Jews in armed partisan activities is also occasionally mentioned.[18]

Quite a number of diaries, letters, and memoranda have survived that pertain to the large concentrations of Jews in Poland, in large part owing to at least three collections that preserve these materials: the Oineg Shabbes (Heb.: Oneg Shabbat) underground archive organized by Emmanuel Ringelblum in Warsaw, some two-thirds of which survived the war, and the much less voluminous collections of Zvi Mersik in Bialystok and Herman Kruk in Vilno. As far as I am aware, very few diaries pertaining to the kresy have survived, and letters exist largely only for the Soviet period, not for the German one, although there are a few. The diaries are tremendously important. One was written by Aryeh Klonicki/Klonitsky (Klonymus), a Hebrew teacher from Pinsk in Polesie, who was in Buczacz, in East Galicia, with his wife, Malvina, when the Germans invaded. They had a baby son, Adam. After one of the murder actions in the ghetto, the couple hid in the fields of a local farmer. The farmer's wife agreed to provide food and some milk for the baby. While hiding in the field, Klonicki wrote a diary, in excellent Hebrew, describing his and his wife's experiences and emotions during that period. They realized that they would not survive and asked the Polish woman to take the child, which she did. They were discovered and murdered, the child grew up as an Ukrainian, and after the war the child refused to return to the Jewish fold. The second diary was written by a man called Beinish (Benjamin) Berkowicz, also apparently a Hebrew teacher, either from Nowogrodek or from one of the neighboring shtetlach. It was written, also in excellent Hebrew, in the spring and summer of 1942, and expresses views about the social and political situation and about the fate of the Jews. The author, an atheist, railed against the belief in a God who was responsible for the horrors of the Holocaust. The diary ends on the day of one of the murder actions in Nowogrodek, in February 1943. The author gave the diary to a Polish acquaintance and asked him to hand it over to a Jewish institution if the Pole survived the war. The Polish person did survive, and he gave the diary to the Jewish Historical Institute in Warsaw in 1946. The presumption was that Berkowicz was killed in the February "action," but according to a document found in the Belorussian National Archives, the group of partisans from the Bielski detachment who attacked a German train included a fighter identified as B. Berkowicz. No person from the Bielski unit by the name of Berkowicz died before the end of the war (there is a list of all the casualties), so it is likely that Berkowicz survived. Efforts to find out what happened to him have failed. The diary is an impressive personal testimony of a person dealing with mass murder and horrific suffering, but it does not add to our knowledge of what happened to the community of which he was a part. Such diaries are crucial to understanding the frame of mind of victims, but they have limited value as regards the general picture.[19]

This leaves us with postwar testimonies, written, oral (taped), and videotaped. Use of testimonies is not popular among historians. The obvious and oft-repeated arguments are that memory is unreliable, and purposeful distortion or worse are always a risk (as shown in the case of the invented memoir of Binjamin Wilkomirsky, whose real name is Bruno Grosjean).[20] Testimonies taken or written down immediately after the war are considered more reliable than those of later years.

Elsewhere I have explained why in my judgment these arguments are unconvincing, but it is worth repeating the discussion here and perhaps somewhat expanding on it. I think that historians have to deal with historical sources, especially those on the Holocaust, in a broad context. How reliable are written documents? The classic example is, as many have pointed out, the so-called Wannsee Protocol, the minutes of a meeting of top German administrative officials at a Wannsee villa in Berlin on January 20, 1942. Those at the meeting discussed the implementation of the so-called Final Solution: the annihilation of the Jews. We now know that the minutes were "cooked"; they were composed by Adolf Eichmann at the behest and under the watchful eye of his boss, Reinhard Heydrich. At Eichmann's trial in Jerusalem, Eichmann testified that what had transpired at that meeting went far beyond what the written minutes contain; although gassing of Jews was not discussed, other details of the mass murders that were already going on and that were planned for the future were. The document is clearly unreliable, although it provides us with a general framework of what was said; Eichmann's oral testimony, twenty years later, seems much more reliable. Similar analyses can be offered regarding events that took place in the kresy. In one instance, a Soviet document supposedly originating from March 1942, signed by a rabbi and relating to the murder of the town's Jews, was submitted to German investigative agencies in the nineteen sixties. It can be shown that the Soviets predated the document to incriminate Germans who were being investigated by German courts and that no rabbi signed any document on the mass murder in Nowogrodek in 1942.[21] This does not mean that the events the document tells us about did not happen more or less as described. But postwar oral testimonies of the mass murder are much more reliable because they can be cross-checked for accuracy.

I do not mean to say that oral testimonies are in principle more reliable than written documents. Generally speaking, contemporary documents are preferable, whether they are reports, letters, or diaries. But written documents have to be analyzed as to their veracity, and this holds true for any documentation. For the Holocaust, there is the additional problem of attempts by Germans and local collaborators to "beautify" (*verschönern*) the murders. A special language was developed, a subspecies of what Victor Klemperer termed Lingua Tertii Imperii—namely, *Sprachregelung* (use of terminology to hide atrocities).[22] The German document speaks to us in a double language and cannot be used without dissection. Yet German documentation provides the basis for the "perpetrators' history," for what the Germans and their collaborators did—who, where, and when. Very rarely do these documents throw light on the question why.

With postwar testimonies we have to be doubly careful. The argument that memory is unreliable is true. But testimonies can be cross-checked against each other. If I have the choice between believing a contemporary written document and trusting the conclusions reached on the same event by cross-checking ten testimonies that agree on an alternative version, I will choose the testimonies. As far as the research on the kresy is concerned, however, there is not much choice: documents are rare, and there are many postwar testimonies.

Postwar testimonies present two other major pitfalls. First, we have the testimonies of only the tiny minority who survived, and their testimonies do not necessarily reflect the experiences of many of those who were killed or died. Second, the testimonies are mostly of people with a middle-class background and not of the vast majority of the poorer members of the Jewish population. The reason is quite simple: people with more property or wealth often managed to save some of it even under the most difficult circumstances, and their bits and bobs were very useful when they tried to find hiding places in the forests or with peasants who wanted to be paid for the food they supplied. Merchants, shopkeepers, and owners of tracts of forests or land had sometimes also developed friendly relations with peasants and others, which could make the difference between death and survival. The survival of middle-class and wealthy people is reflected in the testimonies we have.

The opening of former Soviet archives has propelled research on the Holocaust forward. But not all archives are open or stay open. At the moment of writing (2009), access to Russian archives is limited, access to Belorussian archives is practically nonexistent, and only Ukrainian archives are relatively easily accessible. Western archives are generally open, with the important exception of the Vatican archives—the Vatican has valiantly defended its bastions, and it is only lately that serious efforts are being made there to open its documents from World War II. These must contain a great deal of material pertaining to Poland, especially the Uniate Church in East Galicia and Volhynia, which recognized the bishop of Rome as its head. Whatever we conclude today regarding the shtetlach of the kresy may well undergo revision when these sources become available, as I hope they someday do.

Two

---•—•—•---

THE THIRTIES

According to a census taken in 1931, Poland had a population of 3,133,933 million Jews. Thus, it had the highest percentage of Jews of any country in 1939: about 10 percent of the total population.[1] The number of Jews had grown from 3.1 million in 1931 to 3.3 million in 1939. The percentage was higher in some large cities: in 1931, the Jews in Warsaw accounted for 30 percent of the population; in Lodz, they accounted for 33 percent. But many were still living in smaller towns and townships, and a quarter of Poland's Jews were living in villages. In the northern four provinces of the kresy, including Bialystok and Vilno, nearly 10 percent of the population were Jews—there were 452,000 altogether—and there were even more, around 485,000, in 1939, plus some 875,000 in the two southern, Ukrainian provinces.[2]

A small minority of merchants and industrialists were at the top of the Jewish occupational ladder, but a plurality of Jews eked out a living as craft workers, peddlers, and small traders. Close to 80 percent of Jews employed in "commerce" were peddlers and small shopkeepers employing their own family members—if they had any employees at all. A large number of Jews were industrial workers, although opposition by Polish workers to the employment of Jews forced even Jewish entrepreneurs to hire Poles rather than Jews. About half of the Jews employed in "industry" were self-employed craft workers living on or under the poverty line.[3] At the bottom of the ladder was a growing underclass of people with no visible source of income, the so-called *Luftmenschen* ("people living off thin air"). A small but important group of intellectuals was responsible for the tremendous cultural developments that took place despite the difficult economic circumstances.[4]

Whereas most Jews spoke Yiddish and were culturally embedded in Yiddish cultural life, a growing number of Jews spoke Polish and adapted to and borrowed from Polish culture. Some of these acculturated Jews contributed to Polish cultural achievements, just as Jews elsewhere in Europe often participated prominently in general cultural life. Although many of the acculturated Jews were also very prominent in internal Jewish life, others tried to assimilate—disappear into—gentile Polish society. A small number, primarily among the wealthiest Jews and some prominent intellectuals, converted to Roman Catholicism.[5]

The central issue for Polish Jews in the interwar period was the steady decline in their economic fortunes in the context of the continuing economic crises that hit Poland as a whole. Most of pre–World War I Poland had been under Russian and Austrian rule, and the markets for industrial products from Poland were huge, especially in the vast Russian Empire and only slightly less so in the Habsburg lands. Jewish industrialists in the growing city of Lodz could sell their textiles in Saint Petersburg or Moscow, or for that matter in Kiev or beyond the Urals. Their counterparts in Lwow found markets in Vienna, Prague, and the Balkans. The prewar Russian industry developed at breakneck speed, and both empires were going through the first phases of a capitalist revolution; some areas, such as Bohemia and Moravia in the Habsburg Empire and Saint Petersburg in Russia, had already developed a modern capitalist basis for their economies. The Polish provinces of both empires, especially western Poland in the Russian-controlled areas and parts of East Galicia in Austro-Hungarian Poland, had followed suit.

With Polish independence in 1918, all this broke down. The markets contracted radically, down to the area of the new republic, as the successor states of the defeated empires developed nationalistic, protectionist economic policies. The newly established Soviet Union closed its doors to normal trade with Poland; elsewhere, high customs barriers prevented the flow of trade. Poland's internal market was very constricted because the poor peasants who composed a majority of the population still practiced primitive subsistence agriculture, lacked land, and had little purchasing power. Poland's economy was still largely controlled by a few aristocratic landed families: fewer than 1 percent of the farming units owned 45 percent of the land, and 29 percent of the peasants were landless. The government struggled unsuccessfully with the basic problems of a redistribution of land and a surplus peasant population.[6]

Many among the Jews, most of whom belonged to the lower middle class, did not find employment, and a growing number descended into a poverty-stricken underclass. By the nineteen thirties, roughly one-third of the Jews lived on or below the poverty line, and in some places hunger was a real danger.[7] Contemporary testimonies of foreign visitors substantiate these conclusions. In 1937 the *London Jewish Chronicle* described the Jews of Poland as "a helpless minority sunk in squalid poverty and misery such as can surely be paralleled nowhere on the face of the earth."[8] There was still a middle class, and a small percentage of Jews were upper-middle-class and rich, including wholesale merchants, industrialists, and bankers. But even the intellectuals were underprivileged, because the increasing antisemitism among Poles caused universities to institute a quota system for Jews, and only a minority of young students could afford to get their university degrees abroad.

Although external economic and political circumstances contributed substantially to the increasingly disastrous situation of Polish Jews, the major factor affecting them was probably the growth of an exclusivist Polish nationalism, which developed from about the middle of the nineteenth century. In *Poland's Threatening Other*, Joanna B. Michlic describes and analyzes the growth of this extreme form of nationalism, which was based on Catholic antisemitism but which developed the idea of Jews as the ultimate foreigners, the source of an unassimilable negative influence on Polish life, the reason for the suffering of the Polish people.[9] This view was represented in its most radical form by the Polish intellectual-politician Roman Dmowski (1864–1939). Dmowski's ideology was anti-German, but his radical antisemitism was more important to him than his dislike and suspicion of Germans. He opposed the inclusion of non-Polish elements in interwar Poland and initially even opposed Polish rule in the kresy because the Ukrainians and the Belorussians were the majority in those areas. In interwar Poland, he advocated Polonization of these ethnicities in order to create as purely Polish a state as possible. The Jews, who were not concentrated in one area of Poland but were spread all over the country, were, in his eyes, parasites on the body politic of the Polish people, exploiters of the peasantry, a foreign element with a religion radically different from Polish Catholicism, unabsorbable and therefore an enemy who should be gotten rid of. Poland could never find its proper place in European and world society unless the Jews were excluded from it. This exclusivist ideology saw the Jews as "a distinct race, in the following sense: a group different from the Poles because of their innate, immutable characteristics—physical, mental, emotional and spiritual."[10]

Despite all the denials by Polish nationalists, their view of the Jews came very close to German National Socialist racism, and, in fact, Dmowski came to admire Hitler (while hating the Germans). He was explicitly anti-German and pro-Nazi. Zionism was nothing but the Jewish attempt to rule the world from Palestine—his view here was much in line with views current in the SS, the Nazi police force, in the late thirties. Dmowski's political party, the National Democratic Party—called Endecja from its Polish acronym (its members were the "Endeks")—and its even more radical offshoots represented mainly middle-class Poles and later peasants who had immigrated into Polish towns and sought upward social mobility. The Endeks were led by a highly intelligent group of academically trained individuals and gained a large number of adherents, especially among university students. Indeed, with the exception of a small group of liberal intellectuals, the Polish intelligentsia, especially the younger generation that grew up in the thirties, were mostly supporters of antisemitic views.

The Endecja concentrated on economic issues; it saw the Jews as competitors to be brushed aside; their places in the struggling middle-class were to be taken by ethnic Catholic Poles. The solution for the Jews was emigration, and the Endeks pursued schemes to force Jews from Poland, even convincing the center and center-right political forces to support their position. To make the Jews emigrate was no easy task, given that there were millions of them and that there was nowhere to send them. But, the Polish government of the thirties, especially after 1935, acted vigorously to propagate the idea of a mass emigration of Jews in international fora, chiefly with the League of Nations, with France (with the French government it supported the idea of Jewish emigration to the island of Madagascar), and with Great Britain (with the British government it supported the opening of Palestine to Jewish immigration). In 1938 the Polish government participated at the Evian Conference, convened to find a solution for refugees from Germany, and demanded, along with Romania, that emigration from Romania and Poland also be discussed. In the United States, the Poles negotiated with Jewish organizations, mainly the JDC, to gain their support for the idea of emigration. Desperate for solutions, Polish Jewish representatives were also looking for a way to ease the pressure of anti-Jewish policies by promoting emigration from Poland.

In the meantime, the Endecja advocated and implemented a boycott, primarily against Jewish shopkeepers, peddlers, and merchants but also against doctors, engineers, and academics; again, in the late twenties and especially in the thirties, after 1935, this policy came to be supported by the government. On June 4, 1936, the prime minister, General Felicjan Slawoj-Skladkowski—by no means a radical antisemite—declared in parliament that physical attacks on Jews were to be condemned but that boycotting them was "of course [*owszem*]" all right. The policy of owszem was translated into a radical attack against Jewish attempts at economic survival, and "of course" the boycott inevitably led to physical attacks, then pogroms, symbolized in 1936–1939 by the pogrom in the small, largely Jewish shtetl of Przytyk in central Poland. The kresy were not hit as hard, probably because the Poles were a minority, but there was a pogrom in Brest-Litovsk, in the Belorussian kresy, on May 13, 1937, and the following days. Three hundred fifty Jews were reportedly killed in Poland between 1935 and 1939, many thousands were deprived of their livelihood, and some towns were abandoned by most of the Jewish population. In the industrial city of Czestochowa, a bastion of radical Catholic antisemitism, a local Endek paper published lists of streets on which the Jews had not yet been robbed.[11]

Polish students at universities led another radical form of the boycott. Their aim was to chase out all Jewish students. Apart from engaging in physical attacks that sometimes ended in murder, they succeeded, in some universities, in forcing Jewish students to sit separately on so-called ghetto-benches. As a result, the percentage of Jewish students dropped from 25 percent in 1921–1922 to 8 percent in 1938–1939.[12] As in Germany and Austria in the pre-Hitler period, the universities and, in a wider sense, the intelligentsia were the leaders in antisemitic agitation and policy. Jewish students tried to study abroad, but in most cases finding the money to do so was almost impossible.

The right and the center-right found wide support for their antisemitic policies. A major, relatively moderate journal could write in 1936 that "one should let the Jews be, but eliminate them from the life of Christian society." And separate schools should be instituted "so that our children will not be infected with their lower morality."[13] Even the moderate left, represented by the Stronnictwo Ludowe (SL—Peasant Party, also called Wyzwolenie), supported this approach.[14] The allies of the Jews, the Polska Partia Socjalistyczna (PPS—Socialist Party), advocated Jewish mass emigration. Many, if not most, Jews wanted to leave Poland. The Zionists felt that Jews should concentrate in their ancient homeland of Palestine, and even the ultra-orthodox and violently anti-Zionist ultra-orthodox Agudat Israel (Yid.: Agudas Yisroel) Party came around after 1936 to support emigration to the Holy Land—not to establish a Jewish State or Commonwealth there, or a Jewish majority as a refuge for the Jewish people, as the Zionists demanded, but to establish ultra-orthodoxy in the Holy Land. Only the Jewish Bund Party opposed what it called "emigrationism," and demanded that the Jewish "masses," the proletariat and its allies, seek their future in a socialist Poland that would grant full equality to the Jews, who, in turn, would develop on the basis of this equality their (secular) culture using the Yiddish language.[15] But even the Bund's Polish ally, the socialist PPS, had to be careful not to alienate the workers, among whom antisemitism was spreading. It avoided a too pro-Jewish stand and never agreed to a formal alliance with the Bund.

Interwar Poland was never actually ruled by the Endeks (they split into groups in the twenties and the early thirties), who were the main, radically nationalistic opposition to whatever government was in power after 1926. Before that, coalitions of Endeks with Polish liberals and peasant representatives had formed unstable governments. In 1926 the national hero and chief fighter for Polish independence, Marshal Jozef Pilsudski, overthrew the government by force and instituted an authoritarian regime, which did, however, allow for a form of controlled and rigged elections to a parliament—a lower house, called the *sejm*, and a senate. These bodies exercised some influence, although the reins of power were firmly in Pilsudski's hands. Pilsudski established his own party, Bezpartijny Blok (BB—Nonparty Bloc), which won (rigged) elections. He was no antisemite and acted to prevent anti-Jewish riots. His general policies were oriented toward a re-creation in some form of the old pre-partition Polish Commonwealth, which in the late Middle Ages and early modern times had been a state in which Poles, Lithuanians, Ukrainians, Belorussians, Germans, and Jews had lived together more or less peacefully—although the Jews had always been discriminated against to some extent—in the context of a hegemonic Polish culture. Thus, the national Polish poet, Adam Mickiewicz, opened his great epic poem *Pan Tadeusz* with the words "Lithuania, Lithuania, my fatherland."

Mickiewicz was born in Nowogrodek, a Jewish shtetl that had been at one time the capital of Lithuania and that had a mixed Jewish-Polish-Belorussian-Tatar population. It was the Polish Commonwealth (*Rzeczpospolita*) that had provided a reasonably secure environment for the development of Jewish culture and economic life, despite problems with the Catholic Church and the gentile town burghers. The Jews had fulfilled, as has been pointed out by all the historians dealing with the subject, a vital economic function as intermediaries between the peasantry and the towns, on the one hand, and the aristocratic landowners, on the other hand. This changed with the advent of capitalism, but Pilsudski tried to develop Poland's industry and, at the same time, strive for the re-creation, under the new conditions, of the multiethnic Polish Commonwealth.

His main effort, in the late twenties and early thirties, was directed toward the integration of the Ukrainians, especially in Volhynia; altogether, Ukrainians were the largest national minority, about 5 million people, some 16 percent of the total population. Pilsudski's close collaborator, the artist and intellectual Henryk Jozewski, was nominated to be the governor of Volhynia, and he tried hard to attract the Ukrainians to the Polish Republic, giving them opportunities for national cultural development.[16] The Polish landowners still owned much of the land, however, and opposed his policies designed to aid the local peasantry; and Polish nationalism hampered his efforts.

Radical Ukrainian nationalism was represented by the Organization of Ukrainian Nationalists (OUN). The nationalists founded their movement in 1929 and became predominant in neighboring East Galicia by the late thirties. The major Ukrainian political party, until the mid-thirties at least, was still the moderate nationalist Ukrainian National Democratic Alliance (UNDO—Ukrains'ke

Natsional'ne Demokratychne Ob'iednannia), led by Vasilyi Mudryj. UNDO participated in elections and was relatively friendly to Jews. But in the twenties and the early thirties it was the Communist Party of Western Ukraine that gained the most adherents in Volhynia, because of its slogan advocating radical land reform. Pilsudski's Poland had signed a peace treaty with the Soviets in 1921, which gave Volhynia and East Galicia to the Poles. Pilsudski tried to foment Ukrainian disaffection with the communist regime in eastern (Soviet) Ukraine in hopes of unifying most of Ukraine with Poland, as in the old Commonwealth. But this failed miserably. The Soviets followed a double track: they communized Ukraine and brutally eliminated all political strivings for Ukrainian unification and independence, targeting nationalistic tendencies among Ukrainian communists especially; all Communist Party members who ever so slightly overemphasized Ukrainian culture and language were annihilated in the thirties. In Polish-controlled Volhynia, the Soviets pursued the opposite line: emphasizing Ukrainian culture and political opposition to the Polish landowners and town bureaucrats in order to pry Volhynia away from Poland. Slowly, Ukrainian peasant leaders realized that the Soviet paradise was not what they wanted, and the OUN's influence spread. Pilsudski's death in 1935 ended the dream of a Ukrainian-Polish rapprochement.

In all this, the Jews played a very subordinate role. Jozewski may have wanted them to be a part of his dream of a united Polish-Ukrainian-Jewish society, but the government bureaucrats were increasingly antisemitic, influenced as they were by the Endeks and by movements even further to the right. By the mid-thirties, especially after Pilsudski's death in 1935 (and the Polish-German neutrality treaty of 1934 that preceded it), antisemitic propaganda and the anti-Jewish boycott turned physical. In the kresy, brawls, venomous graffiti, and the like appeared in many places in both the Ukrainian south and the Belorussian north, instigated and perpetrated by Polish louts. In a number of postwar testimonies it is claimed that the Jews' relationships with the Ukrainians and the Belorussians were better then than theirs with the Poles in the towns. The situation was complicated. Polonization of the kresy meant the settlement there—mainly on the land—of Poles, mostly veterans from the time of the struggle for independence. These were the *osadniki*, the "settlers," who were much hated by the local non-Polish populations. Polonization also meant settling Poles, mainly from the western provinces, where radical nationalism was prevalent, as functionaries of various kinds in the shtetlach of the kresy. Thus, local government officials, police officers, and army officers were often Poles who had come to Polonize the shtetlach. The indigenous Poles were usually much more liberal than the newcomers, but the nationalists transferred internal Polish controversies into local anti-Jewish policies. We can see this trend in a number of shtetlach where old-time Polish liberals were mayors of towns and tried to maintain decent relationships with the Jews, but were removed from their posts by the representatives of the central government.

In many of the Polish villages relations seem to have been much better, possibly because there the Jews still fulfilled their traditional middlemen functions and were appreciated because of the usually honest way they handled their trades and because of the low prices they charged. Also, Polish villages in the kresy were always in a minority, their residents surrounded by people of the other ethnicities. Poles constituted 17 percent of the population of Volhynia, and 22 percent of the population of East Galicia; in the more northerly region of Polesie they were proportionately even less of the population, 15 percent, but in the larger towns they came to about half of the population.[17] There was a natural tendency for Polish villagers to view the Jews as another minority, in some ways similar to themselves. This had important consequences during the Holocaust.

Some of the large Jewish entrepreneurs engaged in the lumber trade, owned tracts of forest, and hired local lumberjacks and specialists who floated the lumber down the many rivers in both north and south. Their relations with the locals were generally good; some purely Jewish villages of lumberjacks and small traders also existed in the area.

Polish society in all of Poland included a minority, a very important one, that did not accept the prevalent antisemitism. An element of that minority was the social-democratic movement, represented by the PPS, which usually garnered 12 percent or so of the popular vote until the late thirties, when it grew considerably. The PPS was opposed to antisemitism and maintained careful but, on the whole, friendly relations with the Jewish Bund Party; in some places, Polish-Jewish groups formed to oppose right-wing Polish pogromists. But elements in the PPS were less friendly toward Jews. In 1938, for instance, the PPS refused to demonstrate on May Day together with Bund members. And the smaller Stronnictwo Pracy (Labor Party) represented a centrist movement loyal to the Catholic Church and unfriendly to Jews.[18] The two relatively powerful peasant parties were ambivalent toward Jews, but the more leftist one, SL-Wyzwolenie, opposed antisemitism, at least verbally (although it, too, wanted the Jews to leave Poland). The right-wing peasant party, Piast, led by the charismatic Wincenty Witos (from exile in Czechoslovakia, because he fell afoul of the government), was much more explicitly antisemitic. A liberal-democratic movement among the Polish intelligentsia, including a liberal Catholic group, strove to turn Poland into a real democracy with equal rights for all. In 1939, the liberal-democratic groups coalesced to form the Stronnictwo Demokratyczne (Democratic Party), a small but important non-antisemitic party that maintained itself during the German occupation.

But the overall picture was grim for Jews, because antisemitism was common in the government, especially after 1935, and among the Endeks and the even more extreme rightists, among whom National Socialist propaganda from Germany regarding the so-called Jewish question made some headway. After Pilsudski's death in May 1935, the government party, the Bezpartijny Blok, split into three factions, and it was not until 1936 that a new government party was founded, called Oboz Zjednoczenia Narodowego (OZON—Camp of National Unification). Its policy toward the Jews, formulated originally, in February 1937, by Colonel Adam Koc, a radical nationalist, supported economic discrimination and emigrationism—in effect, the expulsion of Jews from Poland. With the establishment of OZON, an old argument was settled: Dmowski had advocated an exclusivist nationalist line—the "national idea" (*idea narodowa*)—whereas the Pilsudskiites had favored a statist, inclusive line (*idea panstwowa*) that favored an identification of all the ethnicities with the Polish state in return for full equality. Now the heirs of Pilsudski basically accepted Dmowski's ideology. The main line toward the Jews became the Endek line: the idea that the economic and social ills of Poland—the agrarian problem and the weakness of the middle class— could be solved by the elimination of the Jews. Poles would dispossess the Jewish middle class and replace it, thereby causing a productive immigration of peasant masses to towns and cities under the leadership of an upper class of Polish industrialists informed by the achievements of Polish culture and unsoiled by Jewish influences. The parallel between that and Nazi ideology is not difficult to find.[19] However, as the Endecja split into mostly radical nationalist groups like the Radical-National Camp (ONR—Oboz Narodowo-Radykalny, founded in 1934) and groups even further to the right, an ever-stronger fascist tendency became apparent. The government party aimed at attracting the radicalized middle class, and the best way to do that was by radicalizing its anti-Jewish policy.

The influence of the Catholic Church was central. In the public mind, Catholicism was identified with Polishness despite the existence of small islands of Protestant and Orthodox communities. The two most important Catholic figures were the Catholic primate, Augustyn Cardinal Hlond, and the archbishop of Cracow, Prince Adam Sapieha. Both of them and most of the Polish clergy accepted the antisemitic policies of the government and its right-wing Endek critics. On February 29, 1936, Hlond declared it "a fact that the Jews fight against the Catholic Church, that they are free-thinkers, and constitute the vanguard of atheism, of the Bolshevik movement and of revolutionary activity. It is a fact that Jewish influence upon morals is fatal, and their publishers spread pornographic literature. It is true that the Jews are committing frauds, practicing usury and deal in white slavery." But, he said, "let us be just. Not all Jews are like that"; indeed, "it is not permissible to hate anyone. Not even Jews."[20] Such a contradictory and vile list of "facts" would be hard to match; they combine the anticapitalist and antisocialist images of Jews and imply that Jews were a satanic group of people, acting collectively and out to corrupt their gentile neighbors. Hlond's speech is a perfect example of radical, hateful antisemitism (you must not hate anyone, not "even Jews"), one that was accepted in the interwar years by a large percentage of Catholics, especially but not exclusively in Poland.[21]

Increasing poverty in the underclass and the lower middle class, together with other processes of modernization, caused a fairly radical political realignment of the Jewish population. At the beginning of the twentieth century and even in the early twenties, political orthodoxy, represented in the main by the Agudat Israel Party, was the major force on the Jewish political scene, fighting it out with the growing Zionist movement. In the thirties, both the orthodox and the Zionists suffered setbacks. Emigration to Palestine became less and less of a realistic option because the British Mandate, from 1935 on, strictly limited Jewish immigration and also because the Palestinian Jewish community would have been economically unable to absorb large numbers of immigrants into its population — in the late thirties, about half a million — in a half-colonial territory without any serious industrial development. Orthodoxy, for its part, had failed to improve the Jewish condition in Poland despite Agudat Israel's alliance with the government, which had guaranteed the party a preeminent position in many Jewish communities by recognizing Jewish communities as religious communities.[22]

The movement that gained from the relative failure of these two was the Bund.[23] During the thirties, the Bund gradually captured pluralities or majorities in the Jewish communities, especially in the major Jewish centers, Warsaw and Lodz (57 percent). By the end of 1938, the Bund controlled the Jewish community structures in both these cities—a paradoxical situation, for the supposed emphasis of the internal governance of Jewish communities was on organized religious life, and the Bund was fairly radically antireligious. According to one study, 38 percent of the Jews had voted for the Bund in local communal elections by early 1939, as compared to 36 percent for the mutually hostile Zionist factions and 23 percent for political orthodoxy.[24] We should not pay too much attention to the precise percentages, because many Jews did not vote in communal elections, and a number of communities were not included in the survey given a lack of sources. But the trend is clear: a decline in the influence of political orthodoxy and an increase in the power of the Bund. The decline of the influence of Zionism outside the kresy was especially marked: it was a total reversal of the trend in the twenties. The decline was due not only to the effective closing of Palestine. It was also due to the failure of Zionism to find solutions to the economic crisis of Polish Jewry, a failure accompanied by Jewish accommodation to Polish culture. Acculturation was a cul-de-sac because the vast majority of Poles did not accept Jews as part of their community or culture. As Ezra Mendelsohn says, this internal Jewish crisis was the result of "acculturation, economic decline, political divisiveness, [and] the failure of national autonomy and Zionism to solve the Jewish question."[25]

How much did orthodoxy decline? We should be careful not to overstate the case. The emphasis must be on *political* orthodoxy and not on social and behavioral norms. It is said that Jews who voted for the Bund went to *shul* (synagogue) on Saturday mornings, contributed to Zionist funds (the "blue boxes" through which money was collected to buy land for Jews in Palestine) at lunchtime, and demonstrated with the Bund against the rabbis in the afternoons. Most Jewish homes maintained kosher kitchens, whatever the politics of the household. Younger people naturally inclined toward socialism or socialist Zionism, or were indifferent to politics altogether. But most of them went to shul with their parents simply because that was the tradition and because the family stood together (often with great difficulty), especially in the trying circumstances of the thirties.

All these trends were reflected in the kresy. Yet there was a very important difference between the kresy and the rest of Poland. With the exception of Lwow, there was very little industry in the kresy, and consequently there was little in the way of a Jewish working class, the primary basis for membership in the Bund. On the other hand, it was in the kresy that the various Zionist parties and youth movements developed and strengthened their bases. This was especially significant in the area of education. Most shtetlach had Tarbut (Heb.: culture) grade schools, where classes were taught in Hebrew. Religious Zionists also founded a number of "Yavne" grade schools, named for the town in Roman Palestine where, after the destruction of the Second Temple in 70 CE, rabbinical Judaism had its origins. There were only a few Bund grade schools, where classes were taught in Yiddish. A minority of Jewish children—but more in the kresy than elsewhere—studied in these three types of schools, which were supported to a large extent by the Jews themselves. Others studied in Orthodox Talmudic schools and academies (*yeshivot*). Orthodox schools were organized in a network called Khorev (another name for Sinai), but the really innovative aspect was the existence of Orthodox schools for girls, the Beis Yankev (Heb.: Beit Ya'akov) schools, which in 1937 claimed to have 38,000 students. And yet Orthodox schools were declining in number, especially in the kresy. All Jewish schools together had only a minority of Jewish children, though a large minority; a majority of Jews sent their children to Polish governmental schools (*szkoły powszechnie*), sometimes to special governmental schools (*szabasówki*), which had provisions with respect to Shabbat and other Jewish holidays and which taught a minimum of Yiddish and Hebrew. (The szabasówki schools were slowly phased out, leaving just about sixty in existence in 1938.)

Education in Zionist grade schools—there were very few Jewish middle or high schools—was very important in that Zionist movements later found many adherents among that generation of young people. According to reports from a number of places, children spoke modern Hebrew on the streets of the shtet-lach.[26] We do have figures for 1935 for all of Poland: of a total of 523,852 Jewish children registered in various types of educational institutions, 343,671 studied in Polish schools, including the szabasówki. That means that two-thirds of Jewish children did not attend Jewish schools at all. Of the 180,181 children who studied in Jewish schools, the majority attended various types of ultra-orthodox religious schools—more than 100,000. Another 44,780 went to Tarbut schools and 15,923 to Yavne ones. The Bund schools—called CISHO (Yid.: Zentrale Yiddishe Shul-Organizacje—Central Jewish School Organization) schools, after the Bundist educational organization that ran them—had 14,486 attendees, and a smaller network of schools where classes were also taught in Yiddish had 2,343.[27] But, as we have seen, these figures do not reflect the situation in the kresy.

We do have some detailed figures for Volhynia, the center of Zionist influence in the kresy. There were forty Tarbut grade and four Tarbut secondary schools, two Yavne grade schools, two CISHO grade schools, and thirty-one orthodox establishments, including yeshivot. More than half the Jewish children went to Jewish grade schools, and of these, two-thirds went to Zionist schools.[28]

Despite the effectual closing of the gates of Palestine to mass immigration, then, Zionism remained the predominant political movement in the kresy. The Zionists, split as they were into factions, seldom united against their Bundist or orthodox opponents. The predominant Zionist faction, the General Zionists, was itself split between two contending groups, but the General Zionists declined in the thirties. The moderately left-of-center Poalei Zion (Workers of Zion, or Labor Zionists) gained many adherents in the crisis period of the thirties; the Mizrachi (East) religious Zionists were not far behind; and the right-wing Revisionists, who split off from the World Zionist Movement in 1935, gained members at the expense of the center and the left.[29] There are examples of these trends in the kresy. However, the Labor Zionists had less of an impact there than the General Zionists did, perhaps for the same reasons that prevented a significant presence of the Bund. Thus, in Baranowicze (Belorussian: Baranavichi), in the Belorussian area, the prewar community was governed by the General Zionists, and minorities voted for Poalei Zion, Mizrachi, Bund, and Agudat Israel. In Buczacz, the head of the community was Mendel Reich, a religious Zionist, but he faced a strong orthodox minority opposition and other, less important minority groups. In Ukrainian Rokitno, the head of the Jewish community was Aharon Slutzky, a General Zionist; the rabbi was a religious Zionist, a strong minority adhered to Poalei Zion, and practically no one owed allegiance to the Bund or Agudat Israel. A similar situation existed in Sarny, a railway hub not far from Rokitno, where Shmaryahu Gershonok, another General Zionist, was the head of the kahal, and minorities supported Agudat Israel and Poalei Zion. In Baranowicze, Sarny, and Buczacz (and elsewhere) there were also tiny underground groups of Jewish communists, who were persecuted not only by the Polish authorities but also by their fellow Jews. Very similar situations, with local variations, prevailed in practically all the shtetlach of the kresy.

The youth movements had a great deal of influence. It is difficult to find an exact parallel in other ethnic groups or nationalities to the youth movements of the Jews. They developed during the early stages of World War I and were greatly influenced by both the German youth movement Wandervogel, founded in 1896, and the Scouting movement, founded by Lord Robert Baden-Powell after the Boer War, in 1907. In their different ways, these movements emphasized the need for a return to nature and implicitly or explicitly expressed rebellion against the town-centered bourgeois life of members' parents. The English Scouting movement tried to harness these reactions in the service of traditional bourgeois values, but the German variant was much more oppositional, including in its sex education. Among Jews, the ideology of the gentile youth movements combined with the influence of a developing Zionism that strove for the self-definition of Jewish young people as members of a new generation that would seek a Jewish homeland in Palestine.

The first stirrings toward the formation of youth groups occurred in Austro-Hungarian Galicia in 1912–1913, and youth groups developed with the outbreak of war in 1914, mainly among Jewish refugees from Galicia in Vienna. Two groups combined, the Hashomer (The Guardian), and Tzeirei Zion (Zion's Youth), to form Hashomer Hatzair (Heb.: The Young Guardian), which was led, from its beginnings in 1913, by Meir Ya'ari (Wald), a young intellectual from Rzeszow, in West Galicia; the much more charismatic Yakov Chazan, whose family came from Brest-Litovsk, joined soon afterward, but the intellectual leadership remained with Ya'ari. Originally a national scouting movement with religious overtones, Hashomer Hatzair (HH) soon became radically socialist, and the Bolshevik revolution inspired a turn to Marxism. HH followed the Marxist-Zionist thinker Ber Borochov in its attempt to combine radical Marxist socialism (later Marxism-Leninism) with a national or nationalist agenda and a striving for a socialist Jewish homeland in Palestine. HH saw itself as an avant-garde movement that would establish collective settlements (*kibbutzim*) in Palestine as the basis for a socialist community, and it refused to be attached to any political party (until the early nineteen forties), unlike other Zionist youth movements.

Other youth movements quickly formed after HH, at first mainly left-wing ones. The poverty and hopelessness of the Jewish masses in interwar eastern Europe, especially in Poland, encouraged socialist ideologies. Hechalutz (Heb.: The Pioneer) originated in Russia and had to struggle against the anti-Zionism of the communist Soviet Union. Most of the original Russian-Jewish members, mostly in their late teens and early twenties, left for Palestine, were deported to labor camps in Siberia because of their Zionism, or abandoned their ideology and integrated into Soviet society. The movement reemerged in Poland. Hechalutz had the same basic ideology as HH, but in a less radical form. HH was much more ideological; it appealed to young intellectuals and to children of middle-class or even upper-class families; in many cases, the children were rebelling against their bourgeois parents. Hechalutz was more of a populist mass organization, mainly of youth in their twenties. Younger teenagers, mostly of the lower middle class, joined either of two movements: Hechalutz Hatzair (Heb.: The Young Pioneer), which emphasized Hebrew education, or Freiheit (Yid.: Freedom), which emphasized popular Yiddish Zionist culture. In 1938, the two youth movements combined to form Dror (Heb.: Freedom).

Hechalutz became, as early as the mid-twenties, an umbrella organization for socialist-Zionist youth movements because it was composed of slightly older members; and it developed into an umbrella organization for all center-to-left youth groups. HH, Hechalutz Hatzair, and Freiheit (and later Dror) belonged to Hechalutz, as did Gordonia and Akiva. Gordonia, named after Aharon David Gordon, an early Zionist pioneer, was a moderate, non-Marxist, social-democratic Zionist youth movement. Akiva, named after Rabbi Akiva, one of the great rabbinical authorities and a leader in the failed rebellion of Bar Kochba against the Romans in 135 CE, was even further to the center; it was a liberal youth movement with slightly religious overtones whose socialism was based on an interpretation of prophetic ethics.[30] Hechalutz was promoted and directed from Palestine by the Histadruth (Heb.: Organization), the Palestine Jewish Labor Movement. In 1935, Hechalutz claimed 58,800 members in Poland.[31] The left-wing movements were especially strong in the kresy, where they also had many of their agricultural training centers (*hachsharoth*), which prepared young people for emigration to Palestine.

The left-Zionist movements led to the rise of parallel groups. The rightist Betar movement was founded in 1923, inspired by the ideology of Ze'ev (Vladimir) Jabotinsky, founder and leader of the Revisionist Party, which advocated an antisocialist, nationalistic interpretation of Zionism. Betar became a mass movement of young people, vying for supremacy in Jewish communities with the left-wing Zionist groups. Religious Zionists, too, established their own youth movement, originally centered around two groups: the Hashomer Hadati (Heb.: The Religious Guardian) and the Tzeirei Mizrachi (Heb.: The Young Mizrachi). In Palestine, Bnei Akiva (The Sons of Akiva) filled the same role, and during World War II, with the destruction of the European organizations, it became the central youth movement. Its religious-socialist ideology had parallels in the various Christian social and Christian socialist movements that developed in different European countries. Like most of the other movements, Bnei Akiva was seen by adults as guaranteeing the future membership of a political party, in this case the party of the religious Zionists (the Mizrachi).

It is difficult, if not impossible, to estimate the strength of all the Zionist youth movements in eastern Europe in the interwar period. The number fluctuated considerably in response to economic and political crises. Prior to the outbreak of World War II, there may have been, roughly speaking, up to 100,000 teenagers in these movements in Poland and the Baltic States. All of the movements, with the exception of HH and Akiva, were attached to Zionist political parties. But the exception of HH is of some importance. HH members regarded the "adult" parties as untrustworthy representatives of bourgeois or petit-bourgeois values and saw themselves as revolutionaries not only in the political sense but in the social and educational senses as well. They came to advocate a strict commitment to emigration (Heb.: *Aliyah*, or "ascent") to Palestine and settlement there in kibbutzim as a practical way to live a socialist-Zionist life. They developed unique methods of socialist education, too, the result of which was social bonding. The culture of intense comradeship was of tremendous appeal. The other movements copied this approach to a greater or lesser extent. This bonding may partly explain the behavior of the alumni of these youth movements during the Holocaust, especially their prominent role in the Jewish resistance.

Non-Zionist and anti-Zionist Jewish political parties also organized youth movements, especially the Bund, whose youth branch, Tzukunft (Yid.: Future), was founded in Russia in 1923. After the elimination of the Bund by the communists in the Soviet Union, the Polish Bund fostered the development of the

Polish Tzukunft, which was influenced not so much by the Zionists as by the Soviet Komsomol (Communist Youth League) and the Polish (Catholic) Scouting movement, although Tzukunft also adopted some of the characteristics of its Zionist opponents. Tzukunft became a powerful organization and did not always accept the line of its parent organization, although it was seen as the base for the future of the party. Like the Zionist movements it, too, became an important influence on Jewish resistance during the Holocaust—in this case, resistance by the Bund.[32]

Nor could orthodoxy close its eyes to competition from the other movements, but its efforts to organize young followers were rather poor, and nothing resembling the other youth movements developed in non-orthodox surroundings.

In the aftermath of World War I, Jewish youth movements were not the only ones to flourish. I have already mentioned the Komsomol and the Polish Scout movement. There were mutual influences, some hostile, as between the Zionists and the Bundists, on the one hand, and the communists, on the other hand, and some friendly, as between the liberal Catholic wing of the Polish Scouts and the leftist Jewish movements, especially the HH. A peculiar friendship developed between these young, devout Catholics and the Marxist Zionists of the HH. During the Holocaust, one of the Polish Scout groups even served as the messengers and contact persons for the armed Jewish resistance in central Poland and the Vilno ghetto.

A number of the Jewish youth movements were either founded in the kresy or had very strong bases there, and their influence was felt very strongly indeed in the kresy shtetlach in the thirties. The parents were not necessarily enthused by the prospect of their children leaving for Zionist hachsharoth, where they were trained for agricultural labor and sometimes in crafts. The young people yearned to leave for Palestine, and for many parents, who depended on their children for economic survival, this foreboded personal and family disaster. In the end, however, many parents supported their children, and thus the children's ideological and political influence became an important factor in the outlook of the adult Jewish population of the shtetlach. And when the closing of Palestine to Jewish immigration forced many of the graduates of the hachsharoth to return to their families, they found that the hard life in the training centers had prepared them for their families' everyday struggle for existence.

Help from abroad became extremely important for the survival of Polish Jewry in the thirties. An estimated 12–14 percent of the budgets of Jewish communities and organizations came from abroad, whether from social organizations or from private sources, and mainly, of course, from the United States.[33] Without that help, many would have starved.

The overall picture of Jewish life in interwar Poland shows us a Poland that, while not exactly what today would be called a failed state, was in some ways not dissimilar to one. Certainly, it had a functioning bureaucracy, a legal system, law and order enforcement, a large, though antiquated, army; tax collection, and a press that, though under strict censorship laws, was able much of the time to say most of what it wanted. The government functioned, but it was in constant trouble. Poland faced economic, social, and political crises. Its rulers did not really address—and therefore were unable to solve—the main economic and social problem: attracting enough capital, internal or external, to induce an industrialization that, together with an extensive agrarian reform, might have led to the urbanization of the surplus agrarian population—and might possibly have created a vibrant middle class. To us today, it seems that the standard of living could have been raised only in the wake of such developments. Forward-looking policies might have changed the social structure, radically reducing the power of the landowning magnates and the descendants of the gentry (*szlachta*), and with it the centrality of the military, whose officers came from this class. The predominance of exclusivist nationalism, which was based on a no-longer-viable system of social stratification, prevented such reforms and precluded a settlement of the main internal political problem: the national minorities. Dealing with them justly or even-handedly might possibly have provided a balance between the cultural predominance of Polish culture and equal rights and equal opportunities for the minorities. This was the line that Pilsudski tried to implement, but he failed.

The Jews, as a non-territorial minority, were the hardest hit by the failures of the Polish state. Traditional Christian-Catholic antisemitism provided a basis on which the newer nationalistic and increasingly racist variety of Jew-hatred became a central theme in internal Polish politics. The Jews had no way out. They could not emigrate, and their allies among the Polish population were too weak to help. It would be too much to say that there was a Holocaust before the Holocaust, but the Holocaust in Poland was possibly easier for the Germans to implement because the Jews were an oppressed and increasingly vulnerable population, often intensely disliked by their Polish neighbors, before the first German soldier ever crossed the border. In addition, we must remember that all Jewish populations everywhere, certainly in modern times but arguably also before, were factionalized and divided. Nowhere in Europe was there a united Jewish community; there were split and quarrelling Jewish communities, but no effective central representatives, not even in Britain, where a Board of Deputies of British Jews had been founded in the eighteenth century; by the thirties, many Jews were not affiliated with the board. The same applied to the Consistoire, supposedly the highest Jewish authority in France—by the thirties, a majority of Jews in France did not belong to it. In Poland, with the Jews divided between orthodoxy, Bundism, and Zionism, there was no real chance of a united stand. A divided, impoverished, discriminated against, and persecuted minority in a state structure in deep crisis—that was the picture.

The following story is illustrative. Throughout the thirties, the JDC had tried to persuade Polish Jewish groups to establish a central welfare and social organization to, at a minimum, distribute the funds supplied by American Jewry. But Agudat Israel would not cooperate with the Zionists, the Bund would not even dream of collaborating with the religious or Zionist bourgeoisie, and the Zionists could never agree among themselves what to do. The JDC persisted. In the end, after tortuous negotiations, a compromise was reached under the leadership of certain benevolent Jewish industrialists, mainly from Lodz. Two individuals were especially active, a manufacturer named Karol Sachs and a banker named Raphael Szereszewski. A cable was sent to the European head office of the JDC, triumphantly announcing that a committee for social work representing all three main Jewish political groups had been set up. The date of the cable was September 2, 1939, one day after the Germans invaded Poland.[34]

As for the kresy, not all of this applied. Statistically, there were no great differences between shtetlach in the kresy and Jewish communities elsewhere in Poland, but the social reality was different. In memoir after memoir, we can read about well-ordered houses, a normal existence, functioning welfare, a lively cultural and religious life, and the usual bickering between political parties, groups, and individuals. There are no reports of hunger, although there were soup kitchens for the poorest people. The poverty in the kresy was harsh enough, but it was not the grinding poverty of the slums of Warsaw and Lodz, where real hunger was a frequent visitor. Since the testimonies of survivors overwhelmingly reflect the life of the middle or upper-middle class, they have to be used with caution. Typically, they say that the father was a merchant or an owner of a carpentry shop, or that he owned forests or orchards, or that he owned and operated a flour mill or a dairy. Occasionally he was a lawyer, the town rabbi, or a schoolteacher. Seldom do we hear from someone whose father was a shoemaker or a tailor, even though these were the main professions in the shtetl. Even more rarely is the father a peddler, but we know that a high percentage of Jews lived by peddling wares in the villages surrounding the shtetl. Shtetl households observing the Orthodox way of life, where the husband studied the Torah and the wife took care of the family, became scarce.

People from slightly wealthier families remember a happy childhood with caring parents, school, youth movement activities, and so on. Childhood for these middle-class children—most of our witnesses were either children or young people—was good and pleasant. The heavy feeling of hopelessness that was prevalent among Jews appears only indirectly in their testimonies. Where the writers report about others, we also learn of the fear of antisemitism, and the lack of a perceived future. There was no easy way to escape the shtetl, and almost everyone wanted to escape, including those who were better-off. Life was restricted to a small place. We have a mix of contradictory expressions to make sense of. The picture that emerges is of communities struggling for their existence in difficult circumstances but reacting with a strong feeling of solidarity despite the constant quarrels and disagreements; of people with a strong family consciousness and a devotion to Jewish life and culture. Religion was important—young people may not have believed in it very much anymore, but rituals gave a sense of groundedness, of permanence, which was essential to survive in the kresy of the late thirties.

Newspapers were read everywhere in the kresy, and they reported the growing threat from Germany. People were afraid of war, but they were influenced by the propaganda of the Polish authorities and thought that Poland would withstand a German onslaught. The Jews would defend Poland, of course—after all, the alternatives were the Nazis or the communists. People served in the army without shirking, despite the rampant antisemitism there. Yet quite a number of testimonies indicate a gnawing sense of insecurity, of fear, behind the façade of trust in the heroic Polish armed forces.

Then Nazi Germany invaded Poland, and the world as they knew it collapsed.

Three

The Soviet Occupation

The twenty-one months of Soviet rule could be considered the last stage of existence of the *shtetl.*

—*Ben-Cion Pinchuk*

The Ribbentrop-Molotov agreement between Germany and the USSR of August 23, 1939, and its supplementary secret protocol of September 28, determined the areas that the Soviets annexed after they invaded Poland on September 17. By then, the Polish army had in effect been defeated by the Germans, so Polish resistance to the Soviets was unorganized, sporadic, and ineffective where it occurred at all. The area occupied by the Soviets included what are now western Belarus, western Ukraine, and the Bialystok district (today in Poland). Neither the predominantly ethnic Polish areas of that district nor the area outside Vilno, then a predominantly Polish city surrounded by a Lithuanian countryside, are included in our examination of Jewish life. This area (without Bialystok and Vilno) is what I am calling here the kresy.

The Soviet leadership apparently did not wish to control areas that were ethnically mainly Polish but instead saw annexation of the predominantly Belorussian and Ukrainian provinces as the abrogation of what it regarded as the imposed treaty of Riga of 1921, which gave these lands to Poland. According to Polish official figures of 1931, which are probably not very reliable, 13,199,000 people lived in the area, of whom 4,125,000 are said to have been Ukrainians, 1,123,000 Belorussians, 1,108,000 Jews, and 5,274,000 Poles. Other sources put the number of Jews at 1,175,000 or 1,309,000 (see previous chapter). The USSR ceded Vilno and its immediate surroundings to Lithuania in October 1939, and after that cession, there were some 420,000 Jews in the northern Belorussian areas, not counting the refugees from German-occupied Poland. This would leave somewhat fewer than 1,000,000 Jews in the Ukrainian areas—plus the refugees from German-occupied Poland. The number of Poles in the whole of the kresy is probably exaggerated, and the Polish government-in-exile estimated it, more realistically, to have been about roughly 4.5 million (30 percent) of the total population. However imprecise, these figures do provide an approximation of the demographic structure of the kresy.[1]

On and after September 17, with the disintegration of Polish rule and prior to the arrival of Soviet troops in all the towns and villages, there was a period of chaos that differed in length in different places: sometimes a few days passed before the arrival of the Soviets, and sometimes just a few hours. In some places the Polish authorities were still in charge when the Soviets came. In this very brief transition period, some of the local population, especially in the Ukrainian areas, tried to use the lack of efficient administration to loot, in the main Jewish property, and sometimes even to kill. General looting, also by Jews, also occurred in some places. Polish troops, frustrated and furious at the defeat of their country, also occasionally robbed Jews and killed them. Whether anti-Jewish pogroms were permitted to happen depended on the local leadership. In Krzemieniec, in Volhynia, for instance, the Soviets came as late as September 22. Local Ukrainians tried to loot Jewish shops, but the Ukrainian school principal recruited and armed teachers and prevented a pogrom.[2] In Grodno, Belorussia, a large town with 25,000 Jews prior to 1939, about thirty Jews were killed in a pogrom before the Soviets entered. Another pogrom occurred in Ivje, a shtetl near Nowogrodek, with 3,000 Jews.[3] In the shtetl of Zborow (Ukr.: Zboriv), in East Galicia, which probably had fewer than 5,000 Jews in 1939, the Ukrainians tried to instigate a pogrom, but a small group of Jews, armed with one handgun and a knife, organized to resist them; the Jews had a siren sound off, the pogromists feared some kind of military force would oppose them, and they fled. The Soviets arrived the next day.[4] In Dereczin, in the north, which had about 2,000 Jews before the war, Poles—it is unclear whether the Polish army or local people—tried to organize a pogrom, but the local, presumably Catholic priest prevented this from happening.[5]

The Soviet aim had always been a united Ukraine and a united Belarus under communist control: "national in form and socialist in content." The large Polish minority in these areas was a political problem for them. Not so the Jews. Roughly 10 percent of the population were Jews, originally some 1.2 million (a compromise between the figures quoted above), but as a result of the German occupation of western and central Poland, somewhere between 300,000 and 350,000

Jewish refugees, but possibly very many more, arrived in the kresy.[6] From the perspective of Moscow, the enemy was not these Jews but the Poles, the former rulers, so they directed the terror and oppression mainly against the Polish population. Political Sovietization proceeded at breakneck speed, and on November 1 and 2, 1939, respectively, the Ukrainian and the Belorussian areas were accepted—at the "unanimous request" of the inhabitants—into the "family" of the Soviet Union.

The purpose of the Soviet leadership was to make these areas into integral parts of the USSR as quickly as possible. Having the people in the newly acquired areas adapt to a communist-directed society was one aim of the Soviet policy of speedy and radical transformation, but it is fairly certain that fear of Germany contributed to it. The Soviets probably wanted to eliminate any potential internal threats to the new regime that could be utilized by a foreign enemy. Since the official ideological motivation for the occupation was the "liberation" of the "downtrodden" Ukrainian and Belorussian masses from the oppression of the Polish capitalist and landowning classes, and their unification with the already "liberated" socialist nationalities of Ukraine and Belarus, the emphasis was on courting those ethnic groups rather than Poles or Jews. Poles—the deposed rulers, the enemies—had no territorial center in the USSR, and their natural link with the Polish people in what was now German-occupied territory made them into a suspect ethnic group almost a priori. Since, moreover, the administration and officialdom in the area had been almost exclusively in Polish hands, the whole weight of the Soviet terror regime fell primarily on Poles. Yet Poles were a recognized Soviet nationality. They were, at least in theory, entitled to representation, Soviet style, as well as to schools and cultural activities—provided, of course, that they were "proletarians" or peasants, had no record of any anti-Soviet attitude or activity, and were willing to cooperate; in fact, though, large numbers of Poles were later deported simply because they were members of a potentially disloyal ethnicity.

The Jews were in a worse position from that point of view: they were culturally, linguistically, religiously, and ethnically foreign, non-Slavic, and, on top of everything else, socially and economically representative of the capitalist society that the Soviets wanted to replace. The majority of the Jewish people were living outside the USSR, dispersed in capitalist countries. They had no territory of their own, and the artificial Soviet attempt to establish one, in Birobidjan on the Manchurian border, was not successful.[7] As a group, they did not meet most of the conditions for national identity that Stalin had established as early as 1913: a distinct language, a territory, an economic community, and a community of culture. They fulfilled only the last condition.

Contradictory policies regarding the Jews had been followed since the October Revolution of 1917. To propagate communism among the Soviet Jews, most of whom spoke Yiddish, and to counteract Bundist and Zionist tendencies among them, a special Jewish section (*Evsektsia*) of the Soviet Communist Party was set up. In the twenties, Yiddish culture was fostered—among other things, as a counter to Hebrew, which was identified as nationalistic and allied with capitalistic ideology. A new form of Yiddish was introduced—a phonetic form that eliminated the many Hebraisms in the Yiddish language. In the initially large number of Yiddish primary schools—few Yiddish high schools and no Yiddish universities were permitted—mention of Jewish history was either forbidden or distorted, and education was strictly atheistic and consequently violently antireligious. Only certain approved classic authors of Yiddish literature were taught, those who had criticized Jewish life in the nineteenth and early twentieth centuries. That Yiddish schools existed and that contemporary Yiddish authors wrote a number of wonderful literary works in the Soviet environment seemed, nonetheless, to promise some kind of continuation of Jewish life. From the late twenties on, the Jewish "national" settlement in Birobidjan was touted as a solution for those Soviet Jews who wanted to create a Jewish nationality. The contradiction was this: contrary to the ideology propagated by both Lenin and Stalin, who had advocated the end of the Jewish nation, or ethnicity, by assimilation, the authorities in fact treated the Jews as a separate nationality, and Jews had their nationality written into internal Soviet passports.

From the early thirties on, the trend became unmistakable: a return to the original Leninist ideology that saw the Jews as members of a dying ethnic group and worked toward their assimilation into the non-Jewish environment. Toward the end of the thirties, the number of Yiddish schools decreased radically, and Jewish cultural life became more and more constricted, although at the same time persecution of antisemitism in most of its forms remained quite real. The regime was trying to eliminate, as far as possible, all ethnic confrontations and mutual hatreds in order to maintain stability. Ideology dictated an internationalism where, in an increasingly classless society, national problems would die away; supposedly such problems could exist only in a capitalist environment. In practice, Russian nationalism underlay much of internal communist politics.

Soviet policies vis-à-vis the Jews in the kresy unfolded later. At the beginning, Soviet troops that came to occupy the region were welcomed, in many cases enthusiastically, by the Jews. Let me immediately add—not only by the Jews: "Throughout the western Ukraine and western Belarus, in hamlets, villages, and towns, the Red Army was welcomed by smaller or larger, but in any case visible, friendly crowds."[8] In late September, the Polish High Command, its army defeated and retreating to the Romanian border, issued an order to Polish troops in the kresy not to resist the Soviets. Many Poles welcomed the Soviet troops because, among other things, they would protect them from the Belorussians and especially from the Ukrainians. In a some places in East Galicia and Volhynia, Polish officials came out to welcome the Soviets.[9] Other Poles, particularly the poor, thought their lot would improve under communist rule.

The Belorussians saw the Soviets as liberators, and there are reports, especially from the Nowogrodek region, of pogroms by Belorussian peasants against Polish landowners and gentry, and it is claimed that some of the gentry sought refuge with local Jews.[10] A Belorussian political party, which was to all intents and purposes a communist front organization, the Belorussian Peasant and Workers Party (Bel.: Hramada, "Party"), had been active before 1939 and had gained many poor-peasant adherents in an area where illiteracy was widespread, so that sympathy for the Soviets certainly existed.[11]

Ukrainian peasants and a minority of Ukrainian communists, especially in Volhynia, also welcomed the Soviets with bread and salt and banners, sometimes Ukrainian flags, and even crosses.[12] But—let there be no doubt—the Jews were particularly relieved at the sight of the Soviet troops. The main reasons are not far to seek. First, the alternative to Soviet occupation was German rule, and by mid-September 1939, Jews realized that German rule meant violent persecution and terrible suffering, although what we now know as the Holocaust was far from people's imagination. The Germans had occupied some Polish areas, which were then handed over to the Soviets, in accordance with the demarcation of the new borders; in many of those places, the Germans had acted against the local Jews with brutality and sadism and had killed hundreds. In Luboml, a town in Volhynia, the Germans committed atrocities during the brief period before they handed the town over to the Soviets. In Sokal, in Galicia, they tortured the head of the community and forced the town rabbi to dance naked in front of his congregation. In Augustow, in the Bialystok region, they shot dozens of Jews. Mass murder took place in Przemysl, a large town straddling the border between the German and the Soviet areas—it had some 19,400 Jews in 1939—and the local rabbi was killed.[13]

In opposite cases, when Soviets handed over places that were to be occupied by the Germans, they took with them many Jews who feared German occupation.[14] In fact, when these frontier adjustments took place in the southern regions, Jews moved with the Soviets eastward, whereas many Ukrainians moved with the Germans westward.[15] As Jews fled into Soviet-occupied territory, they told their stories to local Jews, so these now knew what they could expect from the Germans. "The Germans would not enter, and that was the most important of all."[16]

But according to some testimonies, the local Jewish population disbelieved the stories the refugees told about German behavior.[17] Many Ukrainians, on the contrary, saw the Germans as the prospective supporters of an independent Ukraine, whereas others, probably a minority, saw the Soviets as liberators from oppressive Polish rule—they believed this despite stories about the deaths by starvation of millions of Ukrainians (*holodomor,* "death by hunger") in the Soviet Ukraine in 1932–1933, stories that had filtered into eastern Poland. In the end, for many Ukrainians, German occupation was preferable to Soviet rule. Belorussians reacted differently: their national consciousness was very much undeveloped, and their relations with Russians had always been good.

The second reason that the Jews welcomed the Soviets so enthusiastically was because they remembered the years of Polish misgovernment and discrimination, the cold and haughty Polish bureaucracy, governmental persecution, antisemitism, and economic boycott. Polish politicians and ideologues later accused the Jews of the kresy—and, by association, all Jews—of betraying Poland in its hour of need, of identifying with the Soviet oppressors. This became the main ideological line of Polish nationalists toward the Jews during World War II both in Poland itself and in the Polish government–in-exile in London; it is repeated in Polish historiography, journalism, and literature to this day.[18] The problem with this argument is that from the perspective of most Jews, interwar Poland was an oppressive regime and could hardly demand loyalty from its badly treated Jewish population. Polish antisemitism did not abate under Soviet occupation—quite the contrary. Anti-Jewish stereotypes and exaggerations persisted; for instance, the Polish underground sent a violently antisemitic report to the Polish authorities in exile on December 8, 1939, accusing the Jews of no less than persecuting the Poles.[19]

Very soon after many Poles had welcomed the Soviets, the mood changed, and from the Polish perspective, the Soviets were just as much an enemy as the Germans. From the Jewish perspective, Nazi Germany was life-threatening, whereas the Soviet Union was merely oppressive. It had some positive aspects, and they could live with it, with some difficulty, despite its destruction of Jewish national culture. In Rowne, Volhynia, a Jew was quoted as saying, "I know who the Bolsheviks are. I know they'll take my property, but I know they will leave me with my life."[20] Another said, "We knew what the Zionist movement could expect from the Soviet regime; we knew it would close the way to Eretz Israel [Palestine] for us, but we also knew that it first of all promised us our lives and, therefore, . . . the whole town came to greet them with flowers."[21] The Zionist leader Moshe Kleinbojm (later, in Palestine: Sneh) quoted a Jew he met in the kresy after the danger of German occupation had passed who had the same reaction: "Until now, we were condemned to death; now our death sentence has been commuted to life imprisonment."[22] Jewish disappointment with the Soviets became more marked, especially among the adult population, as time went on. That feeling is captured by Mendel Sroul from Lutsk, Volhynia—a town with some 18,000 Jews in 1939—whose opinion on being "liberated" by the Soviets was, "I'd rather pass on such a 'liberation,' and I beg of them not to try it on me anymore."[23] Another firsthand witness later said, "The Jews received the Soviet Russians indifferently. Some of them were afraid. It wasn't what we had wanted."[24] This last statement expresses fairly exactly the view of the Jewish survivors of the Soviet regime when the war ended, but not necessarily the view of Jews immediately upon Soviet occupation.

Triumphal arches were set up for the Soviet troops in many shtetlach—not only by Jews, but the Jews were prominent—and flowers were showered on them. In the shtetl of Kovel, Volhynia (13,900 Jews in 1939), Jews "celebrated all night" prior to the Soviet entry and then "greeted [the Red Army] with indescribable enthusiasm."[25] In Baranowicze, in the north (9,000 Jews in 1939), "people kissed the soldiers' dirty boots." In Slonim, also in the north (22,000 Jews in 1939), Jews reportedly said, "The main thing is that we escaped the predatory claws of the Nazi beasts at the very last moment."[26]

If the poorer and younger elements were inclined to be enthusiastic at the arrival of the Soviets, the older and more settled people were considerably less so.[27] Most Jews were, as one acute observer put it, "an impoverished stratum of self-employed craftsmen and tradesmen."[28] Some accepted Soviet propaganda against capitalists and (Polish) bureaucrats; some were skeptical.[29] After a short while, the Soviets recruited volunteers to work in the interior of the Soviet Union, especially in mines and factories in the Donbas and the Caucasus. They promised excellent conditions. Thousands of Jews (possibly 30,000 or as many as 40,000), especially among the refugees, agreed to go and work there.[30] But many tried to come back—the conditions were terrible, nothing came of the promises, and the treatment they received was abominable. Those who managed to return were no longer supporters of the regime.[31]

Many Jews were surprised at the initially excellent behavior of the Soviet troops—they were friendly and polite, and they loved children—for the older generation still remembered the brutal behavior of the Russian troops in World War I. Jewish communists, though few in number, became prominent in the transition to Soviet rule.[32] The Soviet authorities set up workers' committees, on which there were many Jews, to establish control over towns and villages. In Lubcz, in the north, where Jews were a majority, Jews filled all public posts, from chair of the municipality (called the "soviet") to clerks in all the retail shops.[33]

This pattern was repeated in other shtetlach. But in some of these places, the Jews were immediately replaced by non-Jews, as, for instance, in the larger town of Lutsk, where the Jewish mayor was demoted and a Ukrainian from the east took his place.[34] Similarly, in Krzemieniec, Volhynia (8,000 Jews in 1939), the Soviets nominated a Jewish mayor (Moshe Sugan) but quickly replaced him with a Ukrainian.[35] In some places, even where there were clear Jewish majorities, non-Jews were appointed as mayors.[36] Yet Jews joined or set up militias (local police) before or immediately following the Soviet occupation.[37] In some Galician and Volhynian localities Jews accounted for up to 70 percent of the militia membership.[38] These militias confiscated major enterprises and arrested many Polish officials. But the Soviets themselves, mainly the secret police—the NKVD—and the new administration, moved cautiously at first, ordering shops to remain open and their merchandise to be prominently displayed; artisans were to continue their work.

In some respects, Soviet policies toward the Jews were no different from the parallel policies toward the other ethnicities. Immediately upon occupation, banks and industrial establishments were nationalized and all ethnic communal institutions were abolished, as were all political parties and youth movements. Voluntary societies and institutions were eliminated more slowly, during the first few months of the new regime. But all this was not necessarily done by regulations or orders. As far as the Jews were concerned—and the situation of the other nationalities was not very different—only minimal coercion was used. Instead, "communal and cultural life ceased by itself." "Everything vanished as if by itself." Even before the authorities had published a single decree, "the entire structure collapsed of its own."[39] There was no actual decree to abolish the Jewish community, the kahal, it just dissolved and disappeared.[40] The same thing happened with political parties and movements. In the Ukrainian areas, "all political activities of the Jewish parties ceased by themselves. No official prohibition of their activities was pronounced."[41]

The Soviets encountered no difficulty in recruiting Jewish informers; some people were more than willing to denounce other Jews for real or supposed anti-Soviet behavior or simply for having been active in Bundist, Zionist, or religious activities under the previous regime. As a matter of fact, informing on others became something of a profession.[42] As in Nazi Germany, even family members sometimes informed on each other. The old elites—the political and communal leaders, the "bourgeois" intellectuals, and also leaders of the socialist parties, such as the Bund and the Poalei Zion—were removed. The most prominent were arrested, people like Wiktor Alter and Henryk Erlich, leaders of the Bund, who had fled from Warsaw, and leaders of the Zionist parties. Some of those arrested, as well as some prominent wealthy entrepreneurs, were deported to Siberia very early on. Many others became laborers, served as experts in their former establishments, or fled or were evicted and found refuge in outlying villages.[43] Some managed to flee before they could be apprehended, and tried, often successfully, to hide in isolated places. Unlike the elites of the other ethnicities, however, who also were removed from their former positions, Jewish leaders were not replaced. In Ukrainian and Belorussian communities, Ukrainian or Belorussian communists or newfound sympathizers took the place of officials and others who had been removed. But Jewish communal and organized life ceased completely; the old elite was not replaced because there were no communities anymore.

Most communist or pro-communist Jews who at first occupied important positions in the new administrations in the larger and the smaller towns were replaced, after being dismissed or demoted, by Ukrainians and Belorussians, sometimes even Poles. The Soviet authorities preferred Poles to Jews, provided they showed real or pretended pro-Soviet sympathies. On October 6, 1939, "elections" were held to the Belorussian and Ukrainian National Assemblies in the newly occupied regions. The majorities in the assemblies had to belong to these nationalities, but others, to a limited degree, could also take seats. Among the 926 people "elected" to the Belorussian National Assembly, there were 127 Poles (13 percent), who had to participate in the unanimous "request" for the newly occupied area to be absorbed into the Soviet Union. Only 72 Jews (7 percent) were accorded that honor, although about 10 percent of the local population were Jews. The Poles thus "elected" were permitted to address the authorities in Moscow in Polish. Yiddish was not permitted to be used. Among the 1,495 assembly members in western Ukraine, only 20 were Jews, proportionately only a fraction of their number in the general population. The authorities chose the "representatives" for these assemblies, and some very odd things happened as a result. For some reason, Communist Party officials decided that a Jew should represent the shtetl of Kleck (Yid.: Kletsk), in the north (4,000 Jews in 1939). They picked a local man by the name of Joseph Frenkel, who had the right proletarian pedigree and had not been a member of another political movement. But it so happened that he had a major fault: he had studied the Bible and the Talmud. However, once the decision had been made, he was pressured to accept the nomination. He demurred—he was not fit for that honor, he was sick; in other words, he tried to get out of it. In the end, he was nominated. Then local communists protested. How could a person who had studied religion become a member of the assembly? (Stalin had studied at an Orthodox seminary for priests, but that was Stalin, after all.) The party hacks relented—and Frenkel was released from his "job," the public excuse being that he was not healthy.[44] In the town of Rokitno, Volhynia

(2,500–3,000 Jews in 1939), the Soviets picked Mushka Schuster, the half-literate wife of Yehoshua Schuster, a very poor construction worker who was eking out a living working half-time. The couple lived in a backyard hovel. Despite Mushka's protests, she was "elected," sent to Lwow to participate in the charade of the West Ukrainian assembly, and then sent home. When the Germans came, Ukrainian antisemites accused her of being a communist, and she was murdered.[45]

After completion of the various "election" campaigns, after Belorussia and Ukraine were officially annexed, and after the people selected to serve in the Belorussian and Ukrainian Soviets, or chambers of "representatives," most of the leading positions in the new, very large bureaucracy were occupied by easterners (*vostochniki*): Ukrainians, Belorussians, and Russians brought in from the "old" Soviet Union. The Soviets did not trust the locals.

The same process occurred in the educational sphere. Hebrew schools were abolished after a very short transitional period, as were religious schools. The whole large network of Jewish schools underwent a radical transformation: some schools became Yiddish schools, teaching in Soviet Yiddish, as did many former religious institutions, and others became schools teaching in Belorussian, Russian, or Ukrainian. According to the Soviet Constitution, parents could decide what language should be used in the schools their children attended. In fact, Soviet educational propagandists appeared at parents' meetings and "suggested" this or that solution. In almost all cases these suggestions were followed. Often teachers who had for years taught in Hebrew in a Zionist spirit became ardent propagandists for Stalin and the Soviet Union. The alternative for them personally was dismissal or worse. At first, Yiddish schools were favored over Slavic-language schools. There are many examples: in Zhetl (Bel.: Dyatlovo), in the north (4,000 Jews in 1939), the Hebrew school became a Belorussian school, but the Yiddish school remained.[46] In East Galicia, for reasons that are not quite clear, there was a flowering of Yiddish schools—69 existed in 1940—whereas there were only 34 in Volhynia. In these Ukrainian areas, altogether 45,000 students studied in Yiddish schools. In the Belorussian region, there were even more—197 schools. But in 1940 the policy changed: it became clear that the authorities intended the Jews to assimilate, and Yiddish schools were gradually eliminated. By May 1941, only 134 Yiddish schools remained in western Belorussia, among them four secondary schools in Bialystok.[47] By that time, the pressure to close came not just from the Soviet authorities but from many parents, who realized that by sending their children to Yiddish schools, they were foreclosing on the prospect of higher education for them; to attend universities and colleges, children had to have attended Ukrainian or Belorussian schools, or preferably Russian ones. Many Jewish parents now sent their children to such schools. This kind of behavior can be seen as typical of the Jewish minority, perhaps also of other minorities—namely, an attempt to adjust to the whims and policies of the ruling power in order to survive economically and socially. Adjusting is what Jews had been doing since Emancipation (the granting of equal citizenship status to Jews), at the end of the eighteenth century, in all the capitalist countries of their residence: accommodating their language, dress, and customs to the majority population while keeping certain elements of cultural separateness.

Was there any kind of resistance to this elimination of Jewish education? Yes. There was sporadic resistance by the pupils, which was sometimes directed against the teachers, who, under heavy pressure, switched from teaching Hebrew and religion to the Stalinist version of education. Yiddish schools taught Stalinist propaganda in the de-Hebraized version of the Yiddish language; Jewish history and most Yiddish—and all Hebrew—literature were no longer mentioned, never mind taught. In a number of places, students rebelled. In Rokitno, no Jewish children came to classes on Yom Kippur, October 1939, the Day of Atonement, the most important Jewish religious holiday, a day of fasting; then, when forced, they came without books or food. But a year later, in October 1940, the former religious teacher yielded to overwhelming pressure and came to school with a sandwich to eat and denounced Orthodoxy and Zionism, both of which he had been teaching all his working life.[48] In Czortkow, East Galicia, "many members of the youth movements changed their ideology and joined the Komsomol," the communist youth group.[49] In Wlodzimierz (Ukr.: Volodymyr; Yid.: Ludmir), young people organized Bible classes and studied Jewish history on their own.[50] Young people also tried to rescue books when the authorities clamped down on libraries, including school libraries, and confiscated "antirevolutionary" material, such as religious texts, Zionist and Bundist books, and literary works that did not fit in with the Stalinist concept of popular culture.[51] They stole as many of such books as possible. But all these attempts at cultural resistance occurred at the beginning of Soviet rule and died down within months. On the whole, the Soviets managed to force their system of education on the Jewish public without much trouble. By the summer of 1940, their victory was complete.

The Soviet Constitution did not prohibit religious observance; synagogues could, in theory, remain open. But synagogues had to pay very heavy taxes, and rabbis had to pay exorbitant income taxes as well. Antireligious propaganda was ubiquitous, and religious books could not be sold; they were considered religious propaganda, which was forbidden. Religious texts and books were taken out of libraries and destroyed. Very few churches closed: it was much easier to deal with the Jewish minority than with Ukrainians, Belorussians, and Poles. Jewish religious observance became a private affair, circumcision was practiced in private, marriages were consecrated in backrooms and then registered in the relevant governmental offices, and Jewish holidays became ordinary workdays. Schoolchildren had to attend school on the Shabbat, and write, which was against Orthodox prescription. On the main Jewish holidays the authorities provided special entertainment programs to prevent Jewish children from practicing traditional customs. In a number of places, synagogues became, initially at least, centers for voluntary social welfare. Parcels were brought there to be distributed among the very poor, and for a while, until well into 1940, these centers were maintained by remnants of local programs.[52] In the end, they closed as well.[53] Most synagogues become clubs, cinemas, storage places, and the like.[54] Many Jews abandoned religious observances and customs, except, interestingly, for *kashrut*, the dietary laws, because these could be maintained in the privacy of the home. The young generation did not observe even that, by and large.

So: a rich ethnic and religious tradition, which had developed into a distinct culture over many centuries, collapsed like a house of cards within a few weeks of the establishment of totalitarian rule. There was not even token civil resistance; there was very little opposition—basically, only a small minority of teenagers and very elderly people put up a fight—and there were no (public) complaints. Only some synagogues remained open, and they were frequented by older people, for the most part, not young people. The Soviets did not have to use coercion because the communities and communal organizations folded. Can totalitarian regimes eradicate cultures that easily? This is a frightening and worrying thought. Or was the Soviet regime special and unusual? After all, Jewish communal life and Jewish organizations continued to exist for quite a while even in Nazi Germany. But the puzzle is even more complicated, because when the twenty-one months of Soviet rule were over and the Germans arrived, the Jewish communities were quickly reorganized, though on a completely different basis. The leaders who had managed to hide out or find work that satisfied the Soviet authorities, and had therefore not been deported, returned to head the communities under the new German occupiers. Had the old communities been submerged, somehow continuing to exist until later resurrection, or were they completely destroyed, only to be replaced by something entirely new under the Germans?

Let us consider the scandalously easy way the communist regime destroyed an ancient civilization so speedily and effortlessly. How can we explain it? And how can we explain the meekness of the Jewish response, especially when we compare it with the unarmed and armed resistance in many of these shtetlach during the period of annihilation that followed?

I can offer a number of hypothetical answers. One of them is that the Soviets brought new perspectives for the Jews, especially for the young among them. First and foremost, they drove antisemitism underground and were quite serious in their efforts to eliminate interethnic animosities to assure domestic peace and quiet.[55] Often, naturally enough, Jews were emboldened to act against antisemitic behavior. Thus, in Wolkowysk (Volkovysk), Belorussia (probably around 4,000 Jews), the retreating Polish troops staged a pogrom, killing seven Jews, prior to the arrival of the Red Army. When the Soviets arrived, a seventy-year-old Jew armed himself, arrested the chief local instigator of the pogrom, and handed him over to the new authorities. In Rozyszcze, Volhynia (fewer than 4,000 Jews), Jews helped to free a Pole who had helped Jews from an NKVD prison.[56] A possible second explanation for the collapse of Jewish communities is that the Soviets opened new employment prospects to Jews. Now, Jews could become government officials, members of the militia, and experts, managers, and workers in industries that had been closed to them under Polish rule. Free education was suddenly available for all. Jews could study freely at universities and technical schools, something they could only have dreamt of under the Poles. True, all of these new opportunities became available after the Soviets had destroyed Jewish communal life, but their promise was made clear right from the beginning.

On the other side was the terror of repression, the informers, the frightening presence of the NKVD, the prospect of jails and deportation. But there was, I believe, something else as well.

This is hardly the place for a detailed analysis of Stalinist communism and its crystallization as the Soviet regime from the late twenties until the demise of the Soviet Union. But at least one salient feature, relevant to our investigation, may perhaps be mentioned: the peculiar mix of pragmatic, terroristic, and cynical policies in the social, economic, and political spheres, on the one hand, and a basically humanistic ideology, which not insignificant parts of the ruling elite and their followers really believed in, on the other hand. Nowhere is this more evident than in the use, misuse, and manipulation of the Soviet Constitution, the "Great Stalin Constitution" of 1936. It would be hard to surpass that document in terms of liberal thinking and parliamentarianism. Personal rights were guaranteed, freedom of thought and freedom of the press were included, free elections were promised (though not a multiplicity of political parties), and free education was promised to all. Interestingly, schoolchildren were obliged to learn it, often by heart, and it was presented to them as the peak of humanistic political civilization.

The total contradiction between that lesson and what was happening outside the school is obvious. Terror reigned in the shtetlach. There was fear of informers;

fear of bureaucracies that forced people into a straitjacket of work discipline with no right to move freely from one place to another or from one job to another without permission; fear of deportation to Siberia for real or supposed or invented transgressions of the Soviet code. Necessary goods were not available in the government stores, and wages and salaries were not sufficient to hold body and soul together, so people were forced to resort to the black market. Corruption was endemic, so bribes were necessary. The alcoholism of many bureaucrats created another basis for corruption. Yet the system worked, and it produced, and individuals within it took the ideological challenge seriously. In their eyes, they were building a new society that would advance the cause of the ordinary people. They believed in the communist theory, and they trusted the *vozhd*, the leader, Stalin the father.

Reality and ideological theory could not have clashed more radically. The genuine desire to help the poor and the downtrodden, embedded in communist ideology and distorted beyond recognition in day-to-day life in the USSR, was probably rare in other totalitarian or near-totalitarian regimes. Marxism, after all, arose on the basis of middle-class liberalism and rebelled against it; but it acknowledged liberal democracy as its parent, even though it despised liberal democracy and wanted to replace it with the utopia of a classless, and therefore democratic, society. Lenin talked about the withering away of the state, with its monopoly on force; he envisaged the end of history. These utopian ideas were at the heart of a regime that murdered huge masses of people in order to realize them, but many Soviet citizens really adhered to these ideas as forward-looking; they believed they promised individual and collective freedom—after the necessary stage of a dictatorship was passed. They saw the dictatorship itself as the dictatorship of the proletariat, that is, of the vast majority of the people, over a powerful but ultimately vulnerable class enemy. The result of these contradictory tendencies was confusion for many individuals caught up in the Soviet system, especially in the former eastern Poland. This is exemplified by the story of Zev Katz.[57]

They were a family of six: Papa Katz, Mama Katz, an older brother (seventeen), a younger brother (fourteen), young Zev (fifteen), and a sister (six). Zev was fourteen in 1939, when the Germans occupied his town in West Galicia, where his father owned a small manufacturing establishment. The family fled to the Soviet-occupied part of Poland. They were penniless refugees and had to live off their wits. Papa Katz opened a little backroom store, the older brother secured a job, and the three younger children went to a Russian school. Young Zev quickly mastered Russian, and a subject he had to study was the Great Stalin Constitution, one of whose paragraphs dealt with the absolute right of young people to a free education.[58] After school, Zev contributed to the family income, and that meant black market operations for him and other family members. They were caught. The father was arrested, and he almost died in prison. When he was released, the whole family was put on a train and deported to Kazakhstan. In exile, they were placed, still as a family, in a slave-labor camp and forced to fell trees in the wilderness. If they did not fulfill their quota, they did not get food. Conditions were terrible, and the two parents were not healthy and needed medicines. Zev and his brother obtained these by adventurous means. In 1941, young Zev, now sixteen, remembered the Great Stalin Constitution. He somehow got hold of paper and a pencil and wrote a letter to the secretary general of the Communist Party (Bolshevik) of the Soviet Union, Comrade Joseph Vissarionovich Stalin; in the letter, he quoted the provision of the Constitution guaranteeing every young person free education. He said that here, in the forced-labor camp in the wilderness, he was being unconstitutionally deprived of his right to an education as a future Soviet citizen. Even if he were to be given that right, he had to look after his family and could not be separated from them. He asked Comrade Stalin to put things right.

The letter, sent twice by way of drivers whom Zev bribed, actually reached Moscow. Comrade Stalin was (mis)conducting the war and presumably had other worries than dealing with the letter of young Citizen Zev Katz in Kazakhstan. A deputy secretary answered the letter: Yes, he wrote to Zev Katz, you have a point. You are entitled to an education, and we have asked the local administration to set this up. The local civilian bosses wrote to the camp that they had no facilities for Zev Katz. The matter seemed settled, but the camp authorities took no action against Zev or his family, apparently taken aback by the audacity of the young fellow, and they became wary of acting against him.

In August 1941 an agreement was reached between the Soviet Union and the Polish government-in-exile, as a result of which Polish citizens were released from Soviet camps. The inmates of the camp in which the Katz family lived organized a strike—something unheard of in the USSR—to force the camp commander to organize transport to the nearest railway station. The six Katzes were released from the camp and settled in Semipalatinsk, where they survived the war years, partly working, partly studying, partly engaging in black marketeering to make ends meet. After the war, Zev earned a Soviet academic degree, which later helped him to settle in Israel. Reliance on the Constitution probably helped make their survival possible.

The Constitution was ignored in a system based on arbitrariness and terror, but it was respected in the same system, which tried to observe certain norms that had their origin in a totally different, liberal world of equal rights. Soviet totalitarianism was not like Nazism; it paralleled neither fascist regimes nor American, African, or Asian dictatorships. It was sui generis, and people who had their wits about them could exploit the internal contradictions. The destruction of the specifically Jewish culture and of the organizations that gave expression to it was made possible in part because the regime as such did not threaten individuals, provided they did not clash with it in some way or were not denounced; in fact, it promised to improve the situation of individual Jews considerably (in contrast to most of the Polish experience under the Soviets). People gave up their old ways, agreed quietly with the dismantling of the communal life they had been accustomed to, and perhaps gave up their belief systems because of these new prospects.[59]

This brings me to Jan T. Gross, a brilliant historian with original and fascinating ideas whose work on these topics is exemplary.[60] I cannot fully agree with his analysis of the Soviet regime, although some of his arguments are persuasive.[61] Gross talks about the Soviet regime as one in which the state was "privatized." I suppose he means that civil society became atomized or, put differently, that civil society was dissolved by a regime whose main characteristic was the insecurity of the individual, contrary to what I suggested. Every citizen could, at any time, be imprisoned, tortured, put to forced labor, or killed as a result of an anonymous denunciation or a change in economic, social, or personnel policies originating in an impersonal directive, ultimately initiated or approved by the dictator. No independent or private social organization of any kind was permitted. The regime controlled everything, which paradoxically resulted in total control over not very much, for no social group with any kind of autonomy was permitted to exist, and officialdom was riddled with corruption.

Much of Gross's description is accurate, and yet it does not reflect Soviet reality as a whole—and does not really explain the Katz story. Many people, perhaps most, supported the regime, and not just because of terror or indifference. The ideology that claimed to help the poor and downtrodden and promised material and cultural advancement in a utopian future was taken seriously by large numbers of people—and in some places still is. In that ideology, contradictory elements vied for supremacy: brutal terror and a dictatorial greed for power against an originally humanistic and even partly democratic approach. Idealism of an altruistic and humane kind was appealed to, and such appeals often worked; on many occasions there was even productive voluntarism. The Soviet system was in these and other important ways very different from the Nazi one.

We can understand Gross's approach. It stems, it seems, from his impressively detailed analysis of the fate of Poles in the multiethnic kresy under the Soviet regime. Without doubt, the Soviets saw the Poles as the main enemy and, initially at least, instituted a regime of utmost terror against them, much harsher than their treatment of Jews, Ukrainians, or Belorussians. Although proportionately more Jews were deported to Siberia, the arrests, interrogations, torture, and deportation of Poles was far more brutal.[62] From a Polish perspective, the Soviet regime was evil, possibly even worse than the Nazi one. As Gross puts it: "In the process of imposing their power and while striving to make it absolute, Communists don't hesitate to tamper with the biological substance of nations."[63] This amounts to an accusation of genocide, and I think it is only partly correct; even in the case of Soviet policies during World War II toward the Chechens and the Tatars (both of whom *did* collaborate with the German invaders) and the Volga Germans, where such an accusation might be justified, there was no mass murder. Rather, there was violent deportation—today we would use the term "ethnic cleansing." Interestingly, the anti-Polish campaign subsided (it did not disappear) in 1940, and Poles were nominated for various positions in the Soviet administration, possibly because they had the experience and the education that others did not and were found to be of use to the authorities.

As far as Jewish society was concerned, we have to remember that the same policies that bore down on the Jews of the kresy had been imposed on Soviet Jewry since the October Revolution, so the question about the destruction of Jewish communal life must be asked in a more general way. Yet there seems to have been a difference. The liquidation of Jewish culture in what became the USSR after 1917 was not achieved without a fierce social struggle. Jews resisted, and even after the Jewish organizations had been broken up, underground activities and resistance persisted. Not until the late twenties did this resistance finally cease. In comparison, all Jewish life collapsed in the kresy, with only a few, small, mostly left-wing Zionist youth groups trying to survive. In late 1939 and the first half of 1940, these groups sent emissaries from their base in neutral Vilno to (re)organize their movements in the kresy. Some of the emissaries— for example, two from Marxist-Zionist movements, Yosef Kaplan of Hashomer Hatzair and Yitzhak (Antek) Zuckermann of Dror—were to play central roles in the Warsaw Ghetto Uprising of 1943. Kaplan visited six places in the north in early 1940. Yitzhak Zalmanson, a major figure in the Hashomer Hatzair youth movement, organized an illegal gathering of members in November 1939, and then his group published and distributed a small typewritten newsletter. Hashomer Hatzair established underground cells (their number is not clear) in a number of places and engaged in educational activities, rescued Hebrew books from Hebrew schools that had been closed, and read Hebrew literature and poetry.[64] Dror established twenty-five underground cells, and the more liberal, centrist Hanoar Hatzioni did likewise. These movements smuggled older members into

Vilno, in neutral Lithuania (until June 1940), with some early success, but after January–February 1940, that road became increasingly difficult and was eventually closed. Attempts to cross the border into Romania largely failed. The youth movements managed to distribute some bulletins and maintain contact among scattered groups of adherents, but by mid-1940 most of their local leaders were found out and arrested, and most of those were sentenced to long periods of imprisonment.[65] Only some religious life continued, on the margins of normative life under Soviet rule.

I have presented here a number of factors that may help explain the quick extinction of Jewish culture and communal life in the autumn of 1939 in former eastern Poland. But I am not at all satisfied with my own explanations. I am deeply worried as a Jew at the ease with which Jewish culture was destroyed by a totalitarian regime with both attractions and existential threats. I am equally worried as a citizen of the world who wishes to see a multiplicity of cultures and civilizations flourish and who is appalled when an ancient culture is wiped out, even locally, and even though the people who were its carriers were not actually killed.

The internal contradictions that I have pointed out enabled shtetl Jews to survive, and survive quite well, under the Soviet regime.[66] In any case, for the first few months the Soviets encouraged limited private enterprise, much as in the USSR in the twenties with the New Economic Policy (NEP), which had allowed elements of private property and private economic initiative to exist for a time. The policy in the kresy was a kind of neo-NEP. Slightly wealthier people exchanged hidden goods for what they needed.[67] Everyone worked, and some people earned somewhat higher salaries. People without high-enough salaries traded—every trade was "black marketeering," but the main black marketeers were officials, industrial managers, foremen, and army officers, all of whom were supposed to suppress illicit trade. Most of these people had come from the "old" Soviet Union, and they in effect taught the new Soviet citizens how to both be loyal to the regime and act in contravention of its laws and regulations.

In postwar testimonies Jews remembered struggling for food and other essential commodities, but practically all of them also said that they somehow managed, some of them reasonably well. In the small shtetlach it was easier than in the larger towns, because shtetl Jews could barter with peasants in the surrounding countryside. Many had small lots of land themselves, which they were permitted to keep. There they often had a cow or two, fowl, vegetable gardens, and fruit trees. Even former "capitalists" managed to survive reasonably well. An interesting case in point is that of Leib Kronish, of Zborow. Kronish was the former head of the local branch of the religious Zionist movement (Mizrahi) and a member of the local prewar kahal. He, his family, and a few other wealthier people were candidates for deportation; their Soviet passports contained the dreaded paragraph 11, which marked them as dangerous elements. His property was nationalized (he says that the Soviets did not nationalize non-Jewish property, which seems to be patently untrue). But then he managed to be appointed the manager of an organization that collected straw, and he hired some fifty Hasidim (ultraorthodox Jews), who then did not have to work on the Shabbat. He did quite well, until the Germans came.[68]

People did reasonably well, but it is still true that the Jewish middle class was, by and large, ruined by the sudden change in the money system. On January 1, 1940, the Polish zloty, which until then had been legal tender along with the ruble, was abolished, and only the ruble remained. The exchange rate had been about four Soviet rubles to a zloty; now it was one zloty to a ruble, thus disastrously undervaluing the old Polish currency, and people could exchange only a paltry sum of zloty. All savings and all cash reserves were wiped out at one stroke. The hardest hit were the Jews, because the majority of them had been traders, shopkeepers, and artisans. Older people who had been peddlers or small shopkeepers now had a very hard time, for they were branded as capitalists or petite bourgeoisie, and could hardly find work. Another radical social change came about because men who found work still could not feed their families, so most women had to enter the workplace. Families now had to adjust to completely new situations, with traditional gender roles changed or even reversed. There is not enough material to examine this change thoroughly, partly because the Soviet regime only lasted twenty-one months but also because detailed postwar descriptions still await analysis.

And yet, as time went on—that is, in late 1940 and early 1941—Jews came to occupy a Soviet version of their traditional economic position as a middle class, except that now they had equal rights (in a regime where there were in fact no "rights") and possibilities of advancement. Some now worked as low government officials, especially in the financial and supply sectors, some were members of the militias (ordinary police), others worked in government food stores or worked as doctors, some were foremen, engineers, and managers of small and middling industrial establishments, and those who had owned enterprises of their own were often employed as experts in their former establishments. The production and sale of clothes, shoes, furniture, and the like, and the Soviet equivalent of trade were and remained a Jewish specialty. Jews remained members of the Soviet-style lower and middle middle classes. They were definitely underrepresented in the higher echelons of the Soviet bureaucracy. Very few Jews held higher party posts or worked in the secret police, in major administrative jobs, or in the central planning administrations. But a few did, and the non-Jewish population found this abominable. The idea that Jews could, never mind should, be part of the governing circle, even a small number of them, was deemed preposterous and against the natural scheme of things.

Antisemitism had not disappeared; it had been pushed underground, and the equality that the Jews were now enjoying, although it was not full equality, strengthened anti-Jewish sentiment. This sentiment was exacerbated by the opportunities that young Jews—and others, of course—now had: they could study at higher educational institutions, gain academic degrees, and become part of the Soviet elite. Many former members of Zionist youth movements joined the Komsomol and became enthusiastic adherents of the new regime.[69] The period of Soviet rule in the kresy was too brief for trends to develop, but the prospective lines of development were there for all to see, and not everyone liked them. A deeply felt anti-Jewish feeling, based on Christian antisemitism and strengthened by the processes that accompanied the development of capitalism, even in backward areas such as the kresy, could not be overcome by government fiat in twenty-one months. Indeed, it expanded, especially in the Ukrainian south, much less so in the Belorussian north, and exploded when the time came.

During the war, Polish propagandists argued that the Jews were overrepresented in the Soviet bureaucracy, especially in the security forces. Gross, in his analysis, notes that in the actual Polish material, mainly testimonies, "Jews are only infrequently mentioned" as village committee or militia members. Although witnesses say that Jews were ubiquitous in the bureaucracy, when they mention names, the names are not Jewish.[70] Soviet material and testimonies make clear that after the first few weeks or months, people from the "old" USSR were brought in to fill NKVD positions, and while there certainly were Jews among them, there were disproportionately few of them compared to Russians and Ukrainians. Yet the image stuck, with disastrous consequences.

Looking at the Jewish reaction to all this, I am struck by a paradox. At the time, Jews should have realized that many non-Jews held violent antisemitic views, more so in the Ukrainian areas than in the Belorussian ones. But the memoirs of Jewish survivors tell a partly different story. Most of the testimonies are those of people who were then children, adolescents, or young adults. They remember their fellow classmates and their playmates, most of whom were not Poles, because of Polish antisemitism, which seemed to be much stronger than antisemitism among Ukrainians, for instance. In fact, many testimonies from the Ukrainian areas mention close friendships between Jews and Ukrainians, especially when Yiddish schools were closing and more and more Jewish children went to Ukrainian, Belorussian, or Russian schools, providing much more contact between Jews and non-Jews than under the Polish regime.[71] Young people from different ethnic backgrounds were members of the same Komsomol movement, and younger children were members of the junior communist group, the Pioneers; they studied together, played, sang, and danced together, and, at least on the surface, relations seemed to become friendlier than before. The Soviet regime was apparently making progress in its attempt to assimilate Jews to the non-Jewish culture around them.

If the Soviet occupation had not been cut short after twenty-one months, would the younger non-Jewish generation have slowly come to distance itself from traditional anti-Jewish attitudes? Possibly. There is a view, as yet unsubstantiated by detailed research, that, during the war, Ukrainians from the east, where the Soviet regime had held sway since the early twenties, were relatively less prone to antisemitism than Ukrainians in the newly occupied former Polish areas. This does not mean that antisemitism had disappeared in the east—not at all—but it was, by some accounts, less virulent than in the west. The difference may also hold true for the immediate postwar period, and it may possibly hold true to this day, but such thoughts are pure speculation.

The Jewish refugees from German-occupied Poland, somewhere between 300,000 and 500,000 in number, arrived during the fall and winter of 1939–1940. Their experiences had been harrowing, not only as they lived under direct German rule but also as they crossed into Soviet-held territory or were pushed there by the Germans. Between September 1939 and roughly January–February 1940, the general Soviet policy was apparently not to interfere too much with these population movements. As time went on, and especially after very early 1940, the attitudes of the Soviets hardened, and they made efforts not to permit refugees to cross into their territory. The winter of 1939–1940 was exceptionally cold, and individuals and families suffered terrible deprivations as they tried to cross the new borders. Sometimes Soviet soldiers showed pity and allowed refugees in, but not often. Once the refugees had arrived in the kresy, the problems multiplied: they had to obtain lodging and work, and that was very difficult. Refugees who had relatives or close friends in the area could expect help. But the dissolution of Jewish communities meant that those who did not have such help became dependent on individual or Soviet-organized charity. Even where synagogues became unofficial centers offering voluntary help, refugees had to look for work, because being branded as a loiterer was very dangerous—it could lead to arrest and deportation. People therefore accepted any kind of work that was offered, under any conditions. Let me emphasize, though, that the fate of the refugees differed slightly in different localities; in some places, Jews provided spontaneous help, and in other places much less so.

An important question arises: Did the refugees inform local Jews about German brutality toward Jews in Poland? The answer is an unqualified yes. Our testimonies tell of the information that the refugees provided, but some of them also point out that many Jews had a disinclination to believe the horror stories told by the refugees.[72] In any case, most local Jews thought that the Soviet army provided a protective shield that the Germans would be unable to pierce, and this feeling was strengthened by Soviet propaganda.

Because Lithuania remained neutral at first, being occupied by the USSR only in June 1940, a relatively small but qualitatively very important Jewish population managed to escape to the Vilno area, which the Soviets ceded to Lithuania.[73] Some 14,000 Jews escaped to Vilno, that is, to Lithuania. They were composed of three groups: some of the top leadership of Polish Jewish parties and organizations who had fled to eastern Poland and, faced with Soviet rule, continued on to Lithuania; groups of students of ultra-orthodox seminaries and schools, who followed the same path; and about 2,000 members of Zionist youth movements. The latter two groups were joined in Belorussia by their colleagues, chiefly from areas adjacent to the Lithuanian border. Dozens of students and some rabbis fled from places like Baranowicze, where there were two yeshivot of importance. Similarly, a few members of local Zionist youth movements also joined the flight to Lithuania.[74] But the fate of the vast majority of the Jewish refugees who remained in the kresy was determined by Soviet policies: most of them were deported to Siberia.

Deportations are central to our story at this stage. Very large numbers of people were deported to the Gulag or to assigned residencies (for families) in Siberia. According to a Polish document of March 15, 1944, cited by Jan Gross, the total number of displaced Poles was 1.25 million, which included people drafted into the Red Army and job seekers in the "old" Soviet Union.[75] Of these, 900,000 were prisoners or deportees.[76] Imprisoned Poles were treated in the most terrible way. But not only Poles were deported. There were four major waves of deportations to Siberia and northern Russia, starting on February 8, 1940, when mainly Poles were deported. The next waves came on April 13–15 and in June–July of that year, when mainly Jews were the victims, and the last one came just before the German invasion, on June 14–20, 1941.[77]

The method was always the same. Militia and NKVD people, sometimes also army personnel and people from the local administration, came in the wee hours of the night, ordered people out of their beds, gave them from half an hour to two hours, sometimes less, to collect clothing and food and other necessities, and took them, with lorries or horse-driven carts, to railway stations. There, long trains were waiting for them or for prisoners, who were transported there from jails. People were crammed into the railway cars, and the terrible journey to Siberia started. It lasted for weeks. Food and water were very scarce, and no one knew where they were going. People felt utterly helpless. They got sick, and many died on the way. There was no medical help. Some deportations were of men only, some of families with men, some of families without men. Families were thus torn apart, and people had no way to find out where family members had been sent. Men were usually sent to slave-labor camps and gulags. Sometimes families were sent there as well, and sometimes families were sent to remote areas, to villages where they had to make do with whatever work was available and live in appalling conditions and meanwhile look after their children.

According to figures collected in 1943 by the Polish government-in-exile in London, the Soviets deported a total of 800,000 people, a number that fits with the other estimates quoted, and this massive loss changed more than the social and political complexion of the region.[78] It appears that the Soviets wanted also to change the area's demographic structure and strengthen the Belorussian and Ukrainian nationalities by deporting large numbers of Poles and Jews. According to these figures, 52 percent of the deportees were Poles, 30 percent Jews, and 18 percent Belorussians and Ukrainians. But, because the Poles constituted approximately 30 percent of the population and the Jews 10 percent, the number of deported Jews was proportionately much higher than the proportionate number of deported Poles and very much higher than the proportionate number of the other ethnicities. If the Soviets' first target, the Poles, constituted the first wave of deportees almost exclusively, the next two waves were already mixed.[79]

Who were the Jewish deportees? The vast majority of them were the refugees who had entered the kresy fleeing from German-occupied Poland. They got caught in an unenviable situation. On November 16, 1939, the Germans and the Soviets agreed on the terms for an exchange of populations—Germans in the USSR to Germany, Ukrainians and Belorussians in German-occupied Poland to the Soviet Union. On November 29, when the Soviet citizenship law was promulgated in the region, all those who had been living there before the occupation became Soviet citizens. Refugees could opt for Soviet citizenship or become naturalized. But most refugees from the west did not want to become Soviet citizens: they had left their families in German-occupied Poland, and accepting Soviet citizenship would mean a final split with their dear ones, because it was perfectly clear that Soviet citizens would not be allowed to leave the USSR. Quite a number of the refugees were trying to return to the west in order to be with their families despite the news about the Germans' treatment of Jews brought by fleeing refugees, or perhaps precisely because of that. Others preferred to remain in the Soviet area; they sent parcels of food to their relatives on the other side but did not mean to foreclose on the possibility of a family reunion. The agreement with the Germans allowed people on either side of the border to opt to move to the other side. In April 1940 the Soviets utilized that agreement, offering to repatriate Jews who so wished to the German-held side but requiring them, if they did not choose to do so, to accept Soviet citizenship. Faced with this decision, large numbers of Jews chose to return to German territory. They were registered, then picked up by the NKVD, and, in June 1940 (some of them earlier), deported to Siberia. They had proved to the Soviets that they were unreliable elements and enemies of socialism.

Generally, the economic and social situation of the Jewish refugees was much more precarious than that of the locals. As we have seen, they had difficulties in finding jobs, and they were disproportionately represented in black marketeering, because even when they did find employment, they could not live on the wages they earned (unlike the locals, who tended to have accumulated reserves of some kind), nor did they usually have a safety net of close relatives and acquaintances who would help them, unlike the local Jews. Once caught trading on the black market, and being without contacts in the bureaucracy, they were picked up and deported.[80] Only a relatively small proportion of local Jews were deported—prominent prewar local politicians and intellectuals and wealthy individuals. Even most of those managed to stay by taking advantage of the corrupt nature of the regime.

Here is another paradox: deportation turned out to be an escape from murder. Most of the deportees survived; those who escaped deportation were murdered by the Germans.

The Soviet period was brief. It was full of paradoxes, and it poses unanswered historical questions. Those who suffered most—the deportees to Siberia—were the luckiest: most of them survived. Some Jews who had collaborated closely with the Soviets were evacuated with the Soviet officials in the first few weeks of the German invasion. Young Jews had been recruited into the Soviet army before June 1941, but that did not save them later. Other young Jews struggled, not unsuccessfully, to lead normal lives; they studied in various institutions, or they were active in the cultural sphere. Life was dangerous but, for those not put on deportation trains, not terrible.

And then the Germans came.

Four

THE HOLOCAUST IN THE KRESY

German preparations for the attack on the Soviet Union, called Operation Barbarossa, have been treated in detail by many historians. Preparations included the so-called Commissar Order, which mandated the murder of political officers in the Red (Soviet) Army and also a general setting up of special murder units. These units, the *Einsatzgruppen* (EGs—Task Forces), were in the Central Reich Security Office (RSHA), under Reinhard Heydrich, Himmler's chief subordinate and commander, in effect, of the Nazi terror machine. The RSHA was composed of the Criminal Police (KRIPO); the Security Police (SIPO), which included the Gestapo; and the Security Service (SD), which was the intelligence unit of the Nazi Party.

No written orders were given to the EGs, apparently, just oral instructions, but there was definitely talk of getting rid of Jews, though probably no direct order to kill all Jews. Heydrich himself talked to the EG officers, and so did other high RSHA functionaries. On July 2, 1941, ten days after Operation Barbarossa began, Heydrich issued an order to kill Communist Party officials and "others," such as Jews; on the surface, the context appeared to be the fight against communism. Because in the Soviet Union all public functions, as well as trade and industrial or quasi-industrial production, were in the hands of the government and the party, killing party officials in fact meant killing anyone that the German authorities decided was in their way—first and foremost the Jews. The idea behind this order was that the Bolshevik Soviet Union was controlled by Jews, so the major enemy of the Germans were the Jews, who ran that state (and all other countries opposed to Germany). Getting rid of Jewish males was a key way of destroying Bolshevism and ensuring German security. In the early stages of Operation Barbarossa, which began on June 22, the EGs murdered Jewish men wherever they could. We have here the primacy of ideological motivation: the German war against the Soviets was an ideological undertaking, and economic planning was embedded in the ideology. Within that context, the killing of Jews as the supposed mainstay of the Soviet regime became a primary aim.

This interpretation is a matter of controversy. Christian Gerlach, in his book *Kalkulierte Morde*, on the German policies in Belorussia—a masterpiece of historical writing—puts it almost the other way round.[1] Economic factors, in his view, were decisive in the planning and execution of German policies, because Germany needed the vast resources of the Soviet Union for the conduct of the war. Antisemitic and racist motivations formed the background to these policies, he says. Gerlach relied on German documentation, and that documentation undoubtedly reflects the economic factors as being of primary importance.

However, Gerlach does not ask what exactly the Germans wanted to achieve in the war, and why they needed resources. After all, there was no objective need for physical conquest, which in even the most pro-German scenarios would have inevitably destroyed many of the very resources that the Germans wanted to acquire; they could easily have procured raw materials and agricultural products in return for manufactured goods that Germany produced. The Stalinist regime, fearful of a German attack, was willing, between 1939 and 1941, to supply the Germans with everything they wanted, in vast quantities. The Germans did not need to fight the Soviets for that. Today, a much larger number of Germans on a much smaller territory engage in exactly that kind of economic exchange, and they prosper. The "need" for expansion was purely ideological and had nothing to do with economic reality. The ideologists saw Germany as the future major power that would control Europe, and through Europe and with allies, the world. Control of Europe required control of the riches of the Soviet Union. According to this quasi-religious-fundamentalist ideology, the forces that stood against Germany were controlled by the archenemy of the Aryan race: the Jews. If this interpretation is correct, then World War II, with its tens of millions of victims on all sides, was the product of an ideology whose core was antisemitism. Once that ideology dictated territorial expansion by force, economic factors motivated by that ideology became tremendously important. I would therefore argue not only that the Holocaust was ideologically motivated but that World War II itself, instigated and initiated by Nazi Germany, was basically an ideological project, one in which antisemitism played a major role. On this central issue, despite all my admiration for Gerlach's work, I am of a radically different opinion from that advanced by him and by some others.

The military campaign, which began on June 22, 1941, started off with major German victories. The German army attacked on three fronts. In the south, the forces, under Gerd von Rundstedt, comprised forty-two divisions, of which five were Panzer (armored) divisions and three were motorized; they attacked south of the Pripjet Marshes, in the direction of Kiev. North of the Pripjet Marshes, the main German forces were concentrated on the central front; forty-nine divisions, under Fedor von Bock, including nine Panzer divisions and six motorized divisions, were grouped in two Panzer armies; Panzer Group 3 was under Hermann Hoth, and Panzer Group 2 was under Heinz Guderian. The German forces at the northern front were commanded by Wilhelm von Leeb; they consisted of twenty-nine divisions, including three Panzer divisions and two motorized ones, which formed Panzer Group 4, under Erich Hoepner. The Germans attacked with 3 million men (not counting the Romanians and, later, the Hungarians, Finns, and others), 3,580 tanks, 7,184 artillery pieces, and 1,830 airplanes. The kresy were mostly overrun within a couple of weeks by the German armies attacking from the center and the south fronts; only a small area in the northeast held out until August. Much has been written about the lack of understanding by the Soviet High Command, and especially by Stalin, of German plans and German might.[2] In the early stages, Soviet counterattacks were beaten off, with tremendous Soviet losses, but the Germans, too, suffered major losses, and by July the German High Command expressed serious concerns about the attrition in terms of dead and wounded soldiers and matériel. In Belorussia and the Baltic States, the Soviet armies were beaten, surrounded, and liquidated, despite repeated counterattacks.

In the kresy, Brest-Litovsk was taken on June 22, Grodno on June 23, Vilno on June 24, Baranowicze on June 25, Bialystok on June 27, and Minsk on June 28 — there the German army was already beyond the kresy. In the south, Rowne, in Volhynia, was finally taken on June 28, Lwow on July 1, and in mid-July the German army reached the prewar Polish-Soviet border. The Soviet general responsible for defending the Ukrainian areas, Mikhail P. Kirponos, was more successful than his northern comrades; he managed an orderly withdrawal after a major tank battle on June 24–26 in the Rowne area. But elsewhere the disorder and, often, the panic were great.

Before the war, Soviet units were prevented, on Stalin's orders, from taking precautionary military measures. Despite repeated and detailed warnings of an imminent invasion, Stalin and his cronies thought that the Germans would not start a two-front war by invading the Soviet Union and that the warnings were Anglo-American attempts to embroil the Soviet Union in a war with Germany, which would weaken both contestants. Even after the invasion had begun, the political leaders tried, during the first couple of days, to avoid a full-scale war by holding back Soviet forces. When they finally accepted that a full-scale invasion was under way, they ordered Soviet forces to attack without proper preparation and without sufficient fuel, spare parts for tanks, or even ammunition. The result was the slaughter of Soviet soldiers and the destruction of whole divisions. In the first couple of days, more than 2,000 Soviet airplanes were destroyed, either on the ground or in air battles, which eliminated air support for Soviet units for months and left the German Luftwaffe free to do as it pleased. Soviet units were badly led, which was largely the result of Stalin's purges of a very high proportion of military commanders in 1937–1938. Nevertheless, in most places, Soviet soldiers tried to fight back and tenaciously defended their positions. The massing of Soviet soldiers in the frontier areas made it easy for the Germans to cut through them or encircle them and destroy them. But the Soviets continued to fight as the invaders conquered the kresy, and their resistance became stronger and more organized. Still, it was three years before the Red Army reoccupied the kresy.

Soviet soldiers made a determined and suicidal defense of the fort at Brest-Litovsk. The Brest fortifications had been built around 1837, and the Soviets had strengthened them. The town of Brest was conquered on the first day of the Barbarossa invasion, but the fort held out for a month, although it was completely cut off from the retreating Soviet armies. At the end, the decimated garrison was led by Efim M. Fomin, a Jewish NCO, a former violinist. When the ammunition finally gave out and the defenders surrendered, the Germans murdered them all—there were no survivors.

After the first day or two of the invasion, Soviet authority in the kresy collapsed. In some towns hurried attempts were made to recruit people into the army, but as the military framework buckled, most of these recruits were sent home again, or they just left of their own accord. Quite a number of Jews had been called up recently, in the spring, and these soldiers now became part of the hundreds of thousands who fought and either died or were taken prisoner. They had practically no chance to survive. The German orders stated that all Jewish soldiers were to be handed over to the SS, the special Nazi units in charge of intelligence, policing, and extermination mentioned above; as a result, Jews were taken from prisoner-of-war enclosures and murdered. Their comrades often told the Germans who the Jews in their units were, although they knew perfectly well what the fate of these Jews would be. Only rarely did Jews succeed in hiding their identity. In any case, only a small percentage of all Soviet POWs, Jews and non-Jews alike, survived their first year in captivity; an intentionally murderous policy of starvation, exposure to extreme weather, deprivation of medical assistance, and skimpy housing reduced the survival rate drastically. The dead numbered in the millions; there are only a few testimonies relating to Jewish survivors.

The Communist Party and the Soviet government managed to evacuate their officials almost everywhere, often at the very last moment.[3] In July, when eastern Belorussia and Ukraine up to Kiev were the scenes of bitter military struggles, the party left certain trusted cadres behind in order to organize future urban and partisan resistance, but most were soon caught and killed. Many industrial establishments were either evacuated or, if that was impossible, destroyed. Most of the evacuees were easterners from pre-1939 areas and party stalwarts. Jews were among them, but the proportion of Jews among these cadres was quite low—we do not know the exact percentage—so not many Jews were saved in this way. In a few places Soviet officials tried to persuade Jews to leave with them, but in most towns and cities Jews as such were not evacuated.[4] In the panic of war, some Jews, especially young men, tried to escape. Most were overtaken by German troops and had to return to their homes, others were killed trying to escape into the Soviet interior, and yet others, especially in the south, were stopped at the old Polish-Soviet borders by Soviet frontier troops, accused of spreading panic, and sent back. Only a relative few managed to reach the unoccupied areas, and they usually carried on eastward into Soviet Asia: Uzbekistan, Turkmenistan, Kirgizstan, and Kazakhstan.

Beginning on June 14, a week before the invasion, the Soviets launched their fourth main wave of deportations of "class enemies." Quite a number of Jews were deported to Siberia—which saved the lives of many of them—but in the last few days before Operation Barbarossa the main Soviet target was Ukrainian nationalists, or people suspected of nationalism. Many thousands were imprisoned and waited to be deported. When the invasion came, Lavrenti Beria, head of the dreaded NKVD, the Soviet secret police, gave orders to either evacuate the prisoners, by rail or on foot, or kill them. Those orders were followed. Some were deported, mostly on foot—not too many prisoners survived that ordeal. But most of them were murdered—an estimated 30,000—in the prisons that held them. The Germans arrived immediately afterward; they and the Ukrainian nationalists in their tow accused the Jews of having committed the crime, although Jews were among the victims as well. To this day, Ukrainian nationalists accuse the Jews of the slaughter, although those responsible were clearly Russians and Ukrainians from the east; only a smattering of Caucasians, Jews, and others were among the NKVD cadres. Utilizing the fury of the Ukrainian nationalists, the Germans encouraged them to engage in massive killings, in early July, especially in Lwow, where some 5,000 Jews, at least, were killed, but also elsewhere; when the Ukrainians did not show enough initiative, the Germans stepped in and themselves murdered Jews.

In most of the kresy there was a brief interval between the collapse of the

Soviet regime and the entry of German troops, just as there had been between the collapse of the Polish regime and the entry of Soviet troops. Pogroms unrelated to the kind of mass murder that occurred in Lwow broke out, especially in the south, and some people were killed, but the main purpose of the attackers was to steal Jewish property.[5] Occasionally in some shtetlach, Jews made successful attempts to defend themselves, and here and there, local Ukrainian groups or individuals defended Jews. In Kurzeniec, Belorussian townspeople kept peasants from surrounding villages from robbing the Jews, but that was because they saw Jewish property as their own future spoils and did not want to share.[6] After a while, in many cases, the German officers stopped the pogroms to establish some kind of order. One commander, General Karl von Roques, issued an order on July 27 for army personnel not to participate in pogroms.[7]

Many young Jews fled before the advancing German armies. Testimonies suggest that people thought the Germans would endanger the lives of young men but probably not harm women, children, and old people. However, the German advance in the kresy was so swift that the chance of escaping was very low. Escape was largely, too, a matter of luck. Thus, in Belorussia, during the first days of the invasion, whoever fled in the direction of Minsk was caught in the huge pincer movement that captured Minsk on June 28; people who fled in the direction of Mogilev had a better chance of escaping because the German advance in that direction was slower and the Soviet resistance stiffer. In the south, German forces advanced at a slower pace than in the north, and areas in eastern Volhynia were easier to flee from. But Soviet border guards on the former Polish-Soviet border prevented the mainly Jewish refugees from crossing into "old" Soviet areas—at least during the first few days of the war. The guards turned the refugees back, accusing them of anti-Soviet behavior, cowardice, and spreading panic; the great Red Army, they said, would soon turn the Germans back, so the refugees should return home. Testimonies indicate that the old border was not open until after June 26, and then people could run for their lives.[8] Shmuel Spector has calculated that about 5 percent (12,000–13,000 people) of the Jewish population of Volhynia managed to flee into the Soviet interior.[9] In East Galicia and Belorussia the percentage was probably smaller. Those who fled, mostly young men, had a terrible decision to make: leaving their families behind. Sometimes their parents encouraged them to run, and sometimes the parents tried to prevent their escape, fearing what would happen to them in the Soviet interior and fearing, too, that they would be killed by the Germans along the way.[10]

Those who reached the Soviet interior did not necessarily survive. German aerial bombardments took their toll, and life for a refugee in eastern Ukraine or Soviet Central Asia was extremely difficult. Some refugees were overrun by the

Germans later on in eastern Ukraine, others died from disease and malnutrition, and some were recruited into the Red Army—often into labor battalions that had a high casualty rate—and if recruited as Red Army soldiers, they became part of the Soviet war effort and often died or were severely wounded in action. All these dangers notwithstanding, their chances of survival were higher than if they had stayed behind in the kresy.

Many (not all) accept that the Holocaust, the genocide of the Jews, was not preplanned but was prefigured by the potentially genocidal ideology that motivated the National Socialist regime. As late as 1941, there seems to have been no actual murder plan but instead a development of genocidal intent. For the Nazi leadership, as we have seen, the invasion of the Soviet Union was an ideological necessity, and it saw the Bolshevik regime that had to be destroyed as having been set up by a Jewish conspiracy. The Soviet Union was, in that ideological construct, run by the Jews, and beginning with the murder of Jewish men served the double purpose of, first, depriving the Bolsheviks of a central part of their leadership by eliminating Jewish intellectuals and, second, helping to prevent any possible Jewish resistance to German measures. The first wave of massacres was conducted primarily by the four EG units, numbering together about 3,000 men (plus a few women secretaries), by a number of battalions of Order Police (ORPO), numbering several thousand men, and by additional German troops, usually rear units of the army who were responsible for "pacifying" the recently conquered areas, which were put under temporary military command.

On September 1, 1941, the areas of the kresy were handed over to civilian administration, but some rear army units stayed there to strengthen the German presence. The EGs and the ORPO were both part of the SS, and the collaboration of the army and the emerging civilian authorities with the SS murdering teams was very smooth. The EGs were part of the RSHA, whereas the ORPO was run by Kurt Daluege as a separate SS formation—again, however, in full collaboration with Heydrich's units. The organization was complicated, because Himmler also set up a parallel command structure run by the *Höhere SS-und-Polizeiführer* (Higher SS and Police Commanders). These HSSPFs were put in charge of all the SS and police in their respective areas, of which there were two: HSSPF North, and HSSPF South. The relationship between the HSSPFs and Heydrich's RSHA was not always smooth, and the EGs remained, in fact, under Heydrich's command. For the areas of the kresy, the two EGs responsible were "B" and "C," originally under Arthur Nebe ("B"), a brutal police commander (who in 1944 mutated into an anti-Hitler conspirator), and Dr. Dr. Otto Rasch ("C"; he had two doctorates). In addition, Himmler had, under his personal command, a special force of three SS regiments, one cavalry and two motorized,

called the *Kommandostab Reichsführer SS* (KRFSS), who were heavily involved
in the murder of Jews alongside all the other units. The cavalry regiment especially, under Hermann Fegelein, who later became Hitler's brother-in-law—a
relationship that, however, did not protect him from being executed for cowardice during the last days of the Thousand-Year Reich. Fegelein was charged
with annihilating the Jews in the area of the Pripjet Marshes, between Belorussia
and Ukraine. In July and August 1941, Fegelein's regiment murdered more than
14,000 Jews; some units also participated in the mass murder of Jews in the town
of Pinsk, in the same area.

The number of German forces involved in the mass murder ran into the tens
of thousands, far more than the 3,000 men of the EGs. The areas to be covered
were vast, the EGs had to follow the advancing armies, and in many places, especially those that were small or out-of-the-way, they simply did not have enough
men to do the job, even though the Germans could easily augment their strength,
and did when they needed to. Thus, during the first sweep of the kresy, in July
and August 1941, the Germans murdered tens of thousands of Jews, largely men,
concentrating on intellectuals, but the bulk of the Jewish population was left
alive.[11] Many of the prewar Jewish leaders who had survived the Soviet period
without being deported to Siberia were now murdered. They included teachers, rabbis, political activists, medics, lawyers, engineers, and so on, which made
future resistance of any kind much more difficult to organize. A case in point is
the town—not shtetl—of Brest-Litovsk. Some 5,000 men were murdered there
right at the beginning of the German occupation, disrupting families, forcing a
change in gender roles, and upsetting any possible efforts at organizing Jewish
life. That the community nevertheless managed to organize is a matter of some
wonderment.[12]

In accordance with the precedents established in German-occupied Poland
since September 1939, the Germans immediately nominated Jewish councils—Judenräte—which were to be responsible for executing all German orders
promptly and obediently. Penalty for disobedience was death. In fact, however,
in many places, if not most, the Jews themselves chose the Judenräte. The Jews
had no idea what the Germans would later do, and they naturally needed people
to represent them with the new, threatening occupation power. In other places,
especially in the Ukrainian areas, local Ukrainian collaborators took over the administration of towns and townships and proposed to the Germans the nomination of Jews whom they thought would be pliant instruments in their own and
the Germans' hands. Sometimes both these elements mixed. In Kurzeniec, for
instance, a German army officer appeared with the occupiers and called for a
Judenrat to be established. By common consent, the individual chosen to head

the Judenrat was a former sports teacher, a refugee from Vienna named Schatz, whose great advantage was that his mother tongue was German.[13] But in most cases the Judenrat heads were former Jewish community heads or acknowledged leaders of pre-Soviet Jewish political groups. It was as if the Jewish communities, whose internal bonds had been destroyed by the Soviets, were being revived, as if they had risen from the dead. They seemed at first to restart from where they had been when the Soviet occupation had destroyed them. The resurrection was a chimera, however; it immediately became clear that the new Judenräte were to be quite different from the prewar communal authorities, with different tasks and responsibilities. They would have to supply forced labor to the Germans and the local collaborators; they would have to worry about food supply, medical help, and, if possible, even education and social welfare; before the war, Jewish communal administrations had taken care of social welfare only partially. The main problem now would be to keep the community alive physically.

During the first sweep of the EGs, the Germans established rudimentary local police forces that would collaborate with them, but they did not yet equip them with weapons. In some cases, the local police were really a continuation of the ordinary police forces from the Soviet period, usually minus their communist or pro-communist commanders. During the first months of occupation, such local police forces were established in all the towns and villages, and the first mobile police battalions were established alongside them. Both the stationary and the mobile local police forces were called the *Schutzmannschaften* (Protective Police Forces), but the Germans usually referred to them as *Hiwis* (*Hilfswillige*, or "Willing Helpers"). By the winter of 1941–1942, they were beginning to be equipped with firearms and were participating actively in the murder of Jews, often taking over the actual murders from Germans, though in all cases without exception acting under German supervision and under German command. It was the recruitment of local police that enabled the Germans to murder the Jews speedily and efficiently.

From the end of July, the Germans murdered women and children as well as men.[14] Again, there seems to have been no actual order to do so. Once EG "A," under Dr. Walther Stahlecker, which was responsible for murdering people in the Baltic region, began to kill Jewish women and children, other units elsewhere quickly took up the practice, whether they copied what EG A did or whether they started doing it on their own initiative. A consensus arose, on the basis of the shared ideology, that the present generation of Jews in the Soviet Union would be the last one there, which is why women and children were now included in the developing policy of total extermination. On August 26–27, around 16,000 Hungarian Jews, together with local Ukrainian Jews, were executed near Kamenets-

Podolskyi, Ukraine, under the leadership of the HSSPF Friedrich Jeckeln and with the help of, among others, Hungarian troops who held the perimeter of the murder site. On September 23, after the occupation of Kiev, explosions in German-occupied buildings in the city, engineered by Soviet demolition groups, prompted the murder of more than 33,000 Jews—women, men, and children. Germans led by a unit of EG "C" murdered them at Babyi Yar, on the outskirts of Kiev. After that, women and children were not only included but became the main targets. The German administrators and the army realized that they needed Jewish workers, at least for the time being, so the criterion for being left alive (temporarily) was fitness to work. Men now had a greater chance of survival than women or children.

On September 1, 1941, the German civilian administration took over from the military government. That meant a division of the kresy into two *Reichskommissariate* (administrative areas), one of Ukraine, under Erich Koch, an old Nazi Party hack from East Prussia, and one of the combined Baltic and Belorussian area, which the Germans called Ostland, under Hinrich Lohse. Ostland was further divided into so-called *Generalkommissariate*, and Belorussia, now called Weissruthenien, a portion of the former Soviet Belorussia, came under Wilhelm Kube, another party old-timer. Koch, who ruled from Kiev, divided his domain into counties (*Generalbezirke*), one of which was Volhynia-Podolia (German: Wolhynien-Podolien), which consisted of Volhynia and the southern part of the former Soviet Belorussia and included Brest-Litovsk and Kamenets-Podolskyi. The *Generalkommissar* of Volhynia-Podolia was Heinrich Schoene, who had his seat at Brest and then at Lutsk; he subdivided his region into twelve *Gebiete* (areas). The other Ukrainian area in the south, East Galicia, had a different structure. It became a part of the *Generalgouvernement*, the German-occupied territories of Poland, which had a civilian administrator. Kube, the other *Reichskommissar*, ruled first from Rowne and then from Minsk; he subdivided his domain into eleven Gebiete, each headed by a *Gebietskommissar*.

The areas to the rear of the advancing German armies were ruled by a civilian administration in conjunction with the SS—which included, as have seen, the Order Police (ORPO). The SS-and-Police centers that were established were largely manned by former EG personnel. They were organized in the same way as the RSHA that controlled them. Thus, the sections of the area and local command posts reflected the internal RSHA organization, which meant that the Security Police (SIPO), which included the Gestapo in section 4, and the Security Service (SD) dealt with the Jews. The local command posts were called *Aussenstellen* (area posts); Baranowicze, for instance, was an Aussenstelle of the Minsk command, and Buczacz was controlled from the Czortkow Aussenstelle.

The cooperation between the civilian administrators, the SIPO units and the ORPO battalions was perfect. Some of the civilian administrators were, in fact, recruited from the police and the SS; the Gebietskommissar (area governor) Wilhelm Traub in Nowogrodek was an example. In many cases, it was the local civilian governor who initiated the murder of the Jews, and he did that with SIPO, ORPO, available army rear command units, and usually considerable numbers of local collaborationist police and militias. He could then boast that he had made his area *Judenfrei* or *Judenrein*—"free" or "clean" of Jews. There is no evidence from German documentation that this setup was planned; rather, it seems to have developed in response to the ideologically motivated challenges of a genocidal policy directed at the population of the occupied areas—at Belorussians, Poles, Ukrainians, Roma (Gypsies), Czechs, and others—but Jews were the main target. Within that context, economic considerations were very important.

The annihilation of the Jewish population has been described as proceeding in waves, or stages. In the kresy, however, the dates of the various murder "actions," or *Aktionen*—they were called *aktzies* in Yiddish—occur with no clear regularity. Even the harsh Russian winter, which made it difficult to prepare the mass graves into which the shot Jews tumbled, did not always prevent "actions" from taking place. In many places the first major "actions" took place in the late summer, fall, and early winter of 1941. Total annihilation was the fate of the Jews of Hancewicze (Belorussia) in August 1941 and of Horodyszcze (also Belorussia) in the fall. In Kosow Huculski (East Galicia), 2,000 of more than 4,000 Jews were murdered in October. In Nowogrodek, 4,000–5,000 of 6,500 or so Jews were murdered on December 8. In Volhynia, about 25 percent of the Jewish population was murdered in September–October.[15]

Before the early winter, German assessments of the Jews' importance for the economy were contradictory, as we can see from German documentation. On September 17, 1941, an EG "C" report says that killing all the Jews "would render the task of both the economic reconstruction of Ukrainian industry and the reconstruction of municipal administrative centers nearly impossible." But another report by the same EG "C" from November 1941 says that "Jews, needless to say, gave their wholehearted support to the Communists. . . . Only one option presents itself in Volhynia: to exterminate the Jews totally. . . . After all, there is no doubt that they are insignificant as a labor force, but cause great damage as the carriers of the bacillus of Communism." And yet, on April 10, 1942, the Germans argued against the immediate annihilation of Jews because they were "most vital as professional workers and craftsmen."[16] There was a consensus that the Jews had to be killed but there was an argument about the timing. As time wore on, some of the Jewish labor was deemed to be of some importance, and occasionally mass murders were postponed. Workers, men and women alike, were separated from their families; the families were murdered, and the workers were left alive for a while; however, it was clear that all Jews would be killed within a relatively short time.

Most of the Jews of the kresy were murdered between March and December 1942. In March, 3,000 Jews out of 12,000 were murdered in Baranowicze. A second "action" took place in September, and the final annihilation came in December. Only a small number of Baranowicze Jews survived in closed forced-labor camps. In many places, the fact that Jews were needed for forced labor postponed their annihilation. In Buczacz, there was a lull in "actions" between the summer of 1941 and October 1942. The summer of 1942 saw the annihilation of the Jews in a large number of shtetlach. In Krzemieniec (Volhynia), where no major "actions" had taken place since the summer of 1941, all the Jews were murdered in one big massacre in August 1942. Nor had there been any "actions" in Sarny and Rokitno (Volhynia) until both shtetlach were annihilated, all at once, on August 26–27, 1942. The Jews of Kurzeniec were murdered on September 9; before that, smaller "actions" claiming dozens of victims rather than hundreds or more had taken place in the spring.

By the end of 1942, most of the shtetlach in the kresy had been decimated. Jewish labor was still needed, however, and some of the Jews who could still work survived in camps run, in most cases, by the SS or the local civilian administration; in exceptional cases, the army ran the camps. When the Germans had specific labor-intensive projects in mind, Jewish labor became essential. In 1942 they began building a major road, Military Road 4 (Durchgangsstrasse 4) between Lwow and the Crimea to supplement the existing Soviet roads, which could not carry heavy tanks and other similar traffic. The planned route was divided into sections, and labor camps were set up to be run by the Todt labor organization, which was building roads and other essential projects within the Nazi empire. The conditions in these camps were such that the Jewish workers were dying off in huge numbers, requiring the labor force to be constantly replenished from still-existing ghettoes.[17] By early 1943 the shtetlach had been annihilated, and no more Jewish labor could be recruited. The workers died, and the road, whether for that or for other reasons, was never completed. To all who argue for an interpretation of German policies that puts the main emphasis on economic factors we need only show what happened on Military Road 4: the Germans killed off the workers they needed in order to build an essential road. Why? Because their radical antisemitic ideology put the murder of Jews above all economic considerations.

A similar policy was followed elsewhere: saving Jews for labor and then letting them die. In Czortkow and Tluste in East Galicia, for instance, the Germans tried to grow Kox-Agis, a plant out of which they hoped to extract a kind of rubber; rubber was absolutely essential for the German war machine. They established a number of forced-labor camps and put Jews to work. According to one testimony, they established nine camps, especially around the shtetl of Tluste, which had 5,000 Jews in its ghetto in 1942. Jewish men and women were recruited from a number of shtetlach in the general area—for example, from Czortkow, Buczacz, and Kopyczynce. In some of the camps the conditions were almost sufferable, depending on the local commanders, some of whom were older army men, although the SS had formally taken over the camps in September 1942. By 1943 the Germans apparently realized that their plan to grow Kox-Agis was a failure, but they maintained seven (some say nine) of the camps as agricultural enterprises until 1944 because they needed certain agricultural products. Nevertheless, they murdered the Jews in most of these camps. Some of the Jews managed to flee, and there was some physical resistance in the camps, too. In at least one camp, the commander, an army man, protected the Jews until the arrival of the Soviets, saving around a hundred people.[18] Here we can see a combination of economic motives with ideological ones: the ideological motives are evident in the fact that the Jews were murdered despite being economically useful.

Christian Gerlach argues that in Belorussia extermination went faster than it went elsewhere because Jewish labor was unimportant.[19] This may be so in general terms, but labor was needed locally nevertheless. After the Baranowicze ghetto had been liquidated in December 1942, the remaining Jews were employed at the airfield and as suppliers of essential labor to the SD itself, including "private" work done for corrupt SD commanders. In Nowogrodek, craftsmen were still employed until the late summer of 1943 because there was no one else to do the work. The work was still essential when the Jews were murdered. Again and again, we can see that ideologically motivated murder took precedence over economic considerations of any kind.

By early 1943, all the Jews who still survived under German control in the kresy were working in labor camps. As the year wore on, they were murdered. Almost none still survived in early 1944, when the Red Army approached the area. There were some differences between the provinces: Fritz (Friedrich) Katzmann, the SS commander in East Galicia, gave out an order, on April 21, 1943, to kill all the Jews in the area. I have not seen a similar explicit order for Volhynia or Belorussia, although German commanders everywhere were enjoined to do away with the Jews as quickly as feasible, and some meetings were held of high officials where the consensus was the same: namely, that the Jews should be done away with.

The problem of the establishment of ghettoes has been discussed in the historical literature. In East Galicia, ghettoes were established not only in the big city of Lwow but also in larger towns, such as Stanislawow (today, Ivano-Frankivsk), Tarnopol (Ukr.: Ternopil), Stryj, and Kolomya. The same happened in other areas: ghettoes were established in Brest, Slonim (Belorussia), Rowne (Volhynia), and elsewhere in the fall of 1941. But the Germans soon discovered that the establishment of ghettoes had its downside. Because they did not supply the ghettoes with enough food, typhoid epidemics broke out, and the epidemics did not stop at the ghetto walls or fences. Administrative work multiplied, too. In Galicia, Fritz Katzmann ordered that no more ghettoes were to be established without compelling reasons to do so. The same discoveries and responses were repeated elsewhere in the kresy, and no ghettoes were established in many shtetlach, or else ghettoes were established only when annihilation became imminent and the Germans wanted to concentrate the Jews to make the murders easier to accomplish. There were no ghettoes in the small communities of Kosow, Zabie (East Galicia), Kurzeniec (Belorussia), or Rokitno (Volhynia); many similar instances could be listed. But in these and other places, where there were no ghettoes with walls or barbed wire fences, Jews were still forced to concentrate in certain areas, streets, or houses. The establishment or otherwise of ghettoes was therefore a purely pragmatic issue and took place or did not at the Germans' convenience.

Contrary to many other genocides, the genocide of the Jews did not, as a rule, include rape by Germans, because of the strict order, motivated by Nazi racism, for Germans not to have sexual relations with Jews. Occasional sexual harassment apparently occurred in the kresy anyway, although it is difficult to document because of the understandable reluctance of Jewish women survivors to talk about it. Rape by collaborators is documented in some instances.[20]

From the testimonies, we gain an overall impression of the Germans' genocidal policies regarding the Jews that reinforces the impression found in recent literature—namely, that there was close cooperation between the Berlin Center and local initiatives.[21] The local initiatives were the result of a consensus that had developed during the thirties and during the early stages of the war: that somehow—"so oder so," as Hermann Goering put it at the famous November 12, 1938, meeting of top Nazi officials in the wake of the November 9 pogrom known as *Kristallnacht*—the Jews had to "disappear," as Heinrich Himmler, head of the SS, put it later. I use the crucial term "consensus" in its widest possible meaning, as embracing a social attitude shared by most Germans and ranging from a mild anti-Jewish feeling to sadistic murderousness. The mild anti-Jewishness prevented any meaningful opposition to the genocidal intent pushed by the Center, with Hitler himself as the main radicalizing factor.

When we examine the biographies of the local perpetrators, we see that many

of them were radical Nazi Party members with impeccable antisemitic creden-
tials—which is why they were sent to the "east" in the first place. For the RSHA
as a whole, this association between antisemitism and geographical posting has
been worked out very convincingly by Michael Wildt.[22] Sir Ian Kershaw, for his
part, has called the "work" the local initiators did "working toward the Führer,"
which meant that they knew they were acting in the spirit of the Führer, who
would have approved of what they were doing if the relevant information had
reached him. For whatever reason, then—whether to advance their careers, make
material gains, or fulfill deeply felt ideological commitments—these individuals
initiated radical anti-Jewish actions knowing they would be patted on their backs
by appreciative superiors, local, regional, or at the Center. This is clearly reflected
in Himmler's appointment diary for 1941–1942. The SS head took many trips to
inspect his east European empire, meeting with local commanders, approving
radical actions, and initiating more. Here and there, individuals who were found
to be too "soft" were replaced by more radical ones. The general social consensus
enabled them to take murderous action against the Jews in the reasonably justified belief that their work reflected the wish of German society at large. This does
not mean that all of German society or all Germans would have been happy had
they known about the gruesome details of the mass murders; as David Bankier,
Bernward Dörner, and many others have shown, Germans knew generally about
the elimination of the Jews, but the details were less known. A minority of Germans, and no one can tell how many, were distinctly unhappy about the murder
of Jews, Poles, and others. In the east, including the kresy, individual Germans
tried to help and even rescue Jews, but they were an infinitesimally small minority indeed.[23]

The general murderous policy allowed plenty of room for the expression of extreme sadism and brutality. Psychologists tell us that the potential for this kind of
behavior is potentially present with most, perhaps all, humans, but social context
determines whether it is expressed in action or not, and whether individuals will
approve of it when others commit it.

On the whole, therefore, the murder of the Jews was accomplished smoothly,
if messily, in the kresy. In East Galicia, Jews were transported to the death camp
of Belzec, just beyond the northern border of the province, in the Lublin area of
the Generalgouvernement; elsewhere, the Jews were shot where they would fall
into pits or mass graves. Shooting was quick, but caused a mess that locals had
to clear up by covering the pits, dealing with bodies that had somehow been left
outside, and so on. Also, it meant that in most cases, local inhabitants were either
direct witnesses of the mass murder or heard the shots and knew where the mass
graves were located. They still do, or their descendants do. For decades afterward,

local inhabitants dug for the gold that Jews were supposed to have owned and been buried with—in areas where the Jews were at least as poor as their neighbors. Antisemitism is a very hardy weed indeed.

In considering these overall developments, it is crucial to bear in mind the correlation between the development of the war situation and the genocide of the Jews. Mass murders began during the first rapid German advances and were carried out into the fall of 1941 while the German euphoria still held sway—although a few German generals were already aware of the problems ahead and painfully aware of the considerable German losses in men and matériel. After the first big Soviet counteroffensive in the winter threw the German forces back from the gates of Moscow, the murder continued unabated. It continued in the spring of 1942, during the great German advances, nor did it stop when the Germans were defeated at Stalingrad in the winter of 1942–1943. It is important to bear these facts in mind when trying to explain the continued mass slaughter of Jews both during the euphoria of victories and in the face of German setbacks. This found expression in the desire of the Nazi leadership to accomplish the annihilation of the Jews even if Germany was defeated, as Hitler's testament shows. The murder of the Jews was a primary objective in victory or defeat and was pursued under each and every circumstance. The progress of the war certainly influenced the fate of the Jews, but not in correlation with victories. Rather, as the tide of war turned and as German brutalities multiplied, some among the local population began to show more support for the few Jews who were trying to escape or hide (although with others, as will be shown, the opposite happened: the locals wanted to get rid of the Jews because they feared that survivors would incriminate them with the Soviets for having participated in mass murder).

The attitude of the local population was, in any case, absolutely crucial to the survival or otherwise of Jews. During the German advance, when the Ukrainians, Belorussians, and Poles thought that the Soviet Union was collapsing and the Germans were there to stay, any help to Jews would have been taken as opposition to the new, all-powerful masters. The conquered ethnicities had a massive incentive, in any case, to avoid all contact with an unpopular minority destined to be killed. When the Germans withdrew that first winter, from the immediate vicinity of Moscow, the local population wavered. In 1942, during the greatest German victories, attitudes toward Jews hardened again. They softened after Stalingrad, when the return of the Soviet regime became possible, then probable, and finally certain. People feared that the Soviet security service might ask what they did or did not do regarding the victims of the Germans, primarily the Jews. Their anticipation of the Soviet response might have meant either a friendlier attitude toward the surviving Jews or a burning desire to get rid of witnesses who might accuse them of murder and robbery, especially if property that had clearly belonged to Jews was discovered in their possession. We shall see how the attitudes of peasants and, to a lesser extent, townspeople changed in accordance with who they thought would prevail in the armed struggle. The peasants in many of these areas might have been living in primitive conditions, but news spread. As time went on, Soviet partisans, in areas where they were active, informed the local population ever more reliably. Their news had an effect on attitudes toward Jews.

The Soviet partisan movement was late to arrive in the kresy. At first, Soviet soldiers escaping from encirclement or from POW camps made it to the thick forests of Belorussia and Polesie, the border region between Belorussia and Ukraine. Genuine pro-Soviet and Communist Party elements formed a few detachments. The majority of the others, the outlaws, were actually something between ordinary robbers and people fleeing the German occupiers. Ethnically, they were a mixed bunch, with a predominance of Russians, and most of them were anti-Jewish. Because they robbed, killed, and raped Jewish escapees, Jews mostly stayed away from the forests, at least until the spring of 1942. It was only then, and especially from May 1942 on, that an organized Soviet partisan movement emerged, and murderous antisemitism among the partisans diminished. By the summer, significant partisan units had established themselves in a few of the forested areas, and by the winter of 1942 they had spread throughout Belorussia and northern Ukraine. But by then most of the Jews were dead. The small minority that still survived had a chance of finding refuge in the forests as armed partisans or as largely unarmed groups of families and individuals sheltering there. Both groups depended on the goodwill of the surrounding peasantry. In the end, partisans both killed thousands of Jews and rescued thousands of Jews.

All this was true mainly in the north. No Soviet partisan movement developed in central and southern Volhynia, and only small partisan units of this kind developed in East Galicia until close to liberation. Jews fleeing into the woods in these regions had little chance of survival. Ukrainian nationalist partisans in the south and Polish nationalist guerrillas in the north engaged in killings of Jews, making Jewish survival even more difficult.

Liberation came with the Soviet reconquest of parts of Volhynia in February 1944; by March, Soviet forces had also penetrated East Galicia, though German counterattacks forced the Red Army out of some areas they had already liberated. On June 22, 1944, the great Soviet offensive started, and it smashed the German central front completely. By mid-July, the kresy had become "Nazi-frei." Only pitiful remnants of the former Jewish population were left. The Soviets had come too late.

Five

THE SHTETL COMMUNITY AND
ITS LEADERSHIP, 1941–1943

Under German occupation the life span of Jewish communities in the kresy was brief. In most cases, they lasted from the summer of 1941 to the fall or winter of 1942, with some remnants still struggling to keep alive in the first half of 1943. As we have seen, the communities rarely remained whole during even that short period because massacres not only decimated them, often in stages, during that year and a half but also, as the communities lost members, destroyed their economic, social, familial, and cultural fabric—and, most important, their morale. The situation in the kresy differed materially from that in central and western Poland, in Lithuania and Latvia, and in other German-occupied countries. In the large Polish ghettoes especially, there was a period of time during which some type of unarmed Jewish response could develop. In cities like Warsaw and Cracow, up to three years—in Lodz, five years—passed between occupation and annihilation; in the Baltic States and Bialystok, which had been under Soviet rule until June 1941, two years or more passed. In most of these concentrations of Jews, as in smaller towns in central Poland, a response developed that I call Amidah, which in this context meant standing up against the Germans, with or without arms.[1]

In the Warsaw ghetto, Amidah meant efforts to keep life going; but what the leading social, political, and cultural elites aimed at was not just survival but meaningful survival—meaningful in terms of Jewish and universal culture as these elites understood it. As Israel Gutman describes and analyzes this Amidah, it included efforts at producing goods that could be smuggled outside and sold in order to provide sustenance for ghetto inhabitants, smuggling food in, organizing social welfare for adults, running soup kitchens, looking after small children, keeping up orphanages, arranging for education for older children and young adults, organizing medical services on as large a scale as possible, and, finally, trying to maintain cultural activities to keep up morale — lectures, concerts, theater, and so on. Underground literature flourished, both political and nonpolitical — diaries were kept, poems were written, religious treatises were composed. Political parties maintained cohesion by working underground and by publishing journals and other materials. Youth movements, especially Zionist and Bundist ones, kept up a lively intellectual and social life.[2] Similar or parallel efforts were made in Vilno, Bialystok, and Lodz, and similar though perhaps less comprehensive efforts were made in Cracow, Kovno (Kaunas), Sosnowice-Bedzin, Czestochowa, Radom, and elsewhere.

The question has to be asked whether anything like these efforts existed in the shtetlach of the kresy. This is especially so because in historical literature on the Holocaust it is usually assumed that what happened in Warsaw or other large ghettoes was paradigmatic, that much the same thing happened elsewhere. But, as we have seen, the situation in the kresy differed in most ways from the situation farther west, even before the war, never mind after war had broken out. Comparisons have to be made, and parallels and differences worked out. These considerations have general implications as well: we may possibly learn how victims of genocide — in this case, the unprecedented genocide of the Jews — reacted, what they did, and perhaps even what they thought. The Holocaust is relatively much better documented than other genocides, and what we find out about Jews in this particular area, the kresy, under these particular circumstances, may be of universal importance. Every genocide is, after all, specific as to the characteristics of perpetrators and victims, and this is true of every event that is or resembles genocide. Specificity is, in fact, a universal characteristic of all such events, so conclusions drawn from the specific elements of one genocidal situation may have some importance in understanding parallel events with different specificities.

That the Holocaust was a form of genocide is obvious. We do not have to enter into the big debate about what the term "genocide" means. The UN Convention for the Prevention and Punishment of the Crime of Genocide of 1948 is a problematic document, to say the least; but since it was formulated in the wake of World War II and was decisively influenced by the tragedy of the Jews and the Poles, its definitions fit the case of the Holocaust, and we need not bother with definitions any further here. However we define other tragedies before and since the Holocaust that show parallels to what happened to the Jews at the hands of National Socialist Germany and its collaborators, it is also obvious that some, many, or most of these tragedies call for a comparison with the genocide of the Jews. Our examination therefore has two aspects: one specific to the Jews and a universal one. For both, the question of the responses or reactions of the victims is central. Since the victims of mass murder will always outnumber the perpetrators, most of us are more likely to become victims than perpetrators; therefore the reaction of the victims to the threat that confronted them matters to all of us—even if we are more likely to be bystanders than either victims or perpetrators. We need to know how the victims reacted before they knew they were going to be victims and again after they realized that they were being targeted, for discrimination, persecution, and then death. In the Holocaust, the specificity lies in people's being targeted solely because they were Jews: all of them, without exception, anywhere on the globe. That is one of the main reasons why the genocide of the Jews is the most extreme form of this horror.

For group reactions on the part of the victims to genocide to have taken place, there had to be some degree of social cohesion or some meaningful social contacts that would enable reactions or responses to go beyond the individual and her or his family. When we examine responses in the grim reality of the shtetlach under German rule, we find completely contradictory evidence.

Krzemieniec (Yid.: Kremnitz; Ukr.: Kremenets), an ancient town in Volhynia, can serve as an extreme example. The Germans put Jews from surrounding villages in the town; by 1942 it housed 14,000 Jews. We have to remember that the Soviet regime had already pulverized Jewish communities and that all the prewar organizations and cross-fertilizing contacts that connected the people in the community qua community had ceased to exist. When the Germans arrived, they murdered 300–800 Jews in Krzemieniec who were accused of having killed sixty Ukrainians whose bodies were found in the local prison. The Ukrainians had been murdered by the retreating Soviet NKVD, but a *Sonderkommando* of EG "C" responded by killing Jews, to the satisfaction of the Ukrainian population.[3] After a short while, leadership of the Judenrat fell into the hands of criminals and collaborators, and there seems to have been no attempt from among the Jewish population to oppose them, although any opposition would probably have failed in any case, given the brutal rule of the German and Ukrainian authorities.

The ghetto was established in March 1942, but there was terrible starvation even before that. Workers were allotted 250 grams of bread daily, and nonworking people received 75–80; neither amount was enough to keep body and soul together. It is probably safe to say that hunger is what prevented any kind of organized response to the policies of the oppressors. Every day ten to twelve people died of starvation. The ghetto, when it was established, was almost hermetically closed, and although some smuggling of food did take place, the amount was too small to supply the ghetto inhabitants with even minimum sustenance. Only the workers could contact the surrounding Ukrainian population—that could be accomplished as they were escorted to their places of forced labor—but the attitude of the Ukrainians was very negative, and no significant help could be expected from them.

Starving, sick, and dying people were put up in what before the war had been a hotel, and there they just died, in their hundreds.[4] From what we know, a feeling of despondency prevailed, an even worse despair, it seems, than in Lodz, in the west, where starvation also ruled. No Amidah was remotely possible, no educational activities took place, no one cared about orphans, no religious life existed, and seemingly very little, if any, underground political activity went on. No trace of social welfare activity has been found. Anything resembling cultural life could not even have been dreamt of. Only the doctors tried to do their job, but they had no medicines to work with; nevertheless, they managed to avoid any outbreaks of epidemics. They were an exception. Otherwise, there was no social cohesion; Jewish society effectively atomized. Paradoxically, the only organized activity seems to have been an attempt to set up an armed underground, although the evidence is sketchy. There is no reliable documentation for the claim by some survivors that an underground existed, but there is reliable evidence that a small Jewish armed unit, set up by a young Jewish communist, escaped from the ghetto and maintained itself for a short time in the surrounding woods before it was liquidated. An organization must have existed for this group to have armed itself and escaped.[5] Apart from this one group, we can safely say that there was no Amidah in Krzemieniec. The basic reason was hunger. And hunger was the result of planning by the especially brutal and sadistic civilian governor, Fritz Müller, with the active help of the Ukrainian police and urban authorities. The shtetlach all differed from one another, and Krzemieniec is the place where starvation was worst.

Let us look at some other shtetlach. Buczacz, in East Galicia, had a prewar population of 23,000, about 7,500 of whom were Jews.[6] In 1941, after the usual concentration there of Jews from surrounding villages, the Jewish population surpassed 11,000. Buczacz was a famous little place; it had a long history of communal and religious life and was the birthplace of Shmuel Yossef Agnon (Czaczkes), the Israeli who won the Nobel Prize for Literature; Emmanuel Ringelblum, the great Jewish diarist and historian of the Holocaust, who was killed by the Germans in March 1944, in Warsaw; and Simon Wiesenthal, the postwar hunter of Nazi criminals. Part of Sigmund Freud's family hailed from there, too. By the end of the summer of 1941 the Judenrat was led by a corrupt character, a former Hasid, Baruch (Berek) Kramer. Ukrainians filled the positions of town administrators, a small group of German gendarmes served there, and the SIPO came there from their nearby center in Czortkow.[7] The ghetto was not established until the end of 1942, and no "action" occurred between the summer of 1941 and October 1942. Seemingly, therefore, the Jews had some time to develop rudimentary ways to resist without arms. The Judenrat organized a soup kitchen and sent food and some clothing to young men who were sent to forced labor camps in the Czortkow area, where conditions were so terrible that many died.[8] Generally, however, families had to fend for themselves; there was no organized smuggling or other attempts to obtain food. Starvation was not as bad as in Krzemieniec, but that did not mean that the Jewish communal authorities went beyond that one soup kitchen. There was no organized effort to educate children, there was no religious life, there was no attempt to organize social welfare for the poorest, there was no care for orphans and the elderly. The result was almost the same as in Krzemieniec: a far-reaching atomization of the community. After the second "action," in November 1942, in which thousands were transported to the death camp of Belzec—by that time people knew it was a death camp—"there were weddings, balls were organized, dance evenings, there were flirtations. A person ceases to be a human being when the Angel of Death stands at the threshold." Of course, such festivities were the privilege of the few who, often by unsavory means, managed to remain or become wealthy. The vast majority suffered privations, and they did not participate in these activities. "Solidarity and communal togetherness dissolved."[9] There was no social or cultural life except for the rich, but again, paradoxically, as in Krzemieniec, there was a serious attempt to organize armed resistance, here by three separate groups of young people from the town and from other places who had been brought to Buczacz by the Germans.

The information we have for the resisters in Buczacz is much better than what we have for Krzemieniec, so we can say that most of these young people were graduates of prewar Zionist youth movements of the right and the left. They established contact first with a member of the Judenrat who had been a prewar member of the community's elite, as well as with some other Judenrat members, and they procured money to buy arms. The few survivors from these groups have long since passed away, making it impossible now to find out exactly how they organized and to what extent there was a political underground in the shtetl out of which such resistance groups could arise. However, we are dealing here with small groups of young people, and the overall situation of the community did not thereby change: there was no unarmed Amidah, and the community had in effect disintegrated.[10]

A similar situation prevailed in Czortkow, in East Galicia, which had 8,000 Jews in 1941. A popular lawyer, Kruh, headed the first Judenrat, but he and most of the other Judenrat members were murdered in October 1941.[11] The new Judenrat head was Dr. Haim Ebner, universally condemned by the survivors for fully cooperating with the Germans. In the Czortkow area the Germans established a regional Judenrat, to which the local Judenräte were supposed to be subject (in fact, they largely maintained their independence). The regional Judenrat was, generally speaking, like the local Judenräte. In Czortkow, as in Buczacz, there is clear evidence of the dissolution of social cohesion and a lack of almost any Amidah activity. The Judenrat did not initiate local workshops to produce goods that the Germans were interested in, which might have provided the Jews with some form of protection—as occurred in a number of other ghettoes. In fact, stories emerged in Czortkow of parents abandoning their children and of children abandoning their parents. Babies were choked to death because their crying endangered people in hiding—although that did not happen only in Czortkow. A popular Judenrat member, Abraham Belgoraj, who managed to survive, confirms these stories. People starved in Czortkow, and in some of the neighboring, smaller shtetlach, and what had passed for normative behavior prior to the war became well-nigh impossible when people were hungry and community support was absent. Those who survived the war judged most of the Judenräte in the Czortkow area very negatively. The exception was the Judenrat in Skala, a small shtetl in the area: "When they were ordered to act against their conscience, they refused, and as a result they were killed by the Germans."[12]

In Sarny (northern Volhynia) a relatively more popular Judenrat tried to help local Jews as best it could.[13] There is no evidence of attempts to establish education for children, but the religious groups became functional again after the Soviets suppressed them. There was social life and contacts among people, especially the younger generation. There was no central care for orphans and old people, but extended families were of help. There was no actual starvation, although food was scarce, and people helped each other, although the situation deteriorated after a ghetto was established. Relationships with Ukrainians in the surrounding area were not completely severed, and local animosity was not as total as in Krzemieniec, although it was bad enough. In other words, certain elements of Amidah did exist, but we cannot say more than that. No underground political activity seems to have taken place, but during the last days before annihilation, which occurred in August 1942, former Zionist youth movement members tried—and failed—to organize some form of resistance.[14]

There was no ghetto in the small Belorussian shtetl of Kurzeniec, and there was no starvation—the Jews had little vegetable gardens and raised some fowl, and even when the Germans and their collaborators took these away, they could supplement their rations with home-grown food. The local mayor was a friendly Pole, Matoros, who, in one instance, agreed to take a cow owned by a Jewish family rather than letting the cow be taken by the Germans, and he supplied the family with half the milk produced by the cow.[15] Many of the 1,500 local Jews were taken for forced labor in the neighborhood, but those who were left behind somehow made do. A local synagogue continued to function until March 1942, when the very popular rabbi, Moshe Aharon Feldman, was killed by the Belorussians in one of the three small "actions" that terrorized the Jews before the final annihilation on September 9, 1942. There was no attempt to educate children, nor was there organized social welfare, perhaps because in such a small, poor community mutual help came naturally. Social cohesion certainly existed, so we can say that some central elements required for Amidah did exist.[16]

In Volhynian Rokitno, very close to Sarny, social cohesion was not disrupted either. Thus, when the Germans called for "contributions"—a way to rob Jews of their property by demanding forced levies in gold, silver, money, or other forms—Rokitno Jews held town meetings in the synagogue to organize this equitably. Although there was no concentrated effort at education, mutual help and rudimentary social-welfare activities were organized on a voluntary basis. There was no underground political activity, but most of the Jews who escaped from Rokitno joined partisan detachments. Many of these Jewish partisans had a Zionist youth movement background.[17]

Baranowicze, in Belorussia, provides an extremely positive example of Amidah. The Judenrat mobilized a community that the Soviets had destroyed. Education was organized for children below the age of forced labor. The elderly were cared for, as were orphans. Underground political groups met and developed some sort of political life, just as religious people had some sort of organized religious life. After the Jews were forced into a ghetto in December 1941, food was smuggled in with the help of the Judenrat, as were arms for the underground organizations that developed on the basis of prewar Zionist and Bundist groups. The community reconstituted after the flight of the Soviets tried to maintain itself. An extremely popular Judenrat headed by a Zionist merchant, Ovsiei (Yehoshua) Isaakson, and his secretary, Genia Menn, the wife of a refugee from Vilno, led the effort.[18]

The situation in the shtetlach dealt with here and in those that were surveyed but not treated in detail was somewhere between the extremes of Krzemieniec and Baranowicze.[19] We cannot say that communities generally managed to survive as coherent groups, because each situation was unique. Amidah was rudimentary at best, but it did exist in some places—in others it did not. The reasons, as they emerge from the accumulated evidence, are fairly evident. Where there was starvation, that alone was enough to check most Amidah work: hunger inhibits social activities. Starvation aside, much of the leadership and the intelligentsia and many of the young men were murdered at the very beginning of the German occupation by the EGs and others. Later, forced labor sapped the strength of the remaining Jews, both by removing many of the remaining young men and by causing irreparable damage to families and the communal structure. Under these conditions, Amidah was out of the question. And yet it did happen, sometimes sporadically, sometimes effectively, in a number of places.

Thus, despite German oppression, communal activities continued in some shtetlach. Even in Buczacz and in Dubno (Volhynia), children received some private education.[20] Some communities produced *matzoth* (unleavened bread) for Passover. Religiosity increased in some shtetlach, but that also led to the emergence of false messianic hopes.[21] Attempts to provide social welfare were made—for instance, in Miedlyrzecze (Ukr.: Mezhirichi; Yid.: Mezericz), in Volhynia, where the Judenrat used the miserable wages paid to the workers to help provide a soup kitchen for the starving.[22] In Lachwa, a Belorussian shtetl where a rebellion took place later, the community certainly held together, and the Judenrat organized the smuggling of food.[23]

One conclusion may be that forms of Amidah developed in the kresy that bore little resemblance to the forms developed farther to the west and north. Even when destruction overwhelmed communities, some things could still be done: mutual help by individuals, maintenance of customs from better times, and armed resistance by small groups of survivors. Amidah on the model of Warsaw was necessarily an exception, not the rule.

The extreme pressure of German oppression brought, in some places, a return to religious traditions. When Jews were forced to pay "contributions" to the Germans under threat of death, they sometimes turned to the medieval Jewish custom of *kherem*—ostracizing those who did not follow along with the community decision. At the ceremony, which took place in a synagogue, a rabbi and leaders of the community demanded a contribution of each and every one, according to a prepared list, and administered a solemn oath. The shofar (ram's horn) was blown, as on the Jewish holy days, and black candles were lit to curse miscreants who might not fall in line.[24]

Some Judenräte insisted on acting in constant consultation with the Jewish population. Thus, in Glyniany (East Galicia), the Judenrat nominated thirty respected community members to act as a consultative body and would not act without its approval. Similarly, in Bursztyn (East Galicia), the Judenrat head resigned publicly in order to explain to the community the essence of German policies.[25]

Can we generalize? I do not think so.

More contradictory evidence emerges when we examine the Judenräte themselves. When they were first established, in many places the Jews chose and the Germans approved old-time communal functionaries, or else the local non-Jewish authorities proposed names of Judenrat heads to the Germans, who accepted them. There were exceptions: in several shtetlach the Germans nominated the Judenrat chairmen right from the beginning.[26] In those cases, too, Belorussians, Poles, and Ukrainians often proposed well-known local Jewish leaders as Judenrat members.

Let us consider some examples. In Buczacz, the first Judenrat head under German occupation was Mendel Reich, chairman of the prewar community and leader of the local religious Zionist movement. He was well respected, but after just a few weeks, when he realized what the Germans wanted, he resigned; remarkably, the Germans permitted him to resign, and they nominated his deputy, the above-mentioned Baruch Kramer, instead. In Krzemieniec, the first Judenrat head was Ben Zion Katz, former head of the Tarbut Hebrew school and a social activist; when he refused to provide forced labor to the Germans, he was executed, and Jonah Greenberg, the head of the local Bundist group, was nominated instead. Greenberg, faced with German demands, lost his mind. His successor, Buzi Landsberg, tried to commit suicide. All this happened within the first weeks of the occupation. The next head was Dr. Bronfeld, a refugee from Czechoslovakia, a totally corrupt man.

Other examples are more positive. In Baranowicze, Ovsiei Isaakson, who led the successful Amidah effort there, was chosen by the Jews and approved by the Germans. He was a young man, a General Zionist, whose father had gone to Palestine, and Ovsiei had not managed to leave Poland to join him before the war started. In Rokitno, the last prewar chairman of the kahal, Aharon Slutzky, became the Judenrat chairman, by general acclamation. He was and remained a popular figure, heading the Judenrat until the final "action."[27] In Sarny, Shmaryahu Gershonok, a seventy-year-old man, also the prewar community head, also well liked, remained the Judenrat chairman until the end. In Zborow, Yakov Fuchs, a former community chairman, became head of the Judenrat and continued in this position until he was murdered because of suspected links with the resistance. The Judenrat under his leadership was generally judged very positively.[28] The Germans set up both a ghetto and two separate forced labor camps in the township. The Judenrat tried to provide bread to the camps and to help as much as it could. The German accusation that Fuchs maintained contact with a Jewish underground was well founded, and despite the most horrible torture he did not betray the resisters, who finally indeed staged a rebellion.[29]

Yet other examples show negative and positive variations. The head of the Czortkow Judenrat, Dr. Haim Ebner, a former communal activist, became a hated collaborator with the Germans. In Nieswiez (Belorussia), Maghilieff, a refugee from Warsaw, became the Judenrat chairman. He tried to walk the tightrope between German demands and the needs of his adopted community. The Germans killed most of the 4,500 Jews in the shtetl in October 1941 and established a ghetto for the remaining 585 Jews. Maghilieff continued in his post until the ghetto was liquidated—and its residents rebelled—on July 21, 1942. In some places, the local rabbi called meetings to elect a Judenrat.[30]

The first chairmen of the Judenräte in the kresy were nominated much the same way they were nominated in the rest of Poland. In non-kresy Poland, too, as Isaiah Trunk and Aharon Weiss have pointed out, the first Judenrat heads were usually past local community leaders or figures from the various political parties.[31] Even Mordechai Rumkowski, the hated "president" of the Lodz ghetto, had been a General Zionist representative on the communal council before the war, and Adam Czerniakow, the Warsaw Judenrat head, had chaired the Jewish craftsmen's organization in prewar Poland and had been on the board of the Jewish Agency for Palestine as a non-Zionist representative. As in the kresy, in non-kresy Poland and in Lithuania, there were also exceptions. In Vilno, Jacob Gens had been a Revisionist (right-wing Zionist) activist and an officer in the Lithuanian army. By contrast, Dr. Yohanan Elkes, the revered head of the Kovno ghetto, had been a popular medical doctor. Jewish communal representatives had forced him to accept the nomination as head of the Judenrat after the Germans came, at the bidding of the chief rabbi in the city, Avraham Duber Shapira. The kresy fit the general pattern.

After the first Judenrat there often came a second, third, and even fourth. Mostly this happened because the Germans were dissatisfied with the performance of the chairmen, some of whom resisted German demands or tried to wriggle out of them, or became too independent, or acted in a combination of these ways.

For East Galicia and Volhynia we have information for some shtetlach that indicates how the members of the first Judenräte under the Germans were nominated or elected and who they were. We know that thirty-two of forty-four Judenräte for which sufficient figures are available were headed by prewar heads of the communities. We know from relevant testimonies that members of thirty of seventy Judenräte were chosen or elected by the Jews themselves and then approved by the Germans.[32] In at least two instances the Germans appointed a Judenrat because the Jews refused to elect one.[33]

The Judenräte were given impossible tasks to do while facing constant humiliation and death threats. They had to supply people for forced labor; they had to comply with German demands for money and various goods ("contributions"); they had to look after the poor in the community; they had to somehow help those who were sent to forced labor camps in the area, usually young men, who suffered deprivation, hunger, and humiliation while doing backbreaking work; they had to provide medical service, if they could; and they had to negotiate all this with people who usually were brutal murderers, whether German or local. They had no resources, because almost all the communities were poor and had been, in addition, sucked dry by the Soviet administration before the Germans came. When the demand came to hand over gold, wedding rings, other personal jewelry, and religious objects, death was the punishment for failing to comply. Furniture, clothing, and household items followed; and when the Jews were squeezed into ghettoes, their former homes and all they contained were given to their non-Jewish neighbors. Peasants from surrounding villages practically always came with their carts and horses to carry away anything the Jews had owned. Whatever remains of it is in peasant houses in the former kresy to this day.

Some of the Judenräte tried a tactic similar to that employed in many places in central Poland: creating workshops to supply the Germans with products that were needed for the German war effort or for the private enrichment of German officials. This was tried especially in East Galicia (Tarnopol, Drohobycz, Borszchow). It did not, however, make much difference to the welfare or the survival of the Jews.[34]

Rumors, soon hardened into knowledge, spread about the destruction of neighboring shtetlach or the mass murder "actions" that preceded it. Frightened members of Judenräte scurried around seeking some sort of help, but there was none to be had. Survivors are the only source we have regarding the behavior of these communal leaders. Their testimonies reflect purely subjective judgments, and they may not reflect what the survivors thought at the time or immediately after the end of the war, since many of these views were expressed decades later. However, of the few thousand who survived and lived on long enough afterward to testify, almost all spoke about their experiences, so we have literally thousands of testimonies and thus at least an indication of what people generally thought of the Judenräte at the time. Surprisingly, perhaps, the overall opinions of the Judenräte are largely positive. Again and again, the argument is that the Judenrat had no choice but to act as it did. Of course, some of the Judenräte are severely criticized. A major exception to the positive opinions can be found in the testimonies of a number of surviving partisans where they tell us of the opposition of many of the Judenräte to potential resisters. This occurred when the resisters wanted to leave the ghetto or the shtetl for the forest or when they were caught by Judenrat members or informers trying to obtain weapons, either for fighting in the forest or for possible armed resistance in the ghetto itself. The reason for this opposition was the justified fear that if the Germans discovered that some Jews had fled to the forest, they would kill everyone in the shtetl.

We have general estimates of the behavior of Judenräte in East Galicia and Volhynia. Shmuel Spector reached the conclusion, based on testimonies of survivors, that of forty-five Judenräte in Volhynia for which he had sufficient evidence, thirty were judged positively by survivors, and nine were judged negatively. For the rest, the evidence was contradictory. Surprisingly, Spector found similar results for the Jewish police. Survivors gave positive evaluations of police behavior for more than half of the thirty-three shtetlach he examined.[35] In parallel research on the whole southern area (East Galicia and Volhynia), Aharon Weiss found that survivors judged positively forty-five out of seventy-three Judenräte for which enough testimonies were found. The heads of six of these Judenräte committed suicide rather than obey German orders; eighteen were murdered for the same reason; four resigned; two led armed rebellions; and two had close relationships with underground groups that rebelled or organized flight.[36] Twelve heads were judged positively on other grounds; one hid and survived.[37] However, these statistics apply only to the first Judenräte under the Germans. When figures for the second group of Judenräte are considered, whose members were nominated after the deaths of their predecessors, the picture changes radically. Of the thirty-one Judenräte that could be checked, only seven were considered in a positive light by survivors; there were conflicting views of fourteen others, and ten received radically negative evaluations. In most instances, the Judenräte that were viewed negatively were in charge during most of the German occupation.[38]

Because of the subjective nature of the sources, these figures should be taken as a general indication of trends only. The testimonies could have been influenced, after the fact, by peer pressure, the general consensus, or other outside factors and, again, may not necessarily reflect what the witnesses thought at the time of the events themselves. However, both Shmuel Spector and Aharon Weiss put into the "positive" column only those Judenräte for which the opinions of the survivors were unanimous and for which there were a sufficient number of testimonies to support their conclusions.

Positive views range from simple statements of fact to hagiographic exaggerations.[39] Given that nearly all the testimonies postdate the war and given that in the postwar Jewish world the Judenräte were generally considered to have collaborated with the Germans, positive evaluations have to be considered seriously—it required courage to defend a Judenrat. Typical are the evaluations—and there are quite a few—for the Volhynian shtetl of Ostrog (Yid.: Ostra'a). Ostrog had three Judenräte in succession. The first, led by Haim Golfersson, head of the prewar community, was considered to have been very good for the Jewish population, but the members were murdered in August 1941; the second, led by the prewar community secretary, Haim Davidson, lasted for only a month, but it was also considered in a positive light. So was the third, led by a complete outsider, Avraham Kommandant. In fact: "Not a single survivor has a negative word to say about any of the Judenrat chairmen."[40] Is it legitimate to consider negative evaluations as reflective of the actual situation, or is it possible that the postwar anti-Judenrat atmosphere exercised an undue influence over the witnesses, so they ended up conforming to public opinion? I tend to think that negative views, too, reflected real situations, that the negative views are no less genuine than the positive ones. As we have seen, most of the second Judenräte received negative comments.

We can find the whole range of possible behavior modes for Judenräte in different shtetlach. Let us start with three examples that I have already hinted at. In Krzemieniec, after the appointment of Dr. Bronfeld, the refugee from Czechoslovakia, a bitter struggle for supremacy developed between him and Itche (Yitzhak) Diamant, another refugee, from Lodz, and a shady character. Each contender was supported by a different German official in the town: Fritz Müller, head of the civilian administration, and Schumann, head of the gendarmerie. Diamant won, and when he became the Judenrat head, he acquired wealth by robbing the Jews of the remnants of their belongings, by smuggling, and by pursuing similar means. Because of such activities and his relatively luxurious lifestyle, the people he was supposed to lead hated him. In the end, the two Germans became violently hostile toward each other and took revenge on each other by murdering the Jews protected by his opponent. The last Judenrat head in Krzemieniec was yet another refugee from the west, a Dr. Mendel, who had been the head of the ghetto police. Survivors said he was a decent and honest person.[41] This contradicts the common view in the relevant literature that refugees, not having any roots in the communities they now lived in, were usually prone to collaborate with the Germans, although it certainly fits the view of Mendel's two predecessors. Commanders of ghetto police were also generally hated by the Jewish populations because of their collaboration with the Germans and their allies. In the case of Krzemieniec, the last Judenrat head was both a refugee and a policeman and seemed totally untypical in his behavior.

In Buczacz, the second (and last) Judenrat chairman, Kramer, had been a member of an ultra-orthodox sect in his hometown of Czortkow. From available testimonies it may be concluded that his development into a traitor to his people came gradually; here and there he tried to do something to help, as with the Judenrat's effort to send food to people incarcerated in forced labor camps.[42] Furthermore, the Judenrat he headed included some individuals who came in for a limited amount of praise in some survivors' testimonies; one such Judenrat member was Emmanuel Meerengel, the contact for one of the resistance movements.

In smaller communities the relationship between the Judenrat and the population tended to be more positive, because everyone knew everyone else, and the community had been closely organized before the war. It may therefore be more instructive to look at the larger communities, such as Buczacz and Krzemieniec, to find variants of Judenrat behavior. The evaluations of the Sarny Judenrat, for example, lie somewhere between those of the Buczacz and Krzemieniec Judenräte. Shmaryahu Gershonok, a Jew from eastern Belorussia who had fled the Soviet regime, was a well-respected former community chairman. As Judenrat chairman, he surrounded himself with people he thought he could trust, including a refugee from the west (Kalisz), Hermann Neumann, a lawyer who knew German and served as the go-between the Judenrat and Heinz Krökel, the deputy Gebietskommissar and commander of Sarny.[43] The Judenrat under Gershonok dealt with forced labor and "contributions" as best it could, spreading the burden in as egalitarian a way as possible. There were no "actions" between the summer of 1941 and the summer of 1942, but a ghetto was established, and the hostile attitude of the Ukrainian townspeople made survival into a daily struggle. News of mass murders in neighboring shtetlach multiplied, and the ghetto police became the center of a resistance group that planned to burn the ghetto and escape into the nearby thick forest. By the third week of August, the signs of the coming catastrophe became obvious, and the resistance group, with Gershonok's blessing, planned to act, but Neumann reported that the German commander had assured him that nothing would happen. The conspirators decided to desist in order to avoid endangering the whole community.[44]

Nowogrodek (Belorussia) was another complicated case. The first Judenrat was headed by a lawyer, Nahum Zeldowicz, but it did not have any time to develop a policy, because the chairman and some members were murdered after a very short time. A surviving member, another lawyer, by the name of Henryk Ciechanowski, a member of the prewar community council, was appointed chairman. All the survivors who testified saw Ciechanowski as a decent person, but not a very effective one, who tried his best to defend his community. There was nothing he could do when the Germans and their Belorussian and Polish collaborators murdered most in his community on December 8, 1941. Neither there nor in most other communities were the Judenräte asked to specify who should live and who should die—although in Baranowicze the Germans tried, and the Judenrat chairman, Isaakson, refused. The Germans themselves selected the craftsmen and other workers whom they wanted to spare, temporarily. A ghetto was established in the suburb of Pereseika. Jews from small surrounding communities were herded into the ghetto, and the Judenrat had to take care of them. No social welfare, no education, no cultural life could be thought of in the horribly crowded houses filled with hungry people. The Judenrat was helpless; the Jewish police, there and elsewhere called the *Ordnungsdienst* (Order Service), tried to prevent young people from escaping into the nearby forests, fearing that if they were discovered, the whole community would be murdered. People fled nevertheless, and the many survivors do not even complain about the behavior of the police because they say they understood their dilemma. In April 1942, Ciechanowski was murdered, apparently because he had permitted a cow to be brought to the ghetto to supply some milk and ultimately some meat. Survivors had very negative views of his appointed replacement, Haim Isakovicz.[45]

The inhabitants of the Pereseika ghetto were murdered in a second, major "action" on August 7, 1942, and Isakovicz was apparently murdered then, too. The craftsmen and other experts who had been selected out and not massacred were now housed in the regional courthouse, which became the last ghetto in the shtetl. Instead of a Judenrat, the Germans appointed an *Oberjude* (top Jew); his name was Moshe Burstein, and he collaborated with the nascent resistance organization that developed in the new ghetto. Burstein was executed, apparently because the Germans got wind of the preparations that were being made to organize an uprising. A last Oberjude was appointed, Daniel Ostashinski, who had been in charge of the Judenrat labor office responsible for recruitment of forced labor. His reputation there had not been the best, but when he assumed his new position, he became part of the underground and escaped to the partisans in September 1943. In the forest, he was tried for his actions in the ghetto and exonerated.[46]

The extremely positive evaluation that survivors gave to Ovsiei Isaakson and his Judenrat in Baranowicze has already been mentioned. The Judenrat was composed of former community and political activists and, despite its secular makeup, took advice from three nonmembers who were well respected in the community, including the hasidic Slonimer Rebbe, Shlomo David Weinberg, who was living in Baranowicze.[47] The Judenrat engaged in Amidah: education, care for the poor, health services, food smuggling, care for orphans and the elderly. One of the more prominent achievements of the Judenrat was the establishment of a health service, which managed to deal with extreme congestion—12,000 Jews were squeezed into sixty houses, with an average of fifteen persons per room—and prevent the appearance and spread of contagious diseases. The physicians were also used by the Germans to treat local Belorussians, for the number of non-Jewish doctors was very small. All this ended on July 4, 1942, when the Germans collected all the Jewish doctors, with the exception of one (Dr. Zelig Lewinbok, who survived and wrote an important memoir on Baranowicze), who accidentally came late to the assembly point, and murdered them. In typical Nazi fashion, they told the Jews that the doctors had been taken away to do some job, and demanded that the Jews collect food and clothing for them—another way to rob them of more items.

The Jewish police, under Chaim Weltman and later his deputy, Abraham Warshawski, became central to the developing armed Baranowicze underground. The police saw that order was kept, settled the neighborly disputes that were unavoidable in the very crowded ghetto, and looked after cleanliness and sewage—it was a very popular institution in the community. The police were marginally involved in a unique and very telling incident. A man called Muniek Muszynski, a refugee from Czestochowa, in western Poland, was a member of one of the underground groups in the ghetto. He was a daring young man who managed to smuggle arms. At one point, he decided, on his own, to smuggle gunpowder from cartridges into the ghetto; the gunpowder was hidden on a cart. A child saw him hiding the gunpowder and said something to the Belorussian police. The child revealed the identity of the smuggler under torture. Muszynski was caught, and the gunpowder was found. The Germans who got wind of the affair sent two policemen to the go-between between the Judenrat and the Germans, a man by the name of Shmuel Izrael, and demanded Muszynski's arrest. The head of the underground, Eliezer Lidowski, warned Izrael that if the affair was not settled with the Germans, and if Muszynski was in danger of being handed over, the underground, which by then had accumulated weapons, would start shooting. The affair became public knowledge, and frightened ghetto inhabitants started chasing Muszynski; they wanted to deliver him to the Germans and save the ghetto from destruction. Muszynski tried to commit suicide by jumping into a deep well, but the ghetto policemen pulled him out and arrested him. Some of the underground members, seeing no other way out, wanted to start shooting and then flee to the forest, which was only some seventeen kilometers away. After some feverish consultation, Muszynski was instructed by his comrades, through ghetto policemen who were also members of the underground, that if the Gestapo commander (Schlegel) came to take him, he should commit suicide—outside the ghetto—by swallowing poison. Izrael told the Germans that Muszynski had wanted to use the gunpowder to eradicate lice—a very unlikely excuse. He apparently paid them a big bribe. Izrael was acting on behalf the Judenrat, which saw it as its responsibility to save the young man at almost any cost. Muszynski was freed, and the affair hushed up.[48]

This incident was an almost exact repetition of incidents that happened in

Minsk and in Vilno. In Minsk, Germans identified the central figure in the underground, Hersh Smolar (under his assumed name of Stolarski), as a communist resister (which he was) and demanded that the Judenrat deliver him to them alive, or else they would destroy the ghetto. Instead, the Judenrat found the corpse of a Jewish man who had been killed that day; they destroyed the corpse's face, shoved Smolar's false identity card in the name of Stolarski into the corpse's trousers, and delivered the corpse to the Germans, saying that it was Stolarski. In the meantime, Smolar/Stolarski was hiding in the hospital. The Germans found the identity card and apparently decided to believe the story. Smolar was saved.

In Vilno, a Lithuanian communist identified the head of the underground, Itzik Wittenberg, to the Germans after being tortured until he revealed Wittenberg's name. The head of the Judenrat, Jacob Gens, was told to deliver Wittenberg or face the destruction of the ghetto. Gens asked Wittenberg for a midnight meeting and secretly brought Lithuanian police to arrest him. The underground freed him by force before the Lithuanians managed to escort him out of the ghetto. Wittenberg was hidden, but the population of the ghetto got wind of the affair and began to hunt out and beat up members of the underground—it was not very difficult to find them in the small ghetto. By delivering Wittenberg to the Germans they hoped to avoid the destruction of the ghetto. The underground had to choose between giving up their commander and having to resist the ghetto Jews with arms. In the end, the decision was left to the ghetto communist cell to which Wittenberg belonged. The cell members decided that Wittenberg should give himself up and equipped him with a portion of cyanide. Wittenberg reluctantly accepted the verdict and proudly walked to the ghetto gate, with the Jewish population watching silently. He was taken to the prison, where he committed suicide.

The parallel situations in the three ghettos were handled in three different ways: in Vilno, the Judenrat head betrayed the underground activist, who was then was forced to give himself up because of pressure from a frightened population; in Minsk, the Judenrat found a way to mislead the Germans and saved the resister; and in Baranowicze, the Judenrat saved the resister by bribing the Germans. These amounted to two approaches: betrayal, in Vilno, or determined action to rescue the endangered person, in Minsk and Baranowicze. Clearly, the decisions were the result of the different character of the actors and of luck; in Minsk and Baranowicze the character of the Judenrat and its head were of decisive importance.[49]

Isaakson and Genia Menn, his secretary, were murdered in March 1942 because they refused to prepare a list of old people, who were obviously slated to be killed. His replacement was Shmuel Jankielewicz, former owner of a bicycle shop, who carried on in the spirit of Isaakson. During the "action" of September 1942, when the Germans separated the nonworking, "superfluous" Jews from the working ones and concentrated them in a separate section of the ghetto, Jankielewicz organized the smuggling of people from the doomed part of the ghetto into the other. When his own wife and child were caught in the attempt, he escaped to the partisans. He was replaced by a refugee from the Lithuanian town of Suwalki, Mendel Goldberg, who died while escaping from the labor camp where he was held to the forest. Here we have a pattern of behavior that stands not only in contrast to patterns we have seen elsewhere but occurred in the same town with three successive Judenrat heads, the first a former social activist, the second an ordinary shopkeeper, and the last a refugee from Lithuania.[50]

Different types of behavior occur under extreme stress, and we can find examples in various parts of the kresy. In Dereczin (Belorussia), the head of the Judenrat committed suicide when, in April 1942, the decree came that the Jews would move into a ghetto.[51] In Korets (Volhynia), the Judenrat head. Moshe Krasnostavski, committed suicide by burning his house and causing the ghetto to burn, rather than fleeing to the partisans; he said he would not abandon those who could not flee.[52] Other cases were similar to these. Yet the Judenrat of Borszchow (East Galicia) was, according to one testimony, "no more than an instrument of the Germans"; even there, however, one of its members, a man by the name of Soifer, "tried to do whatever he could to protect" the witness and others.[53]

We must conclude that generalizations about the behavior of the Judenräte and their chairmen are not possible. Nor are easy explanations possible as to why some Jewish communities stayed together and others disintegrated. After all, the Germans pursued the same policies everywhere, with but minimal differences among them. The surrounding populations were overwhelmingly antisemitic everywhere. The Jews were the same kind of people everywhere, with the same social, cultural, and political backgrounds and the same types of attitudes. Surprisingly, though, places near to one another had differences. Nowogrodek and Baranowicze are but fifty kilometers apart, for instance. In Nowogrodek, the Jewish community was, to all intents and purposes, atomized, and only very weak elements of Amidah existed, under a weak and inefficient Judenrat, with its head judged positively only because it was felt that he was helpless in any case. Baranowicze had an active Judenrat that succeeded in keeping the community going, in the most difficult circumstances, until the final destruction. Why the different behavior patterns?

Factors usually thought to be secondary in historical analyses seem to have been of major importance in these cases. First of all, and most important, we have to consider the character of the leaders, although it is true that their appointment by the Germans or with German approval had an important impact. Ciechanowski, Reich, Bronfeld, Kramer, Diamant, Gershonok, Jankielewicz, Slutzky, Isaakson, and all the others had different characters, and not as a result of preexisting local conditions, as far as I can see. It was by chance that Bronfeld and Diamant managed to ingratiate themselves with the Germans in Krzemieniec, just as it was by chance that the Jews of Baranowicze managed to force Isaakson, against his will, to accept the leadership position; it was even more by chance that Jankielewicz, a complete outsider, was appointed head of the Judenrat after the death of Isaakson. Kramer was appointed deputy head in Buczacz, apparently with Mendel Reich's consent (possibly because both of them were religious), and turned out to be the monster he was only with time. Character and chance therefore played central roles—I can already see the wagging fingers of historians who place their emphasis on economic, social and political factors and relegate character and chance to memoirs and other literature.

Another factor is no less important: luck or the lack of it. Luck is not the same thing as chance. Fuchs in Zborow was discovered to be in touch with the underground; that was bad luck, and it influenced the way the community was murdered. In Rokitno, as we shall see, Aharon Slutzky escaped and survived because, luckily, the community, already gathered in preparation for deportation to be annihilated, was warned by a courageous woman of the looming deadly danger (see chapter 7). Slutzky had nothing to do with his survival; in this case, it was a matter of both chance and luck. The overall processes that caused the annihilation of the shtetlach were caused by ideological, economic, political and other factors, but the behavior of the victims and their leadership groups was determined to a not inconsiderable extent by character and chance. And the survival of those who managed to stay alive until the end of the German occupation was due to no small extent to simple luck. Practically all the survivors had intimate brushes with death, and they knew and remembered later that it was luck that enabled them to survive. Some of them thought it had been the work of God, but most knew better: the same God, if he existed, had failed to protect their loved ones.

Six

THE NEIGHBORS

Very few shtetlach had an all-Jewish population. Almost all of them had local non-Jewish residents forming between 20 percent and 70 percent of the township's population. And all shtetlach were surrounded by peasants, who farmed the very extensive lands of the kresy. As we know, in the north the Jews' non-Jewish neighbors were mostly Belorussians; besides a large Polish minority, there were some Russians, Lithuanians, and Tatars. In the south, the neighbors were mainly Ukrainians, with a minority of Poles and with some Czechs and Germans. In the middle, in the swampy areas of Polesie, the ethnic identity of the peasants was not clear, nor was it important to them; they usually called themselves "locals" (*tunajsze*) or Poleshchuks and spoke a dialect somewhere between Ukrainian and Belorussian.

If I may generalize, the attitude toward Jews ranged, for most of these neighbors, from indifference to suspicion to hostility, although this varied by area. The background is well known: Many Jews had been brought or had come to the kresy at the bidding of Polish, Lithuanian, or other local landowners, mostly during the time of the Polish-Lithuanian Commonwealth, in the late Middle Ages and the early modern period, to serve as middlemen between them and the peasantry, and to work as craftsmen. Some Jews had heard of the economic opportunities while living elsewhere in Poland and had come to live in better and more secure surroundings, where the landowners had good economic reasons to defend the Jews against the Catholic and Orthodox Churches and against peasant uprisings. The peasants often saw the Jews as oppressors who did the bidding of the pans (lords); the Jews were often responsible for collecting taxes and were given the right to own pubs, where peasants got drunk on cheap alcohol. On the other hand, Jews supplied the peasants with basic goods produced by Jewish craftsmen in the towns, and bought from them their products. Jews and peasants tended to need each other economically, although their social and cultural lives were completely different and separate: there was little, if any, social contact between the groups.

The mercantile relationships were often quite friendly, because the Jews knew they had to avoid overcharging or underpaying in order to make a living off the peasants. At the same time, the Jews were exploited and economically squeezed by the pans. Sometimes, the exploitation of the Jews by the pans and consequently the exploitation of the peasants by the Jews, or simply the bitter enmity of the peasants for the landowners, reached a boiling point, and rebellions occurred. The victims were mainly the Jews — because the landowners usually managed to get away in time — until the soldiers came who suppressed the rebellions, and then the victims were the peasants.

Religion played a role in local attitudes. The Christian churches added their ideological-theological venom, introduced anti-Jewish superstitions, and perpetuated an anti-Jewish feeling. On occasion, however, the opposite result was reached: Jews were seen as the people of God, in accordance with the Bible, especially by such antiestablishment minority movements as the Old Believers and Baptists-Mennonites. Ethnic minorities, too, tended to be less anti-Jewish and were sometimes decidedly pro-Jewish: this is true of some of the Polish peasant minorities in Volhynia and East Galicia and of Volhynian Czechs. These minorities generally felt that the Jews, like themselves, were threatened by the majority populations. The non-Jewish town burghers who often competed with the Jews in the areas of trade and crafts absorbed Christian antisemitic attitudes, with the help of the priests of the different Christian denominations.

Who were more anti-Jewish, the townspeople or the peasants, is a moot point. According to many survivors, the townspeople seemed to be worse during the Holocaust. The testimonies of survivors are occasionally contradictory, however. After all, no one could have survived without getting some help from non-Jews. On the other hand, we do not have testimonies from those who were betrayed by non-Jews, or denounced or killed by them. After the war, and especially after decades had elapsed, no non-Jew could be found in the vast area of the kresy who admitted to having killed, tortured, betrayed, or denounced Jews. They all claimed to have had only friendly feelings toward their Jewish neighbors. If all those who later claimed that they had helped Jews had really done so, many more thousands of Jews would have survived. But neither can we rely, without careful analysis, on survivors who said that "the Ukrainians were worse than the Germans," that all Poles were antisemites, and so on — and there certainly are many such testimonies. When we look more closely, we have to differentiate between regions, groups, professions, backgrounds, and other variables.

Buczacz can serve as an example of the difficulties we encounter in the story of interethnic relationships in the kresy. The area around the town was populated by a Ukrainian majority and a Polish minority, and the relations between the two before the war were strained. Under the Germans, the Ukrainian police in the town itself were murderously antisemitic, and they aided the Germans in the "actions." The first "action" occurred on October 17, 1942, and it was reputedly led by Hans Krüger, the SS officer who had started the process of mass murder in the whole area of the Generalgouvernement by murdering at least 10,000 Jews in Stanislawow (in East Galicia) on October 12, 1941. In Buczacz, Jews were herded to the railway station and sent to the Belzec death camp. The people who did the herding of the 1,600 victims and who murdered 200 more on the streets of the town were the Ukrainian police. They repeated their exertions in the second "action," of November 27, which was reputedly instigated by Ukrainian doctors fearing the spread of typhoid from the Jewish to the non-Jewish inhabitants; some 2,700 Jews fell victim this time. In December the ghetto was established, and the Ukrainian police guarded it; they also murdered many Jews in numerous small incidents in the two following months. In a third "action," on February 2, 1943, Germans and Ukrainians shared the task of murdering 3,600 Jews on a hill (the Fedor) just outside the shtetl. A fourth "action," on April 13, 1943, in which 3,000 Jews from Buczacz and neighboring shtetlach and villages were murdered, was accomplished the same way. Right until May 15, when the town was declared Judenrein, purified of Jews, Ukrainian police murdered the Jewish people from their town alongside the Germans. Yet, as we have seen, the Ukrainian mayor tried to help Jews as much as he could.[1]

Jews from Buczacz fled to the countryside. The Polish villages in the area, themselves besieged by an increasingly hostile and murderous Ukrainian nationalist militia, adherents of Stefan Bandera—and hence called the *Banderovtsy*—were in a number of cases friendly to Jewish escapees from the town.[2] But they were not the only ones, it seems; a small, indeterminate number of Ukrainian peasants also rescued Jews. On March 23, 1944, the Red Army liberated Buczacz, and about 600 Jewish survivors returned to the town. However, the large German forces north of Buczacz broke out of their encirclement, rejoined the main German army, counterattacked, and retook the town a week later. The Jewish survivors were completely helpless. Most were killed by the Germans and the townspeople. Only sixty-five had survived when the Soviets retook Buczacz, on July 21, while destroying the German center army in a campaign that started on June 22 and ended in early August at the gates of Warsaw. Had this final disaster not happened and had the Soviet army not withdrawn after first taking the town, the Buczacz Jews would have had the highest rate of survival in East Galicia:

something like 8–9 percent. Non-Jews must have helped the 600 people. Probably more than one gentile family was needed to rescue a single Jew or a Jewish family, because usually the fugitives had to move from one place to another when their previous temporary abode became unsafe. If we assume, for the sake of argument, that Poles rescued half of them and Ukrainians the other half—an assumption that may not be very far from the truth—possibly 1,000 Ukrainians must have helped Jews to survive. In addition, others must have helped Jews who were killed, or perhaps the rescuers themselves did not survive, in which case we have no chance of finding evidence of their deeds. Taken together, the number of Ukrainian rescuers would still be a very small proportion of the Ukrainian population, but it would disallow the conclusion so often heard in testimonies that "the Ukrainians were worse than the Germans."[3]

Let us compare Buczacz with Krzemieniec, where not a single Ukrainian has even been investigated, never mind recognized, as a possible rescuer. The recognized rescuers there were three Russians. The "action" that annihilated almost all the Jews of Krzemieniec on August 11, 1942, was conducted by Ukrainian Schutzmannbattallion 102, under German command. The Ukrainian citizens of the town participated in the liquidation of their Jewish neighbors and looted what was left in their houses, although a fire, whose origin is not quite clear, burned down most of the ghetto immediately after the Jews were led out of it to be killed. The Germans kept 1,200 selected Jewish workers alive for a very short time before the same forces, Ukrainians under German command, killed them.[4]

How can we explain the difference in the behavior of the non-Jews in those two cases? After all, both central Volhynia (where Krzemieniec was located) and East Galicia (Buczacz) were populated by the same ethnic group, the Ukrainians. German policies were the same, and the previous relationships between the Jews and their neighbors had been more or less the same, too. Most of the local population in both places supported Ukrainian nationalists by 1942–1943. There were no Soviet partisans in central Volhynia at all, and few in East Galicia, and even those few were not there until late in 1942. One difference may stem from the lack of a significant Polish minority in central Volhynia and the presence of one in East Galicia and northern Volhynia. But that could have had the opposite effect from the one we see here. By 1943 the Poles were being exterminated by their Ukrainian neighbors in all of the southern kresy. The Ukrainian nationalists, the Banderovtsy, often saw the Poles as protectors of Jews, which may have been why Ukrainians there did not help Jews. The Orthodox Church, which was violently antisemitic, was strong in Volhynia. In East Galicia it was the Catholic Uniate Church, under the leadership of Archbishop Prince Andrej Szeptyskyi of Lwow, that was predominant among Ukrainians; Szeptyskyi, who had welcomed the Germans when they occupied the area, now instructed his priests and monks—his brother was in charge of the monasteries in the area—to help Jews. No currently available evidence suggests that the archbishop's policy influenced his flock, but it is possible, and it may be an explanation. Beyond that, we are again reduced to resorting to explanations that involve character and chance— this time the character of the peasants. To put it bluntly, I have no satisfactory explanation.

When we examine survivors' testimonies regarding their rescue at the hands of Poles, Belorussians, and Ukrainians, we have always to remember that the number of survivors and rescuers was pitifully small. Observers have a natural tendency to give undue weight to the numbers of rescuers when dealing with the Holocaust. And yet the stories are important: they counter the story of the genocide and therefore have both specific and universal importance.

The stories of the rescues have a number of recurring themes. As Jews realized what was in store for them, those who still owned more than the clothes on their backs deposited their possessions with non-Jewish friends, real and supposed, and neighbors, in the hope that if they survived, they could reclaim their property—clothes, mainly, sometimes pieces of furniture or family memorabilia, and occasionally sums of money and jewelry. In fact, the attempts to save possessions backfired, because many of the non-Jews with whom these things were deposited now had a very real incentive to see that their owners were killed and would not come back and reclaim their belongings.

Another theme also involved Jewish money. When Jews looked for peasants who would agree to hide them, the peasants usually demanded payment for the food they would supply to the Jews. Jews were then hidden in barns, cowsheds, pigsties, or, less often, lofts, and sometimes in holes dug in the ground, either in peasants' yards or in the peasants' fields. The Jews paid whatever they had, as long as they had it, and got very small amounts of food for it. When the money ran out, as it inevitably did if the Jews hid in 1942—liberation, after all, did not come until early 1944—the peasants very often turned the Jews in to the nearest police station, and they occasionally killed the Jews themselves—especially when the peasant who hid the Jews was the same person with whom the Jew had deposited his or her possessions. We know of these cases second-hand, again because the Jews to whom this happened could not tell us about it. But such transactions and betrayals were common knowledge, and before the return of the Soviets became inevitable, peasants sometimes boasted about killing Jews. Postwar Soviet investigations also provide some evidence. Finally, when the Soviets approached, peasants, especially in some East Galician areas, feverishly sought out the last Jews in order to kill them so they would not tell the Soviets what had happened to the Jews at the hands of non-Jewish neighbors.

Most of the stories we have from survivors relate to the peasants—and, very rarely, the townspeople—who continued to hide Jews even after they could no longer get any money from them, and to the peasants who from the start did not ask for any money. Those were the real rescuers, whom Yad Vashem in Israel honors as "Righteous." They were few in number, but it is they who enable us to teach about the Holocaust. Without them the Holocaust would be a tale of unrelieved horror, and we cannot teach people, especially young people, a tale of unrelieved horror; the stories will be rejected, and no humane lesson will be learnt. The existence of rescuers who were not paid for their pains but did their rescue work at great sacrifice and at great risk not only to themselves but to their families shows that there was a way out, though a very hard one. The genocide was thus not inevitable, and the perpetrators and their active and passive collaborators were not the only people involved. We have to remember, as I have repeatedly said on other occasions, that our moral problem with the Holocaust—and in this the Holocaust does not differ from other genocides—is not that the murderers were inhuman but that they were human, just like ourselves, and that we human beings are prone to the kind of murderousness they evinced. The rescuers, few as they were, show that we have another possibility within us as well.

Hiding Jews was extremely risky. Non-Jews helping and hiding Jews were liable to be executed, together with their families. If they were peasants, their farmsteads were burned down as well, as a warning to others who might wish to help Jews. Such punishments happened regularly, in fact. It was one thing for a peasant man to endanger himself by hiding a Jewish escapee. It was quite another thing for a peasant man to endanger his wife and children and perhaps other close relatives. It was also very common for "nice" neighbors of peasants to denounce them when they suspected them of hiding Jews. Besides being wary of the Germans and their helpers and watching out for their own neighbors, rescuers had to contend with material issues—getting food, providing hiding space, dealing with emergencies of a medical nature. If rescuers got more food than was normally needed for their own families, they came under suspicion of hiding Jews. The whole venture was nerve-racking and terribly dangerous, and not many people could be expected to undertake the task. On top of that, in the Ukrainian areas, the Ukrainian nationalist forces were seeking out Jews in order to kill them; later some of the Poles sought them out, too. Ukrainian nationalists murdered every peasant they found who was hiding Jews, and the peasant's family as well, just as the Germans did. It was not easy to stand up against all these threats, and we can't help but wonder how we would have behaved if we were faced with a similar situation. Let me emphasize again and again that rescuers in eastern Europe were unusually courageous individuals.[5]

What were their motivations? We have already discussed those who did it for payment. Researchers have investigated a number of motives. Some people of strong religious convictions saved Jews because of what they believed to be a divine command; some rescuers were radical opponents of the German rule; some—including in the areas we are investigating—were Soviet patriots with strong political convictions; some were people who had developed friendly relations with Jews generally or with specific Jews and their families, who did not renege on these relationships when trouble came; and some people simply (simply?) thought that it was their duty to save other human beings who were in desperate need.[6] All these motivations were represented among rescuers; none seems to have been predominant. All efforts to find patterns of behavior based on backgrounds or social factors of one kind or another have, I think, ended in failure. I believe that the common underlying factor was a very basic instinct that is found in all of us. Just as there is an instinct that ultimately leads to murder, there is an instinct to regard another person as a valuable asset: a rescuer may gain friendship or an opportunity to feel satisfaction at having done a good deed or to feel hopeful about a world to come. It appears to be that instinct that leads people to commit acts that we understand as selflessness or as heroic manifestations of friendship.[7]

Ukrainian nationalists and their murderous attitude toward Jews are a problem not only of historical research but also of present-day identity politics in Ukraine. The contemporary Westward-looking Ukrainian government regards itself, probably rightly, as the heir of OUN, the Organization of Ukrainian Nationalists. OUN, first under Andrej Melnik and then under the influence of Stepan Bandera (who, for most of the time from 1941 on, was a prisoner of the Germans), developed a violent, exclusionary, and murderous policy. In advance of the German invasion, special units of the OUN (*pokhilny grupy*—advance units) penetrated Soviet Ukraine and prepared those whom they managed to reach for the kind of anti-Polish, anti-Jewish, anti-Soviet, and pro-German policy that they had adopted. It was they who agitated for the murder of Jews as a revenge for the killing of Ukrainian nationalists by the Soviet NKVD.

One of their emissaries was a former stone-quarry owner and engineer from Dubno (Volhynia), Maxim Borovets. He had had not unfriendly ties with some Jews from Rokitno and had been arrested by the Poles for his radical nationalism. However, he succeeded in getting himself appointed by the Soviets to manage a stone quarry near Sarny. He at first tried to see whether the Soviets would support

Ukrainian nationalism; when that did not happen, he became a pro-German agitator. When the Germans invaded, he joined them with a band of armed supporters, and they appointed him to be the first commander of the Ukrainian militia in the Sarny district; the radically pro-German Orthodox bishop Polikarp of Lutsk (also in Volhynia) helped him gain the appointment. Borovets called himself Taras Bulba, after the hero of one of Nikolai Gogol's books, and his supporters became known as the *Bulbovtsy*. They went out to kill Soviet army stragglers in the thick forests of northern Ukraine and southern Polesie—and Jews. They killed all the Jews in the township of Olevsk, which is within the pre-1939 borders of the USSR. In November 1941, the Germans ordered him to disband his group; on the face of it, he complied, but then the Bulbovtsy withdrew to a base he had established in his ancestral village of Borovoye (Sarny region). In February 1942, he offered to establish a unit to fight the growing Soviet partisan movement, and when the Germans refused his offer, he set up his own partisan units.

A competition arose between the Bulbovtsy and units of the Bandera nationalists, who had also abandoned the Germans; they did so because they were disappointed by the German policy of not recognizing the right of the Ukrainians to self-government. Both groups were based in forests, and both now called themselves the Ukrainska Povstan'ska Armia (UPA—Ukrainian Insurgent Army). By 1942, there were 4,000 Bulbovtsy in northern Ukraine who fought against Soviet or quasi-Soviet partisans and killed all the Jews they could find. In late 1942, they began murdering Poles in local Polish villages. By March 1943, some 6,000 Ukrainians in German-controlled militias had abandoned their German masters and joined the two forest UPAs. This was the heyday of the murder of Jewish escapees in the forests and Jews hiding with Ukrainian and Polish peasants.

In firefights with Soviet partisans in mid-1943, the Bulbovtsy sustained heavy losses and were forced to join the Bandera units, the Banderovtsy. The Banderovtsy had no competition in central and southern Volhynia, and they were much more numerous and powerful than either the small Soviet groups in East Galicia (including Polish communist groups) or the Polish units of the Armia Krajowa (AK), the army of the Polish resistance, which was controlled, at least in theory, by the government-in-exile in London. The Banderovtsy worked the family lands during the daytime in the agricultural season and formed their units at night to roam the forests and attack opponents: Poles, Jews, pro-Soviet Ukrainians, and more moderate Ukrainians. If Jews escaping from ghettoes and shtetlach in these areas went into the forests, the Banderovtsy would kill them. They often went there nevertheless, and hid in dugouts, usually unarmed, in the hope that they would not be found. Their only other hope was to find a peasant who would agree to hide them. After the war, the Soviets caught Borovets and executed him. The

Bulbovtsy and the Banderovtsy had killed many thousands of Jews—no one can say how many.

The story of Petro (Piotr) Ilnitsky exemplifies a Ukrainian rescuer. Ilnitsky was a peasant living in the mountain village of Rostoczki above the shtetl of Bole-chow, in East Galicia. Because Bolechow had some important industries, the Germans maintained a Jewish labor force there until the late spring of 1943. Ilnitsky had good contacts with Jews from the township, and when the Germans began annihilating Jews in the area, the Kessler family of six persons fled to him. This was in October 1942. The Kesslers made a dugout in the forest to live in—a *zemlianka*, or "earth home"—and Ilnitsky supplied them with food. As long as they could, they paid for it, and when the money gave out, Ilnitsky looked for someone who could pay for the food. He found the family of Bernard Löw, who agreed to come to the forest with some money. But a day before the planned escape, Bernard Löw was murdered, and his wife and daughter arrived at Ilnit-sky's without any money. Ilnitsky took them to the dugout nevertheless, and went back to Bolechow, where he found Moses Grünschlag, a timber merchant with some money who had already lost his wife and one child but still had two sons. They left for the forest in August 1943, and Ilnitsky sent them to the dugout, too. Thirty-seven more Jews were hiding in the forest some distance away from the Kessler-Grünschlag hideout. They were careless, and Ukrainian peasants found them and killed all the Jews except for five who made it to the Kessler-Grünschlag dugout. Now there were sixteen people for Ilnitsky to supply with food, and the money they had was insufficient.

Ilnitsky was a widower living with his five children and a housekeeper, with whom he had fathered another child. The Jews in hiding often could not get food from him, especially in the winter, because their footsteps would be discovered in the snow, and were often starving. They had to wait for opportunities to fetch food. When they finally got to Ilnitsky, he gave them what he had accumulated in the meantime. He sold piglets in faraway places and bought provisions there because his neighbors were suspicious of him, and if they had known for certain that he was hiding and helping Jews, they would have killed the Jews and prob-ably him as well. Banderovtsy tried to persuade him to tell them where he was hiding Jews. They beat him up, but he did not tell them. His children helped him—they were in the know. To dispel the neighbors' suspicions, Ilnitsky sent his older son, Vasily, to join the Banderovtsy; obviously, someone who sent his son to the Banderovtsy could not be hiding Jews. He had two brothers, who opposed his actions, and he had to persuade them not to denounce him.

In the end, seven out of the sixteen Jews that he was supporting survived. The others died in the hideout because of the impossible conditions there. After liberation, the Soviet forces killed Vasily as a Banderovets. Despite that terrible blow, Ilnitsky did not regret what he had done; he explained his actions by saying that the New Testament obliged him to help people in need. After liberation, the Soviet authorities exiled the villagers of Rostoczki to Kazakhstan because they had supported the Banderovtsy. Ilnitsky and his family were exiled with the rest and did not return from exile until a number of years later. He and his older surviving son, Mikhailo, received help from the people he had rescued for the rest of his life, and he and his family were recognized as Righteous by Yad Vashem. As the story shows, the rescuers faced problems, and the Jews had to show initiative to find the Ilnitskys among the peasants—clearly, there were only a few.[8]

An example that shows the contradictory attitude of the Ukrainian peasants toward the Jews during the period of murder and flight is contained in the story of Ruchama Oliker of Berezowo, in northern Volhynia, a small village with a few dozen Jews. She and her family fled into the countryside. As Oliker tells the story, "A peasant saw us and began to yell: 'Come, cross [the river] to here, where are you going? There is a peasant family nearby that will immediately deliver you to the police.' He knew my uncle and my father. At first we were afraid that he might eventually deliver us [to the police] himself, but he crossed the river in a boat and explained: 'Come, cross over to this area. There are some more Jews here. Don't stay here. The moment someone sees you [here], they will hand you over to the Germans.' The peasant, Stefan, helped us a lot and encouraged us. For some time we stayed in his haystack. We used to bury ourselves in the hay. He brought us potatoes. He did not have any bread. Then he used to say to us: 'Go into the forest for a while, try to go to the other peasant. You can perhaps stay with him for a while—he was afraid—but if he does not accept you, return to me.' He also brought me the information that my family had fled to the forest. They were there ten days, but my mother and my brother became ill. That happened on the eve of Yom Kippur [1942]. They made a fire, baked potatoes, and prepared for the fast. Just then a peasant passed by. He went to the village and brought antisemitic peasants (not policemen). They bound them and took them, and thus they took them to the police in Berezowo. All night they were held there in the cells and the next day the policemen shot them. Quite a number of people fled from Berezowo, but in the end there were almost no survivors, because the peasants denounced them in return for a kilo of salt. . . . My sister escaped to a peasant whom we had helped for years. He sat her down to eat and sent his wife to bring policemen."[9] We gather that the peasants were very poor (Stefan did not have any bread), that most of them hated Jews, and that they denounced Jews to the police—even the peasant whom the family had helped did so after he had given his victim something to eat. The testimony mentions exact dates (eve of

Yom Kippur) but not the names of the peasants. Such stories can be multiplied many times.

Some Jews were saved by Old Believers. The Jews sometimes erroneously called them *Subbotniki*, or Shabbat observers, because many of them used to keep the Jewish Shabbat rather than the Christian Sabbath, but the real Subbotniki were another sect of Russian Christians, some of whom had converted to Judaism early in the twentieth century and some of whom were among the first Jewish settlers in Palestine. In Poland, Old Believers' villages were usually found in the Polesian swamps, far away from other villages. The story of Yitzhak Goren may serve as an example of the kind of odyssey that Jews had to undertake in these remote places, as well as of the attitude the Old Believers had toward Jews.[10] Yitzhak's family lived in the shtetl of Wysock (6,500 Jews in 1939), far north of the Sarny-Kiev railway, on the border between Volhynia and Belorussia, in the marshes of the Pripjet tributaries, three of which passed through or near the township. Yitzhak's father was a master log-cabin builder, who had learned his trade in Boston early in the twentieth century while trying to make a living as a new immigrant to the United States. Family ties and obligations caused him to return to Wysock. He married and had three children: Leibl, born in 1925, Yitzhak, born in 1931, and Miriam, probably born in 1935. The family made a decent living, considering the circumstances, for the father's skills were much needed in the area. Yitzhak does not tell us much about his prewar life, but it emerges from the testimony that he must have gone to a Polish school and, under the Soviets, to a Ukrainian one, because he could speak and, more important, read both languages. When the Soviets came, nothing much changed for the family. The father's profession classified them as "proletarians," and they suffered no disadvantages. The fact that many local Jewish businessmen, politicians, and refugees were deported to Siberia affected them morally perhaps, but not materially.

Then the Germans came, and it soon became clear that life was very unsafe. A ghetto was established, but the father could still provide some food because his skills were needed. By 1942, their situation had become untenable. Leibl, the older brother, and a friend armed themselves with a knife and perhaps also a firearm of sorts. The mother was killed. Together with some relatives and friends, the father and his sons and daughter escaped from the ghetto. They waded in the shallow river (it must have been summer), the older brother carrying his younger siblings on his back. The company split, and the Goren family went into the forest alone. They found a friendly peasant on an isolated farm who helped them at first, but they could not stay there, and they went deeper into the forest. They kept alive by stealing potatoes from fields and collecting berries in the forest. Leibl left them, declaring that he would find partisans and join them in order to take revenge. Winter came, and the father fell ill. The smaller children could not save him, and he died. The two children had to dig a grave in the hard winter soil and cover his body with earth and snow. Leibl, now an armed partisan, appeared. He took the two children to separate villages and put them up with peasants, threatening that if the peasants did not care for them properly, he would return and kill them and their families.

Yitzhak, now renamed Grisha—apparently they did not tell the peasants that they were Jews—worked for the farmer, but after some time, rumors began to spread of German and collaborationist units surveying every village to find hidden Jews. The eleven- or twelve-year-old boy decided to flee, and he left for the forest. He does not remember how long the wandering in the forest lasted—certainly weeks. Finally he came upon a cluster of wooden huts, a tiny village in the middle of the forest. He knocked at the first door, and an older woman opened it, with "a bright face, as though some kind of holiness was shining through it." He said he was an orphan, and she did not ask any questions. He got food, a place to sleep, and some primitive clothing. He worked in exchange—mainly, he led the cattle out to pasture. Most of the villagers were Old Believers, and none of them could read or write. The person who had read the Bible to the group until then had died, and they had no one to take his place. It turned out that the woman who had accepted him was the elder of the community. Yitzhak/Grisha ("Grechko") soon became, in effect, the village priest: he read the Bible to the people, who mainly concentrated on the Old Testament. They slaughtered animals (pigs) according to the laws of kosher butchering, kept Saturday as the Sabbath, and led lives according to a strict interpretation of the biblical commands. They did not ask where the boy had come from—what interested them was whether he knew when the End of Days would come. "I accepted their creed," he says. No wonder.

Yitzhak Goren stayed there until March 1945—the area had been liberated in early 1944, but the villagers had no idea that that had happened, because they were completely isolated from the world. In March some Soviet officials came to the isolated village because they had identified it on a map. They were friendly—after all, the villagers were the classic "proletarian laborers" the Soviets were supporting. Yitzhak went back to the village where Leibl had placed his sister and found her still there; she did not want to leave, because she had been accepted by the peasant family as one of their own, and it appears that she, too, had accepted the religion of her rescuers. But she went with her brother, and they returned to Wysock. Yitzhak became the mascot of the Soviet unit, commanded by a Jewish officer, that was stationed in the township. He received a uniform and was there when the war ended, on May 9, 1945. The two children then traveled to Sarny to stay with some distant family members, and the boy went to school. The decisive moment came when a Jewish Communist Party official, a woman, offered him entry into the Komsomol and a bright future in the Soviet Union, and, at the same time, a Jewish survivor, a photographer, advised him and his sister to flee to Poland. He chose the latter option, and they went, illegally, to Poland, where the two had another stroke of luck—they found Leibl, and together the three made their way to Palestine.

This, it may be argued, is an exceptional story, not a symptomatic one. In response, let me say that about 2 percent of the original 1.3 million Jews in the kresy survived. Because they survived in many different ways, none of the stories they tell can be considered symptomatic for all or even most of them. There were basically three ways of survival or rescue: (1) hiding or living with non-Jews, (2) surviving in unarmed or poorly armed family camps in the forests, or (3) surviving as members of partisan units. The Goren case comes under the first rubric and is, in some ways, a typical case of rescue by someone or several someones in a minority group. Still, each case is different from every other case, even within a more general category; each survivor story has characteristics that are not shared by others.

Hardly a survivor in the southern provinces was not rescued or helped by a Ukrainian Baptist-Mennonite. These Baptists probably were around 7,000 in number, but they were spread all over the area, especially in Volhynia—but also in Belorussia—and Jews met them as they fled from their persecutors. There is no research on this religious minority in prewar eastern Poland, and we know very little about them. They seem to have been converted by German Mennonites who had settled in Volhynia in the late eighteenth and early nineteenth centuries; they certainly followed Mennonite customs and rites, as we can tell from the survivors' stories. Their emphasis on the Old Testament led them to see the Jews as God's Chosen People; and since rescuing a Jew was certain to lead to an afterlife in Paradise after death, they did all they could to rescue Jews. One problem we have with rescuers generally and with Baptists-Mennonites in particular is that very often survivors did not remember the names of their rescuers, or remembered only their Christian names and not their family names, and thus we are not able to identify or recognize them. The number of rescuers is therefore considerably larger than the number who were recognized as such by grateful postwar Jews. On the other hand, postcommunist regimes in eastern Europe tend to identify as rescuers some whose actions cannot be proved, which makes me wonder how many of them really helped and how many were recognized by the postcommunist regimes on false pretenses. Yad Vashem, by contrast, has very strict criteria for recognizing Righteous rescuers, so we can be reasonably certain that people recognized as rescuers by that organization really are heroes.[11]

There are many stories about Baptists—whom the Jews and others called *Shtundists*, a name that probably derives from a German term (*Stunde* means "hour" in German). A few examples will suffice. A group of Jewish partisans in the forests, pursued by the Germans, were rescued by three Baptists who led them through the Polesian swamps.[12] According to another, apparently very reliable testimony, that of Yitzhak Surowitch of Rokitno, who escaped into the Polesian marshes, he and his family found refuge with a Baptist peasant.[13] The peasant, Surowitch says, "got sick with fear, but he said that we would be killed anyway [if he did not save them], so come in, and if the bad times come, we will all suffer together."[14] There were individual Baptists-Mennonites all over the kresy, including East Galicia. Antos Suchinski ("Anatoshu"), a very poor man, rescued Jews in Zborow.[15]

Sometimes German individuals or small groups rescued Jews. We know of two such cases in Krzemieniec, and they are worth describing. In one of them, a Jew by the name of Ben Rotter was made to work in a German army unit near the town. The soldiers became friendly with him and protected him for a while, but they were found out and Rotter had to flee; he managed to join a Polish anti-Ukrainian defense unit and survived. Another man, Michael Kaplan, was employed in a field telephone unit of the German army and traveled with it to various locations. He, too, was protected by the soldiers.[16] In Rokitno, a German, probably a gendarme and possibly a communist, provided food for Mordechai Shulner and his family.[17] A particularly poignant story from Sarny is that of a German named Paul Rüdiger, from Cologne, who rescued Feige Schwartz on the day of the mass murder at Sarny (August 27, 1942). With the help of another German, whose name we do not know, he protected her from German patrols that night. He then found a Polish woman in the town whom he promised to support if she saved Feige and another Jewish girl. He kept his promise, providing food for the three until he was sent to the front. He and Feige Schwartz survived the war.[18] Also in Sarny, an "elderly" German, possibly a worker in the Todt organization, who supervised some Jewish workers, carried Moshe Goldman, who was accidentally injured, to his home, called for medical help, helped out with food, and visited Goldman a number of times until he got well.[19] There are similar stories from other shtetlach in Volhynia, but very few from East Galicia.[20]

In the north, too, individual German helped Jews. One of them, Hugo Armann, headed a small military section providing space on railway wagons for wounded German soldiers returning home. He hid six Jews in his house in Baranowicze, contacted Eduard Chacza, a Polish rescuer, and saw to it that the six reached the forest. He also supplied ten rifles and ammunition to Jews who were working for the SD and planning to escape to the forest. When, after the war, he was asked why he had done it, he gave the answer typical of so many rescuers: "It was humane assistance, that goes without saying."[21] What is no less interesting is that up to ten German soldiers were aware of what he was doing and did not turn him in.

There were other Germans like that. According to one testimony, two German soldiers warned a Jewish family in Baranowicze that they would be killed by the Germans, and other testimonies mention German communists who had deserted from the German army and fought in the ranks of the partisans.[22] German historiography on the Holocaust and on the German army in the east has never dealt with these or similar cases. It is difficult to estimate how many individuals were involved. But stories like these can be documented for many places, especially in Brest-Litovsk and other places in the north.

Poles also helped and hid Jews. Their friendlier attitude toward Jews where Poles were a threatened minority can be documented for both Volhynia and East Galicia. In Volhynia alone, according to one source, there were 745 Polish villages, mainly in the northern part of the area.[23] Three Polish villages were near Rokitno, and a fourth, mixed Polish-Ukrainian village was next to a large forest. Many of the Jews who fled from Rokitno on the day the Jews there were liquidated turned to these villages for help. They stayed in the forest nearby, and during the nights they went to the Polish villagers, who provided them with food. Often, too, Jews worked for the farmers and received something in return. It is difficult to establish the number of Jews who were helped in this way, but it must have amounted to well over a hundred. One peasant especially, Juzek (Jozef) Zaleski, is remembered fondly by survivors. The unusual element in the story is that in the summer of 1942 an anti-German underground organization arose in the villages, led by the local priest, Ludwik Wolodarczyk, and the schoolteacher, Felicja Masojada. They got in touch with Soviet partisan detachments early in 1943, especially with a Soviet Polish one led by Roman Satanowski (after the war it came out that he was a Jew). They directed Jews to these Soviet partisans—a Catholic priest directing Jews to Soviet communist partisans! In the fall of 1943, the Banderovtsy turned against these villages, burnt and destroyed them, and killed many of the peasants. Masojada was caught while traveling to Rokitno and brutally murdered, and Wolodarczyk was burned in his church.[24] The surviving Polish villagers joined the Jews in the forest and tried to survive alongside them. There were other such Polish oases in Volhynia.[25] Testimonies about individual Poles rescuing or helping Jews exist for Sarny as well. Anna Studzynska, for one, is recorded as having saved a bloodied Torah scroll from a dying beadle.[26] Of course, not all Polish villagers behaved with such courage, and there is also evidence of hostility.

For East Galicia we have similar stories. Moshe Schwartz of Buczacz was already on a train to the death camp of Belzec when his father managed to break through a window on the train, and both of them jumped to freedom. The boy broke a leg, and the father carried him on his back. The mother, who was in another car, also jumped, and they met in the Polish village of Medwedowce, where the Polish farmer Mieczyslaw Wychorek, hid them — without payment — from March 1943 until liberation.[27] Another, rather well-known case is that related by Alicia Appleman-Jurman in her memoir.[28] She tells the story of a Polish village, Wojciechowka, where a joint Polish-Jewish armed group was put together to defend the village from the Banderovtsy (another Polish village, Nowosiolka, is mentioned in the same context). But even more interesting is her story of an epileptic Polish aristocrat living alone in a wooden barrack in the forest who rescued not only her but a number of other Jews; he managed to feed them and protect them from the nearby Ukrainian villagers. She calls him uncle (*wujciu*), a term of endearment that he certainly deserved. He is not the only Polish aristocrat mentioned in the testimonies — a number of them are.[29] Appleman-Jurman's stories are sometimes tinged with what appears to be hindsight, but not in this case, for she is telling the story not only of herself but of others. In Kosow Huculski, to give another example, a Polish clerk in the labor office warned the Jews of an impending "action."[30] Many such stories are reported from East Galicia.[31]

But, in East Galicia as in Volhynia, other testimonies point in the opposite direction. Thus, one of the resistance groups in Buczacz tried to join a Polish partisan group in the forest. The partisan group, which was led by a man called Niedzwiecki and which belonged to the Armia Krajowa, tried to kill those in the resistance group, and they had to flee for their lives. Another armed Jewish group killed a Polish woman (no name is given) who had betrayed Jews to the Germans.[32] In Zborow, there was armed resistance to the Germans during the liquidation of those in the last forced labor camp there, and the survivors of that rebellion managed to flee into the adjacent forests. But they were not safe. "A few days before the return of the Soviets, Polish murderers surrounded the forest and killed many of those hiding there, including my brother Lulu [Pfeffer]."[33] More stories like that can be told.

Two further stories from the same shtetl of Zborow (6,000 Jews in 1941) can be documented. One is told in a most unusual memoir, written by Sabina Schweid, daughter of the Zborow Judenrat head, Yakov (Janek) Fuchs.[34] The Germans set up two forced labor camps in Zborow, into which they placed people from the shtetl and from other places, and when they liquidated the Jews in the local ghetto (which was maintained for only a couple of months in any case), they moved some of its inhabitants to these camps. In one of the camps, ruled over by an obnoxious German by the name of Klaus, a resistance group was organized. It managed to offer some armed resistance, and a number of the inmates of the camp escaped. The Germans accused Fuchs—rightly—of supporting the resisters. He was horribly tortured before he was murdered, but did not betray any of the rebels. Janek Fuchs, according to almost all of the testimonies of the few survivors, was a truly heroic person. He did what he could to keep as many of the Jews of Zborow alive for as long as possible by bribing Germans and local officials and tried to maintain a semblance of community life.

The rescuer of Sabina Fuchs-Schweid, her mother, Yonka, and five other family members was a very unusual Ukrainian, Anton Bigus, whose story is very much worth telling. Bigus was born in the village of Prisowce, near Zborow. Before World War I, his parents decided to emigrate to Brazil, but the ship on which they traveled sank, and only little Anton, aged eight, survived. He grew up in an orphanage, where he was maltreated, until he fled at the age of fourteen. He pretended he was older and joined the French Foreign Legion, for a while serving in North Africa. But he acquired both a taste for alcohol, and a dislike of mosquitoes and heat, so he volunteered for the French army, in the early stages of World War I. After spending a wonderful time in Paris on the way to the front, he was sent to fight the Germans, was taken prisoner, and learned German, in addition to the Portuguese and French that he already knew. He probably fled to Russia before returning to Paris, where he married a French woman and had two children with her. But the settled life did not appeal to him, and he did not much like to work. Nevertheless, he became a sailor on a merchant ship and spent occasional furloughs in Paris. When life at sea turned out to be too strenuous for him, he settled in Paris as a professional thief. After a companion betrayed him, he fled to Poland. In Warsaw, he met and lived with a Ukrainian prostitute and her son, both of whom, coincidentally, hailed from his village of Prisowce.

Bigus stayed in Warsaw until the outbreak of World War II, probably working as a thief again. When the Soviets occupied East Galicia, he saw his opportunity—he returned to the home of his birth and, as a true proletarian, received from the Soviets a peasant house and some land outside the village. The house had been confiscated from a Jewish "bourgeois." His "wife" worked the land, milked the two cows, and kept the rabbit farm that she developed while Bigus drank and sometimes worked. He was bored and sought adventure. He offered to hide the Fuchs family, in return for dollars, of course, to support his drinking habit. Fuchs accepted the offer for his wife, daughter, and five more female relatives, and Bigus hid them on his farm. He kept them there until, in early 1944, the money ran out. Mrs. Fuchs gave him the remaining clothes and a little jewelry she had brought with her, but that was the end. Bigus, convinced she was hiding more, staged an attack by Ukrainians—in fact, these were people fleeing from the advancing Soviets whom Bigus had paid to "discover" the Jews in hiding. These Ukrainians searched the frightened Jews, but found nothing. Bigus then told the Jews to get off his farm because they had been discovered. This was in the middle of winter, and it was freezing cold, but the women had no choice. They began walking away. Bigus ran after them and brought them first to his "wife's" brother and then back to his farm even though he no longer received any money from them. Sabina was sent to a Polish acquaintance, who kept her until the Russians came.

A very odd friendship had developed between the twelve-year-old Sabina and the drunkard, thief, and cheater with a violent temper. Bigus needed company. He had read literature in a number of languages and was a complete outsider in his Ukrainian environment. His discussions with the Jewish girl provided him with both the companionship that he sorely missed and a sense of purpose. During the course of their time together, he told her the story of his life, and she transcribed it as retold here. Bigus was not above robbing Jewish women of their last possessions, as we have seen; he chased them away, then ran after them to rescue them. His character combined brutality and criminality with tenderness and a peculiar, but apparently strong, feeling of responsibility toward his wards.[35] There were more rescuers like him in other places.

The second rescue story from Zborow is that of Leib Kronish, a relatively wealthy man who had been the local representative of the Mizrahi religious Zionist party on the communal council. Under the Soviets, he maintained himself despite the fact that he was a "capitalist," partly by bribing officials with vodka and partly by organizing an artel (cooperative) that collected and utilized straw. For the artel he employed Hasidic Jews who did not want to work on the Shabbat and managed to hide that fact from the authorities. When the Germans came, Kronish hid, thus saving himself from the first massacre, of men. A cousin of his made preparations for armed resistance, but neither the name nor the date is mentioned in the records. As a member of the Judenrat, Kronish was responsible for the Jews' relations with the Ukrainian police. He claimed that the local commander was friendly to Jews, providing some food and releasing prisoners. And he described Fuchs, head of the Judenrat, in glowing terms.

After the second "action" in Zborow, on August 28, 1942, Kronish left his protected job with a friendly Pole because he realized that protection by anyone was no longer possible. In early 1943, Kronish fled to a peasant in a nearby village, but the peasant became scared of hiding a Jew, so Kronish turned to another peasant, a Pole, Fedko Potorsky, an old acquaintance. The peasant asked his priest, Jan Pawlicky, for advice. Pawlicky—who is mentioned in a number of testimonies as a very courageous defender of Jews, apparently for a mixture of humanitarian, political, and religious motives—told the peasant to hide Jews. The peasant had to provide for nine people: Kronish's family and a friend of theirs. A hole was dug in a cabbage field outside the peasant's house, and the Jews hid there. The peasant, his wife, or his mother brought them food at night. In the dugout, Kronish maintained strict discipline. He taught his daughter and a niece history, mathematics, and Jewish tradition despite the terrible conditions in a rain-soaked field. They were accidentally discovered, apparently in late 1943, by a hunter and his dog. The man did not betray them, but the dugout was no longer secure, and the oncoming (second) winter became unbearable. The peasant dug another hiding place, under his pigsty in his backyard, and there it was warmer.

In early 1944, the Zborow area became a battlefield between the advancing Soviets and the Germans, and the peasant's house was taken over for a German command post. The Jews had to move again, back to the cabbage field, in the middle of the Polish winter, but there was no choice, for the Germans began digging trenches in the peasant's backyard, and they would have been discovered. At one point, the peasant came to the dugout and told Kronish that he (Potorsky) and his family were being forcefully evacuated to Germany; he brought extra food for the Jews but had to leave. After a few days, the hidden Jews heard two people talking over their dugout, in Russian. One of them said: "What beautiful cabbage" (Kakaya kharoshaya kapusta), and the family urged Kronish to go out since the Russians were there. But Kronish said no, fearing that these might be Russians collaborating with the German army who would immediately kill any Jews. The people hiding in the dugout waited another couple of days. Then the cover of the dugout was lifted, and the peasant stood outside: he and his family had fled from the evacuation train and come back. His first concern was to see whether his charges had survived. He brought food and said the Russians had come.[36] Kronish died in the United States in 1973.[37]

Kronish's story is authenticated by the independent testimony of his niece, Lena Adler, given more than twenty years after his death, and it is also mentioned by Sabina Schweid.[38] Adler mentions other rescuers: a Ukrainian, probably a peasant, by the name of Kukulsky, and an unnamed Polish family of two brothers and their mother. The Kronish story is important because of aspects that it shares with a number of similar testimonies: the rescuer endangered himself and his family after the money gave out; he kept the Jews hidden and supplied them with food while Germans were using his farmstead for a command post;

and finally, after he had escaped from the deportation train, he rushed back to release the hidden family. Potorsky's consultation with the priest indicates that he was probably motivated primarily by religious feelings, but there must have been a deep humanitarian impulse as well. Many other rescue stories show a similar combination of motives—sometimes political convictions took the place of religious ones.

Lest I give the wrong impression of a multitude of rescuers, let me note that the number of survivors from Zborow was thirty-three.

The priest whom the peasant consulted was not typical. The attitude of the Catholic and Orthodox priests toward the Jews was contradictory. However, in East Galicia, there are a number of stories about help being given by Catholic (Polish) priests, such as Jan Pawlicky in Zborow.[39] Similar evidence comes from Volhynia.[40]

Ukrainians gave aid to Jews, too, as we know from the story of Petro Ilnitsky, but his is not the only story by far. Near Buczacz, a Ukrainian peasant, Mikolai Zacharczuk, and his Polish wife saved the life of Yisrael Gelbert.[41] A Ukrainian farmer near Buczacz saved Rachel Halperin, a small girl, born in 1938, together with her parents. He hid them even after his farm had been searched by Germans because of a denunciation by a neighbor—and the family had not been discovered. However, when the Germans returned after the first liberation, in March 1944, the father was killed when he tried to bring food to the family. The mother died of sorrow after the final liberation in July. The girl, who told her story in an orphanage after the war, could no longer remember the name of the Ukrainian rescuer.[42]

Some testimonies emphasize help given to Jews by very poor Ukrainians. Sarah Kirshenbaum relates the story of a poor Ukrainian woman (with rich relatives) by the name of Johanka.[43] Sarah hid in a heap of manure, and Johanka brought her food for three months, until a German found her and wounded her, but then said, "Man muss die Frau leben lassen" (One has to leave this woman alive). Sarah moved to a swamp, and Johanka continued to support her and her husband. Sarah later fled to a Polish village, where she said she had fled from the Ukrainians, and a good woman (a "Jewish mother") kept her alive.

Buczacz survivors tell a particularly important story of the Basilian (Greek Catholic, therefore Ukrainian) monastery there, which reputedly saved the local synagogue's Torah scrolls. If this is true, as it seems to be, then there is possibly some connection with the work of Archbishop Szeptyskyi mentioned above.[44]

However, the evidence of Ukrainian hostility certainly predominates. This is true of Sarny and Rokitno and certainly of Krzemieniec, as well as Buczacz, Czortkow, and a large number of other places that I checked.

Relationships between Jews and others in the south differed from relationships between Jews and others in northern Volhynia and Polesie, and then again from relationships in the Belorussian areas. In Polesie, there were islands of Czech peasants and Baptists-Mennonites, as well as of Old Believers, mainly in isolated villages and farmsteads in the forests and marshes. Although there are stories of betrayals and hostility, there are also—more frequently, it seems, than farther south—stories of aid to fleeing Jews. Ukrainian nationalism did not take hold as much there, although bands of Banderovtsy roamed the area's forests, killing Jews. Each village and shtetl in the area has a different story, and to get the flavor of these, let me tell two.

Berezowo was not a shtetl but a village (*dorf*). It lies forty-five kilometers north of Rokitno, in the Polesian swamps. Eighteen Jewish families lived there among some 500–600 non-Jews whose ethnic identity was unclear to them. These others were probably Ukrainian and Belorussian, or just "locals." The older generation of Jews were practically illiterate, just able to read the prayer book phonetically, without understanding the Hebrew words. In the thirties, the slightly wealthier families began sending their children to the Tarbut school (instruction in He-brew) in Rokitno, and since the village did not have a synagogue, they used to meet for services in the house of the Jewish elder Israel Berezowski. For four to five months after the Soviet retreat, "we did not see any Germans at all," but later sixty Ukrainian policemen came to supervise that whole area. They murdered a whole Jewish community in another village, Wojkiewicze, thirty kilometers away. But there were also local policemen, and these protected the Jews from the Ro-kitno Ukrainians. A Jew by the name of Brick became the Jewish representative. In the end, however, the Ukrainians gathered 303 Jews in Berezowo. In the late summer of 1942, the Berezowo Jews learned about the "action" of August 26 in Rokitno. However, the Ukrainian commander had by that time understood that his unit was being used by the Germans to do their dirty work, and he refused to murder the local Jews. So German troops came. This was in September 1942, when there were only a few partisans in the forests. Nevertheless, many Bere-zowo Jews fled there; the Germans murdered the others. The number in either group is unclear.[45]

The other story, also from the Polesie area, exemplifies the complications that were typical when people hid or rescued Jews. It is based on the testimonies of two brothers, Moshe and Issaschar Trossman. They testified several times, and I was in a position to cross-check their testimonies and thus arrive at something that probably can be taken as true.[46] The Trossmans were a family of five, parents plus three children—the brothers had a younger sister. Before the "action" in Ro-kitno on August 26, 1942, they had arranged to flee if something untoward happened, and if separated, they would try to reach their ancestral village of Glinna, deep in the swamps. On the day of the "action" mother and daughter were separated from the male members of the family. The father and the two sons made their way north into the Polesian area—the father had had a dairy before the war and had sold cheeses and other products in the larger towns in the area, so he knew his way in the forests. They met a Soviet partisan detachment (of Medvedev), who sent them northward; after a series of complicated adventures, they finally reached Glinna. To their great joy, they found the mother and the daughter already there. The family hid in the forest with some Baptists-Mennonites. Glinna, so they say, had a small synagogue, reputedly hundreds of years old. The village was situated on the banks of a river that was used for trade, mainly in wood. The local Ukrainians were not friendly, but Glinna was far from anywhere else, and the few Jews there ultimately joined a Soviet partisan detachment (led by an NKVD man, Pleskonosov) that accepted Jews. After the partisans killed a Ukrainian farmer who had denounced Jews to the Ukrainian militia, the attitude toward Jews changed for the better. Germans were hardly seen in the area at all.

Now for the Belorussian area, where the Poles, in a minority there, were much less prone to be friendly to the Jews than Poles in the south were, probably for two reasons. First, Germans nominated quite a number of Poles to serve as local officials and members of the German-sponsored militia—for instance, in Nowogrodek. Second, after a while the Polish AK established its underground organization there, and the AK was against Jews and actively killed them. The region had been an Endek bastion prior to the war—villages such as Jedwabne, where Poles murdered Jews after the beginning of the German invasion, were just to the west of the area—and the local Catholic clergy encouraged radically anti-semitic feelings. The AK tried to keep the area as part of a future Poland and therefore became involved in fighting the Soviet partisans after earlier attempts at collaboration with the Soviets had failed: the Soviet Union had no intention of returning any part of what was now western Belarus to the Poles. For the Jews, the Soviet partisans were the only hope for survival, and they fought with the Soviets against the AK. Polish antisemitism and the political situation combined to make for bitter enmity between the AK and the Jews.[47]

Even here, there were exceptions, of course. The desperately poor Polish family of Franciszek Bobrowski, called the "dog catchers" by their neighbors, eked out a living by catching and skinning stray dogs. They were shunned by the residents of Nowogrodek and lived a distance away. Jews fleeing from the Nowogrodek ghetto made contact with the family, as did a Jewish partisan detachment (the Bielskis). As a result, the dog catchers' family hut became a meeting and transit point for fleeing Jews. The Bobrowskis helped many Jews, probably dozens, if not more, but the Germans caught them just before the German retreat in July 1944. Most of the family members were burned alive in their shack, with the exception of one daughter, who was sent away to Germany for forced labor. She survived, and received the title of "Righteous" from Yad Vashem in the name of her family.[48] Other testimonies tell of individual Poles who saved or tried to save Jews, some of whom received recognition as being Righteous, and some of whom should have received that recognition but for various reasons did not.

Unfortunately, the Polish attitude was not generally so helpful. Polish foremen brutalized Jewish forced laborers in the ghetto workshops, Poles served the Germans on the town's police force, and most Poles refused to hide Jews. As already mentioned, so-called White Poles, members of AK detachments, regularly disarmed and murdered Jews in the forests of western Belorussia and the Vilno region. And yet we have the amazing story of Eduard Chacza, of Baranowicze. Chacza was born in 1918, in western Poland; he was a married man and apparently a coal miner. After he moved to Baranowicze, he became the custodian of the local Catholic cemetery. He seems to have had some contacts with Jews before the war, and these did not break off after the Germans came. During the first "action," in March 1942, he rescued a man called Arkadi Lipkin and his brother, and helped them to reach the forest. He later rescued two women and Shmuel Jankielewicz, head of the Judenrat. The women were scared at first, thinking he might deliver them into the hands of the Germans, until he brought them to the forest. He saved people by hiding them in the mortuary of the cemetery, where the Germans did not enter, supplying them with some bare essentials, and showing them how to reach the forest. He increased the number of Jews he rescued, and in early 1943 he rescued a group of thirty-five, some of the last Jews in the local SD camp. He alone was responsible for saving the lives of between 60 and 150 people. After the war he did not record his testimony, apparently because his literacy was very limited, but many survivors testified that he had saved them. When no more Jews were left in the town, he served as an intelligence contact for the partisans until he was caught in November 1943, imprisoned, tortured, and sent to a number of concentration camps—we do not know which ones or exactly when. But he survived, and Yad Vashem made him one of the first recipients of the Righteous award (1962). Chacza was a very simple though intelligent person. It is rumored that before the war he had had his brushes with the law for thievery. Some rescuers were like that: they were people with asocial tendencies who rescued people (Oskar Schindler is a good example of exactly that). There is no doubt—Chacza was a hero, whatever his past.[49]

There appears to be much truth in statements found both in the literature and in testimonies that, by comparison, the attitude of Belorussian peasants to Jews was slightly better than the attitude of their Ukrainian neighbors to Jews. Stories abound of betrayal and cruelty by Belorussian peasants, but the stories that involved help extended to Jews are more frequent than in the south. The small shtetl of Kurzeniec can serve as a case in point. The Belorussian police, set up by the Germans, have been described as the dregs of humanity. The first "action," on October 14, 1941, took fifty-four victims. The Germans organized it, but the Belorussian police helped. In the second one, on March 5, 1942, thirteen Jews were killed, probably at the instigation of the local police. Soon afterward, on March 27, thirty-two Jews were killed, this time more clearly at the instigation of the Belorussians.

In a Belorussian village in the area, Wolkowczyzna, there was, on the other hand, the family of the peasant Ivan Siroczyn, who was a friend of the Jews. The surrounding peasants were anti-German—a meeting of partisans took place in the village church. When the Judenrat in Kurzeniec opposed support for the partisan movement and threatened the father of an underground member, Siroczyn went to the Judenrat member responsible, brandished a revolver, and said he would shoot any Judenrat member who prevented Jews from working with the underground. The first Soviet partisan detachment in the whole area was set up by a Russian officer who had been rescued by a young Jew from Kurzeniec, and the Belorussians in it saw the Jews as allies. One of them, a man by the name of Matskewicz, was sent to serve in the police as a spy, and he actively helped Jews. In some of the villages local peasants even encouraged the Jews to leave for the forests. "Go that way, and may God be with you," said a farmer from the village of Voronietz to fleeing Jews.[50] "The villagers' attitude to us was good," testified one woman who fled from the shtetl.[51]

So we again find different attitudes reflected in the testimonies of survivors, and we could heap on more stories on both sides. The following story may exemplify the kinds of attitudes in that region: a Kurzeniec woman by the name of Feige-Leah Sarles hid in the forest with the help of local peasants, but she was caught and then tortured to reveal the names of the peasants who had helped her. She refused to reveal any names and died at the hands of her torturers. The peasants found her body and buried her, and her grave became a center of worship—she was perceived as a martyr.[52]

A very important case of a Belorussian peasant aiding Jews is that of Konstanty Kozlowski and his family. Kozlowski had a farm thirteen kilometers from Nowogrodek. He had had connections with Jews before the war and had developed friendships with some of them. When Tuvia Bielski organized his partisan detachment a few dozen kilometers away from the town in the late spring of 1942 (see below), Kozlowski began offering fleeing Jews a temporary haven and a point where they could be picked up by the Bielski partisans. The farm was away from the road and quite isolated. Kozlowski operated for about two years as the main transit point for Jews fleeing to the forest and must have saved hundreds of Jews. He was never found out, and survived the war to be recognized as Righteous by Yad Vashem.[53] One of the important conclusions that we can draw from his story is the great difference that determined action by just one individual and his family can make to the lives of a large number of people.

The Germans did not have much trouble recruiting local intellectuals to serve them from among Belorussian townspeople. In Baranowicze, the first mayor was an antisemite by the name of Sobolewski, and the second was a physician, Dr. Voitenko. Voitenko had been friendly to the Jews, but in the fall of 1941 he changed his tune and advocated the establishment of a ghetto. When informed that its establishment might lead to the spread of disease, he replied that it did not matter, because any Jew who fell ill would be shot at once.[54] Jews in Barano-wicze, as in many other places, entrusted belongings to Belorussian "friends," only to be afraid to ask for them back because the Belorussians threatened to denounce them to the Germans. Indeed, in some cases Belorussian townsmen got rid of former Jewish competitors or other people with whom they had had some kind of falling out by denouncing them as communists, which led to their immediate execution. During the "actions," Belorussian youths ran amok in the ghetto, plundering and beating Jews, or handing them over to the police and the Germans to be killed. Still, according to existing evidence, some Belorussians brought food to the ghetto inhabitants.[55]

Perhaps one of the most telling examples of the complicated relationship be-tween Belorussians and Jews in the kresy is contained in the story of a survivor, Joseph Halpern.[56] In September 1939, Halpern was a lonely sixteen-year-old refu-gee from the west living in Belorussia. He wanted to go to school, but the Soviet authorities informed him that he had been designated as a schoolteacher in a Belorussian village of illiterates. He protested, but to no avail. He was sent to the village, having quickly mastered the Cyrillic script and picked up enough Belo-russian to make do; he was already fluent in Polish. The peasants were very happy to have someone to teach their children to read and to write. They provided him with a wooden barrack, benches, tables, and a blackboard. They even supplied some chalk. After he began to teach the young children, he looked for space for them to play during breaks. But the land around the improvised schoolhouse belonged to the only rich peasant in the village, a man by the name of Bobko, who had a young son, Sergei; the Bobkos strenuously resisted having a small plot taken away for a playground, but the peasants threatened to inform on them to the authorities, who would brand them as kulaks and deport them. The Bobkos reluctantly yielded, but they hated the young Jew who had caused them to lose valuable property.

When the Germans came, Halpern wanted to run, although the peasants said they would protect him; but there were the Bobkos, and they would take revenge on Halpern if they could. Together with a young Belorussian friend, Halpern escaped to Baranowicze, where he presented himself to a town clerk as a Polish refugee who had lost his papers. Having obtained papers using an assumed name, he looked for work. A Belorussian collaborator had acquired some land that had belonged to a Soviet *sovkhoz* (government farm) and was looking for an expert manager. Young Halpern pretended to be such an expert and got the job. The estate was quite a distance away from the town, on the edge of a thick forest. Halpern quickly learned the ropes and ran the farm to the satisfaction of his employer, even making a profit. He made contact with a group of partisans in the forest and began supplying them with necessities. These he obtained by illicitly trading the products of the farm he was managing. He became rather cocky, and the Belorussian police caught him once, traveling with his horse and cart with some sacks of sugar, and accused him of black marketeering. They arrested him and threw him into the Baranowicze jail. Periodically, a commission consisting of a German and a Belorussian came to inspect the jail and determine the fate of the inmates.

In the meantime, Sergei Bobko had joined the Belorussian police and had been sent to serve at the concentration camp of Koldyczewo, a short distance from Baranowicze, where Poles and Belorussians who were suspected of anti-German activities, sometimes correctly, as well as Jews, were held, tortured, and murdered. Bobko rose through the ranks and became the feared deputy commander of the camp. He proved himself to be a brutal torturer and murderer, with quite a number of lives on his conscience, and thus endeared himself to the Germans.

When the commission came to the Baranowicze jail, Halpern went to the head jailer, confessed to being a Jew, and begged to be freed. If the commission had told him to remove his pants, which was likely, he would, in any case, have been discovered to be a Jew and would have been shot immediately. The commander said that it was too late; he had already reported him as a black marketeer under his assumed name, and all he could suggest was that he not go to the German commissioner but try to see the Belorussian commissioner, in the hope of finding more understanding there. Halpern followed the advice—he did not have much choice—and went to the room of the Belorussian. When he opened the door, there, on the other side of the table, sat Sergei Bobko. Bobko immediately recognized Halpern, and Halpern reports a moment of tense silence. Then

Bobko told Halpern to get the hell out of there; the next time they met, it would mean the end of the young Jew. Halpern ran from the jail, escaped into the forest, and survived as a partisan.

After the war, Halpern went to Poland and for a while lived in Lodz (at the time of this writing he is alive and well and lives in Israel). Bobko had been caught by the Soviets, and because he had been responsible for the killing of a number of Poles, he was put on trial in Poznan, together with other war criminals. In his defense he said that he had saved the life of a Jew called Joseph Halpern. "Where did this Halpern live?" asked the prosecution. Bobko had no idea. However, the Polish police looked for Halpern and, lo and behold, found him in Lodz and brought him to the trial as a witness. He was confronted with Bobko and was asked whether Bobko had saved his life. Halpern replied in the affirmative. All the other defendants were hanged. Bobko received a life sentence, and after a number of years he was released.[57]

Saul Friedlander once wrote a book about the anti-Nazi SS-man Kurt Gerstein, the man who tried to warn the neutral countries and the Allies about the death camp of Belzec and, in order to do so, agreed to transport poison gas to the camp. The book is called *The Ambiguity of Good*.[58] The story about Bobko and Halpern is not only about Belorussians and Jews but also about the ambiguity of evil. How do you judge an evil person who saved a life?

The different attitudes of the local population will become even more clear when we discuss the relationships of Jews and non-Jews in the partisan movement, but for now let me summarize the testimonies we have—and there are quite a few for the five Belorussian places I investigated in detail (Baranowicze, Kurzeniec, Dereczin, Mir, and Nowogrodek)—and say that it was easier to find Belorussian peasants than Ukrainians who were willing to help Jews. The reasons are not far to seek: Belorussian nationalism was much weaker than the Ukrainian brand, meaning much less of a confrontational attitude toward minorities. The differences in living standards between Belorussian townspeople and peasants, on the one hand, and their Jewish counterparts, on the other hand, were also rather small. In the small shtetlach of the forest region Jews lived not that much differently, from an economic point of view, from their Belorussian neighbors, despite that unbridgeable social and cultural gap. Many village Jews were also versed in the way life was conducted in those parts. According to Jewish testimonies, village Jews knew how to milk cows, how to thresh grain, how to dig potatoes, and how to drink samogon, the local brand of vodka, in respectable quantities. On top of that, many Jews knew the forest paths as peddlers and tradesmen and experts in tree felling. For many Belorussians, the real difference was not so much between Jew and non-Jew as between townspeople, who did not know how to live in the countryside, and "our people," who did, and with whom they could identify. On the negative side was the influence of Christian antisemitism propagated by the Orthodox Church and the old antagonism of peasants to merchants and traders, which solidified in the perception, in many minds, that the Jews, who looked different, lived in their own communities, spoke another language, and espoused another religion, were rich exploiters and that every opportunity should be used to despoil them. These conflicting attitudes found their expression during the crisis of the war years.

German policies had a significant effect. Originally, as Christian Gerlach has shown, the Germans saw in Belorussia a primitive and unproductive area that should receive as little food and other resources as possible; in effect, they advocated a policy of starving millions of people to death—first and foremost the Jews, of course, but also many Belorussians.[59] There was no intention to keep up programs of industrialization initiated by the Soviets, and only those industries were to be kept going that served the immediate military and civilian needs of the Germans. Belorussian agriculture was seen as useless, and the Germans had no compunction in doing away with the peasants if they resisted or even if they did not cooperate fully. The development of the Soviet partisan movement caused the Germans to respond with increasingly violent and brutal efforts to eliminate the partisans in major military expeditions. All of these attempts failed, and the Germans decided, as again Gerlach shows very clearly, to destroy villages and annihilate their populations, leaving alive only those who were fit for work and deporting them to Germany for labor. They did that in a very big way, causing many villagers to take a radical anti-German stance, which in turn tended to reduce somewhat the existing antisemitic attitudes, for Jews and Belorussians now faced a common enemy. We should remember, however, that Belorussians still often attacked and killed Jews who were seeking refuge in their midst.

In Ukraine the memory of the holodomor, the starving and killing of "kulaks," the supposedly wealthy peasants, in the early thirties by the Stalin regime, had created an initial willingness on the part of a large majority to cooperate with the Germans; in the Belorussian area this willingness was much less marked, and although there was massive opposition to the Soviet kolkhoz system, there was also, in the late thirties, a growing acceptance of the Soviet regime and an identification with it, including among the peasants. There were, to be sure, "red villages" in Ukraine, but there were many more of them in the north. And we must not forget that, as in the south, the progress of the war affected the behavior of the local population. The problem was that when the Jews desperately needed the help of their neighbors, the Germans were advancing and seemed all-powerful; by the time the tide had turned, many fewer Jews were around to seek such help, if any were left at all. This point, which I have made before, is true for the whole kresy and forms the background to any understanding of the Jewish tragedy.

A limited number of Jews saved themselves by obtaining "Aryan" papers or using other subterfuges to register for labor in Germany as Poles, Belorussians, or Ukrainians. There are a number of testimonies of survivors who worked in Germany without being discovered. We have to assume that some—and we do not know their number—were betrayed or found out by the Germans and killed.[60]

A comparison between what happened in the Polish kresy and what happened in other European countries under German control makes it very clear that the attitude of the host populations to the Jews was one of the main determinants of the Jews' fate. This is true of most genocidal events, certainly of the killing in Rwanda and the Armenian genocide. In the genocide of the Jews, survival and rescue rates were highest in countries like Denmark, where almost all Jews survived; Bulgaria (with the exception of Bulgarian-controlled Thrace and Macedonia), where all Jews survived; France, where three-quarters of the Jewish population survived; and Belgium, where over a half did. By contrast, the survival rate in Lithuania and Latvia was below 5 percent. The populations of Denmark and Bulgaria opposed the annihilation policy of the Germans, and there was also massive opposition in the French-speaking part of Belgium and among many of the French, including significant parts of the Catholic hierarchy and all the Huguenot clergy. The same is true of Italy. In the Baltic republics, on the other hand, there was massive collaboration with the Germans. Exceptions existed, of course. Despite the Serbs' radical opposition to German rule and a basically friendly attitude on the part of most Serbs, almost all Serbian Jews were killed because of the nature of German rule there. Generally, however, given that the same German policies were enacted in all of German-controlled Europe, the survival of Jews depended heavily on the attitude of the population around them.

In Poland, and more especially in the kresy, the overwhelming attitude of the population, with the exceptions that I have mentioned, was indifferent at best, and mostly hostile. That sealed the fate of the Jews. It also impacted Jewish efforts to maintain some sort of organized community life, because even that was very difficult without support from outside, whether by enabling food to reach the Jews—a basic requirement—or by supplying moral support and opposition to the Germans. By the time opposition crystallized, first in the Belorussian areas and then in Ukraine, the Jews were gone. Jan T. Gross's famous study of the killing of the Jews of the shtetl of Jedwabne by their Polish neighbors could just as easily have been written about shtetlach throughout the kresy; and, as Gross has shown, there were Righteous rescuers even in Jedwabne.[61] Neighbors . . .

Seven

REBELS AND PARTISANS

We have seen that during 1941 and 1942, when the Jews of the kresy were being murdered, the Soviet partisan movement was still in its infancy. In the southern, Ukrainian parts of the kresy Soviet partisan activity was still limited even in 1943, for the Ukrainian nationalists (OUN) and their army (UPA) were very active there, and its anti-Soviet stance was bolstered by very efficient propaganda. In central and southern Volhynia there were practically no Soviet partisans at all; in East Galicia there were some. Jewish underground and resistance activities in these areas were, almost by definition, acts of desperation. The Jews had little chance of survival. In the south, efforts to survive were mostly a matter of finding hiding places with friendly neighbors. When that was impossible, people fled to the forests and tried to survive by begging or stealing food from peasants on the edge of the woods or in forest villages. Geographically, these areas were only lightly forested, though with some denser patches; they mainly consisted of fertile regions of undulating farmland and no high mountains; the landscape was not at all like that of Polesie and Belorussia to the north, with their thick forests and swamps. The southern forests were penetrable, and paths and roads led through them.

Our topic for the south is twofold: resistance in the shtetlach and survival and resistance in the forests. Besides family camps in the forests, rare armed groups in those very same forests tried to maintain themselves somehow. The differences between East Galicia and Volhynia are very important. East Galicia had a larger Polish minority than Volhynia did, and was the original breeding ground for the UPA, the Ukrainian nationalist armed forces, the Banderovtsy and the Bulbovtsy. Northern Volhynia, basically the area north of the Kovel-Kiev railway, was part of the Ukrainian-Belorussian border region known as Polesie, and it was topographically very different from the other Ukrainian regions. It was there that Soviet partisans developed an impressive presence after the summer of 1942.

For the Jews, armed resistance in the shtetlach was a matter of last resort, sometimes leading to rebellions and attempts to flee into the surrounding areas. Only a widespread anti-German resistance movement could have helped them, but that did not exist in the southern kresy. Underground resistance groups were always small, sometimes very small, groups of mainly young people who banded together in order to sell their lives at as great a price as they could. There is no hard and fast rule about this: In places where we would have expected resistance to crystallize, nothing happened. In places where resistance was a totally hopeless undertaking, it nevertheless took place. Thus, we might have expected resistance in Kosow Huculski, a shtetl in the foothills of the Carpathian Mountains. The population in that area was partly of Hucul origin. The Huculs are an ethnic group somewhere between Ukrainians and Poles, and in the mountains they still talked about the Jewish saint who had roamed there 200 years ago. Indeed, the Besht (Israel Baal-Shem Tov), founder of the Hasidic movement, had spent time in those mountains during the first half of the eighteenth century. Whether a Jewish partisan group could have survived in the Carpathian Mountains is an unanswerable question. There were no Soviet partisan groups there at all; just a raid from Belorussia took place. In fact, the Jews made no attempt either to organize a resistance group in the shtetl or to flee to the mountains in order to fight. Zionist youth movements had existed there, and the Judenrat received positive marks (although a book was written against it in the postwar era), but no type of group resistance was organized.

Buczacz was not far away from Kosow, and it had a similar Jewish population and similar neighbors. The Judenrat there was not a popular one, as we have seen, and the community was disorganized, atomized. Yet three underground movements arose in Buczacz. The larger of the three seems to have been organized by a group of young people, many of them from the shtetl of Tlumacz, who were graduates of Betar, the rightist Zionist youth movement, who had been forced to come to Buczacz, and by refugees from the town of Horodenka, as well as by local residents. Others had been members of different Zionist youth movements as well (Gordonia and Noar Tzioni). The head of the group, E. Bazan-Worman, who survived, claims a large membership for his group, but his estimate is probably exaggerated. The members of the group had contacts with Judenrat members, as well as with the police, into which they infiltrated some of their followers. Until March 1943, they desisted from action because they feared that all the residents of the ghetto would be murdered if they did so. Feeling responsible for non-combatants created a dilemma for many such groups in the kresy (and elsewhere). When the remnants of the ghetto population were deported from Buczacz to surviving nearby ghettoes—in order to be liquidated there—the Bazan group split, and some of them tried to foment uprisings in the ghettoes to which they had been sent, but these attempts failed. The main group fled to the forest of Puzniki, not far from the shtetl, and maintained itself there until liberation. They were partly armed and defended themselves against the Banderovtsy, but they did not engage in any other armed actions. Peasants belonging to the Old Believers' sect helped them.

The two other underground groups were smaller. One, led by Ozio Friedlander, attacked local collaborators with the Nazis and even tried to assassinate a local German civilian governor (but failed). There is some evidence to the effect that these actions against collaborators caused some peasants to hide Jews and not betray them, for fear of Jewish revenge. Some members of this group also survived, having joined Polish peasants defending themselves against the Banderovtsy. The third group, led by a Jew called Wizinger, had access to a radio receiver and disseminated information; members of this group are apparently the ones who finally offered armed resistance in Buczacz itself, sometime in June or July 1943, when the place where they holed up was attacked by Ukrainian police who were liquidating the last people in the ghetto. All the resisters, except for Wizinger, who survived, were killed in a shootout. The testimonies are largely indirect, based on information from local non-Jews, but they converge.[1]

There were resistance groups in many other shtetlach in East Galicia and central Volhynia—in fact, there are reports of resistance groups in forty shtetlach, and of fifty breakouts in attempts to flee from the ghettoes.[2] In Zborow (East Galicia), a group organized resistance in the forced labor camp that the Germans erected in town, as well as a firefight with Germans and Ukrainians who came to liquidate the camp on June 5, 1943. Two armed groups that escaped from the nearby ghetto of Zloczow and two more from Czortkow—all of them in East Galicia—were annihilated by German forces. There were mass flights from at least five or six more places; another group, in the same area, was accepted into the Armia Krajowa—a rare occurrence—and a number of its members survived.[3] There were twenty such forest groups in Volhynia, and fifteen in East Galicia, and their main armed activity was against local collaborators who had killed Jews. A very small number of such groups managed to find and join Soviet partisans, who were themselves outnumbered and outgunned by Ukrainian and Polish anti-Soviet nationalists and, of course, by the Germans. Occasionally, we hear of armed action against Germans: a group of Jewish resisters attacked the German police station in the East Galician township of Bursztyn; a group of escapees from Stanislawow (not a shtetl but a large town) led by a woman, Anda Luft, fought the Germans until Luft was killed (November 15, 1942). Apparently only one group, in the Tarnopol area of East Galicia, managed to survive as a fighting group, in the relatively dense Grzymalow forest, until the Soviets liberated the area.[4]

Tuczyn, in central Volhynia, was a small shtetl with 3,000 Jews; the other half of the population consisted of Ukrainians, plus Polish and German minorities. Prior to the German onslaught, relations between the Jews and the surrounding Ukrainian peasants seemed to be positive. However, two days prior to the German occupation, the Ukrainians of the township and the peasants of the surrounding region enacted a violent pogrom. It turned into an orgy of murder, in which an estimated sixty Jews were killed. Tuczyn was the center of a leather industry—that is, a number of workshops processed leather, an important economic fact appreciated by the Germans. A Jewish entrepreneur from central Poland, by the name of Gross, persuaded the Germans to permit these workshops to exist, which provided protection for the workers and their families. The Judenrat head was Getzel Schwartzmann, a graduate of one of the Zionist youth movements. In the year during which the Jews of Tuczyn existed under German rule, the Ukrainians were murderous. The area's predominant political-military force was the Banderovtsy, and that meant that Jews (and Poles) were, as a rule, killed whenever the opportunity arose. A Ukrainian physician in the shtetl, a Dr. Bortanowsky, was friendly, as was a Russian nurse who helped him. No testimony mentions any other friendly locals. By the summer of 1942, the Germans had concentrated Jews from the surrounding areas in Tuczyn, whose Jewish population grew to 6,000.

For the Germans in Tuczyn, as everywhere else, ideological considerations triumphed over economic ones, and on September 19, 1942, Jews were forced into a ghetto in preparation for their liquidation. Schwartzmann labored under no illusions, and a group of young Jews began to acquire arms. They had five rifles, some handguns, and a number of hand grenades. On September 24, the Ukrainians and the Germans surrounded the ghetto; a German commander offered to take a group of healthy young men as workers, but Schwartzmann refused. He called a meeting in a synagogue and told the Jews to burn the ghetto and try to escape to the Postomit forests, twenty kilometers away, in the hope of finding partisans. Four groups of resisters were organized, kerosene was acquired, and people were instructed how to burn their houses. When the Germans penetrated into the ghetto and opened fire, the few who had weapons responded, and in the commotion, the ghetto inhabitants set fire to their houses. Many people jumped into their burning houses, including the rabbi of the town. Others tried to escape into the forest. An estimated 2,000 people managed to flee; the rest

were killed or burned on the spot. Schwartzmann was killed. The escapees included a high proportion of women, children, and elderly people, most of whom
were caught and killed by Ukrainians armed with axes and pitchforks. Others
tried to survive in the forest, but there was no food, and many, in desperation, returned to Tuczyn, only to be killed by the Ukrainians and the Germans. A group
of sixty men, led by the organizer of the underground in Tuczyn, Nachum Bi-
linsky, managed to acquire eleven rifles; they sought partisans toward the north
but failed to find any. Only one Soviet partisan unit operated in Volhynia north
of Tuczyn, namely the otriad of Dmitry N. Medvedev. A few escapees managed
to go further north, into Polesie, where they joined partisan detachments. At the
end of the war, twenty survivors emerged from the forest, including a handful
of people hidden by friendly Ukrainian peasants, including at least one Baptist-
Mennonite family.[5]

The importance of this particular rebellion and mass escape lies, it seems, in
the fact that it did not help the Jews. The small number of survivors is proof that
given the violent enmity of the Ukrainians, survival was hardly likely. The leaders
of the rebellion were apparently aware of that; their decision to rebel was a measure of the depth of their desperation. The absence of Soviet partisans underlines
this conclusion: Soviet partisans provided the only real hope that more than a
handful would survive, and there were no partisans in the area.

How does one explain the violent hatred of the Ukrainians in the area? We can
only guess at factors: the presence of the murderously nationalistic Banderovtsy,
greed, and an ancient animosity that had exploded in the seventeenth and eighteenth centuries and had never really been forgotten (I refer to the rebellions of
1648 and 1748, first of Bogdan Chmielnicki and then of the Haidamaks, which
cost very large numbers of Jews their lives). The violence of neighbors against
neighbors, resulting in robbery and murder, seems to be a general possibility that
becomes actualized when the circumstances are "right." We have seen similar
events in Bosnia, Rwanda, and elsewhere.[6] In fact, the more familiar neighbors
are with the future victims, the more brutal and sadistic is their behavior. The fate
of the shtetlach in these regions therefore exemplifies a general trend in genocidal situations.

Interestingly, the usually murderous policies of the Volhynian Banderovtsy
were not so murderous in two cases. One was in the area of Rechitsa, east of
Kostopol, in central Volhynia, where the local UPA (the Banderovtsy) employed
400 Jews as craftsmen and workers in other occupations useful to the UPA—doctors, nurses, and so on. In the other case, the local UPA commander, one Stepan
Polishuk, protected 50 Kovel Jews. No independent documentation throws light
on these cases, and we can only guess why these cases were exceptional: the

Rechitsa case seems to have been the result of cold-blooded economic calculation, and the Kovel case was seemingly the result of a personal relationship between Polishuk and Jews, perhaps these particular Jews.[7]

A Soviet partisan movement, led by local Ukrainian and Polish communists, developed only in northern Volhynia. Remnants of local Jewish populations joined these units, which were basically not anti-Jewish. They operated along the border between Ukraine and Belorussia. The most important commanders were Anton Brinski, Vasili A. Begma, Alexei F. Fyodorov, and, further north, in the Belorussian area, Alexandr N. Saburov. They all were either neutral toward Jews or protected them to a degree; in any case, they did not object to Jews qua Jews joining their units.[8]

There was even one Jewish partisan unit in the Rowne area (central Volhynia). It hailed from Korets, a small shtetl west of Rowne (6,000 Jews in 1941). After an "action" on May 12, 1942, an underground group of some twenty members arose, and a first handgun was acquired. The Judenrat decided to commit suicide and burn the ghetto at the next "action." On September 24 (the ghetto was liquidated immediately afterward), a group of resisters, led by Moshe Gildenman ("Dyadya Misha" [Uncle Misha]), who was more than fifty years old, left the ghetto. They met up with Medvedev and his unit, but Medvedev could not or would not accept them. Then they ran into a large number of escapees from Rokitno and penetrated further into the Polesie region. Friendly locals—the Poleshchuks—treated them well. The Jews joined the brigade of Alexandr Saburov. The Jewish unit was at first broken up, but Dyadya Misha organized a new group that contained a large number of Jews and led it until liberation. This Jewish unit was part of Saburov's brigade.[9] Again, we see that if Jews managed to get into the Polesie area, they had a chance of joining partisan units. The commanders in Dyadya Misha's group were generally supportive of his efforts. They included mainly Ukrainian communist commanders and some Poles.

We must not think in terms of a mass movement of Jewish partisans in the Ukrainian areas. The number of Jews who managed to join Soviet partisans was, according to a fairly reliable estimate, not more than 2,500—nearly exactly 1 percent of the prewar number of Jews. Of these, some 1,500 survived.[10] But the figure for the total number of Soviet partisans in all of Volhynia is not very impressive either: according to Soviet accounts, the total number at the end of 1943, just before the liberation of Volhynia by the Red Army, was 13,710. The 2,500 Jews amounted to about 18 percent, if the figures are more or less correct. The difference between Volhynia, especially the central and southern parts, and Polesie and Belorussia could not be more pronounced. The total number of survivors in Volhynia is estimated at about 3,500, or about 1.5 percent of all Jews in prewar

Volhynia. The number who fled the ghettos is estimated at 40,000, which means that we may guess (and it is no more than a guess) that 9 percent of these escapees survived. Clearly, the decisive factor was the hostility of their neighbors.[11]

In the northern parts of the kresy we find, again, local resistance groups, escapes to the forests, and Jews in partisan units. Shalom Cholawsky lists more than sixty shtetlach for which there is fairly solid evidence of resistance groups. Many of these tried to flee to the forests and swamps, where there were Soviet partisans.[12] What is very peculiar is the lack of serious historical investigation of the Belorussian partisan movement that would enable us to deal more thoroughly with the context in which these Jewish attempts at resistance took place. We would have expected postwar Soviet policies to have led Soviet historians to attempt an in-depth analysis of this main Soviet partisan movement during the war. However, apart from statistics and lists of names of the main commanders and names of units, no such analysis has been made, notwithstanding the flood of memoirs from commanders and ordinary partisans and the wealth of documents in archives. It is not my task in the present book to attempt to fill the gap, because I am concerned here with only a fraction of that movement, namely the Jews, first in resistance groups and then in the partisan movement. But it is impossible to deal with the Jews apart from the general context, so some comments are in order here.

The first Soviet detachments in Polesie started to organize very soon after the area had been occupied by the Germans, but these beginnings occurred in the eastern part of Polesie, which had been Soviet before 1939 and which therefore falls outside our area of investigation. The first partisan detachment there was set up by a Communist Party man, Vasily Z. Kurezh (nom de guerre: Komarov). He penetrated into western Polesie only gradually. In the formerly Polish areas, the first Soviet detachments were formed in August 1941, but they were weak. Most of the so-called partisans were, as in the south, escaped POWs, soldiers who had been cut off from their units, and they easily turned into bandits who killed and robbed to survive. Jews escaping into the forests often met with these bands, and if they were lucky, they were disarmed, their possessions, usually their boots to start with, were taken from them, and they were abandoned. If they were not lucky, they were killed. In many cases, those who survived their encounter with bandits had to return to the ghetto. They had no alternative. This discouraged those in the ghetto who planned any kind of resistance. And yet, as Cholawsky documents, in the vast majority of shtetlach groups of young people planned resistance and often managed to collect some weapons.[13]

The situation changed in early 1942. Soviet parachutists and small units that had made it through the front lines began to transform a chaotic situation into

a semblance of order. Such emissaries from the unoccupied Soviet Union belonged to either the Red Army intelligence service, the Communist Party, or the
NKVD. One of these NKVD groups, with more than 100 men, was commanded
by Dmitry N. Medvedev, who also roamed with his group into central Volhynia.
I mentioned him above. His assignment was mainly to gather information about
German military targets. In February 1942, the Soviet counteroffensive that had
started in November 1941 halted, but the Soviets had opened a gap in the German lines in an area thick with forests and swamps. Known as the Surazh Gap,
it was in the Briansk area, and the Germans could not control it. The Soviets infiltrated groups of trained men through the gap to strengthen the partisan operations. Civilians and wounded partisans were sent in the opposite direction. Until
the Germans managed to close the gap in September 1942, Jews were among the
civilians who were led to safety through that area.

In May 1942, a Central Command of the Partisan Forces was established,
nominally under Marshal Kliment E. Voroshilov—no great brain or great organizer—but in fact under Panteleimon K. Ponomarenko, secretary of the Belorussian Communist Party. Discipline was introduced, and as a result, attacks on
Jews diminished, although Ponomarenko was no great friend of Jews. The reason
for the reduction of antisemitic actions was probably the Soviet desire to present
a united front and avoid interethnic quarrels. They also wanted to fight German
propaganda, which constantly repeated the story that the Jews ruled the USSR
and were the movers and shakers in the partisans' struggle. This propaganda appears to have had some influence among Soviet partisans, and the Soviets were
eager to uproot such sentiments. I have not found any Jews among the top partisan commanders sent from the Soviet Union (Medvedev had a Jewish mother,
but this was probably not known at the time, except to the NKVD, which had
sent him), and it was perhaps intentional.

After the Center was established, small units were united into larger military
bodies, commanded by officers appointed by Moscow. All this was possible because of two main factors: one, the geographical reality of huge, impenetrable
forests and extensive swamps, which were ideal for partisan warfare, and, two,
the brutal German policies directed against the local population, which caused
many people to identify with the Soviet partisans. The first German setbacks in
the winter of 1941–1942 buoyed the partisans and their supporters; after the German defeat at Stalingrad everything changed. But, as we already know, it was
not until mid-1942 that the forests of Belorussia and Polesie were home to large
forces of Soviet partisans, and by that time most of the Jews had been killed or
were being killed. Only the remnants of the Jews had a chance of fighting back
or forming "family camps"—that is what they were called, although hardly any

complete families managed to escape. The family groups that tried to survive in forest hideouts were largely unarmed and depended on food from the area's peasants or from armed partisans who agreed to protect them. This is reflected in official Soviet figures. The Soviets claimed that there were 374,000 partisans in Belorussia in 1944, including 45,000 women. Of these, 92,000 were in family camps, presumably meaning those family camps that were protected by the official partisan groups, or were an integral part of partisan units (such as the Bielski and Zorin groups—see below). Family camps (in effect, dugouts in the forests) that were not protected by partisans appear not to have been included. We have to remember that as German policies toward the local population grew more brutal, and the danger of deportation to Germany loomed ever larger, more and more non-Jewish villagers fled into the forests. They, and not the Jews, were the vast majority of the protected family-camp population.

The German response to the partisans was famously brutal. There were major German efforts to annihilate the partisans in the thick forests of Belorussia—west and east—and northern Ukraine, as well as Russian areas farther east. At least nine major German offensives were launched in areas in or near the kresy, with appropriate names attached to them, from "Bamberg" in March–April 1942 to "Hermann" in July–August 1943. Because all of them failed to achieve their goals, the Germans destroyed large numbers of villages adjoining partisan areas and killed hundreds of thousands of Belorussians.[14]

The policy of Soviet partisan units regarding Jews differed from one unit to the other. In most cases, they rejected unarmed Jews and left them to fend for themselves; bandits killed many of these Jews. Soviet units also killed Jews, partly to acquire their possessions, partly to get rid of unwanted witnesses, and partly to eliminate competition for the little food the peasants on the edge of the forest could supply. Many former Red Army soldiers, Russians and others, turned out to be extremely antisemitic. It is clear, from the many testimonies, that the twenty years of Soviet propaganda that had pilloried antisemitism as a reactionary relic had not had the desired effect on a portion of the Soviet population; what percentage, it is impossible to even guess. On the other hand, most of the top Soviet commanders tended to suppress these views in their units, if only because they caused unwanted tension and strife.

One leader had an outstandingly objective and basically pro-Jewish attitude: Vasily Y. Chernishev (nom de guerre: Platon). In late 1942, Chernishev took over the command of the partisan units in the Baranowicze-Naliboki area, which included many units with Jewish partisans, including the Bielski group. Other leaders, such as Anton Brinski in northern Volhynia and Polesie, and Vasili A. Begma in the Rowne area, also established large units that included a growing number of partisan detachments (otriady), many with significant Jewish minorities. This relatively positive change became obvious after September 1942, when an order from the Central Command instructed commanders that the protection of the civilian population was part of their mission.

The best-known partisan commander was Sidor (Sidyr) A. Kovpak, a Ukrainian veteran of the Civil War of 1918–1922. At a meeting of the main partisan commanders that took place in Moscow between August 3 and September 2, 1942, it was decided that Kovpak, with the support of Saburov, would launch a daring raid from Belorussia southward. The targets were the oil fields of the Drohobycz (Ukr.: Drogobycz) region of East Galicia. Kovpak's brigade, 1,500 men and women, started off in June 1943 and succeeded in rebuffing German efforts to stop them. They reached their targets and caused considerable damage. However, in the face of overwhelming German superiority, they had to disperse and make their way back to Belorussia in small units. On their way back, Kovpak's units liberated a couple of Jewish forced labor camps, including the one at Skalat, in East Galicia, and the one on the planned DG4 road at Kamionka, in the general area of Tarnopol (Ukr.: Ternopil) and Czortkow. Some eighty Jews were permitted to join the partisans, even though some of the subaltern officers were no friends of Jews, nor were the partisan units equipped to handle larger numbers of people, and they usually demanded that Jews who joined them be equipped with weapons—a difficult precondition. The Jews, having no ready access to arms, had to capture or buy them. It seems that quite a number of Jews served with Kovpak. The number is impossible to establish, but the impression from testimonies is of 150–200 Jews, or perhaps 10 percent of the total.

Another major partisan brigade was that of Aleksandr N. Saburov, which also tried to stage a raid from its Belorussian base into Volhynia, but it was much less successful. A second raid by Kovpak's forces (he himself no longer commanded them), in early 1944, was also less than successful. Saburov's forces penetrated northern Volhynia and Polesie in other campaigns, and some of his units accepted Jews.[15]

Estimating the number of Jewish partisans in Belorussia is extremely difficult. Cholawsky believes there to have been at least 23,000, and that may indeed approximate the real figure. The overwhelming majority came from the shtetlach. Whether his total includes the thousands that tried to survive in family camps is not clear, but let us assume so. The conclusion is obvious: Soviet and other partisans rescued thousands of Jews and gave them the opportunity to take revenge on those who had murdered their loved ones. Soviet and other partisans also murdered many, perhaps even thousands, of Jews, just as the Germans and their collaborators did.[16]

Here I should possibly add a more general comment on the context in which all this took place. Very clearly, the remnants of the Jewish populations, not only in the kresy but all over eastern Europe, and in fact in all of Europe, were rescued by the Red Army. It was the Red Army that defeated Nazi Germany, although the Western powers certainly contributed to that defeat. Soviet forces used American trucks and a quantity of weapons supplied by the Anglo-Americans; the bombing of Germany helped a great deal, and the defeat of the Germans in the Middle East and the invasion, first of Italy, then of western Europe, contributed a share. But the brunt of the battles were not borne by the Western powers. It was the Soviets, under communist rule, who produced the thousands of tanks and airplanes and guns and mines and small arms and all the rest. It was the Soviets who slugged it out in their destroyed country against a brutal and conscienceless enemy. It was they who lost millions of soldiers and many millions of civilians, partly because of the incompetence of their leaders but partly in terrible battles that were well planned on the Soviet side in the later stages of the war. Had it not been for the Soviet soldiers, including the many antisemites among them, there would have been no Jewish survivors anywhere in Europe. In fact, there would have been no Israel either. It is a fact that a totalitarian, brutal, corrupt communist regime won the war against the enemy of humankind, against the worst regime that had ever disgraced this planet, and in so doing enabled at least some Jews to survive and tell their story. It is also a fact that communists, by and large, rescued Jews, treated them fairly, and protected many unarmed Jews. This was done mainly for ideological reasons; it was the result of indoctrination that had taken place over the twenty years of communist rule in the USSR prior to World War II. The contradictions between the Soviets' actions and the totalitarian and brutal character of the Soviet regime still have to be investigated—as does the contradiction between communist behavior during the war and the wave of antisemitic propaganda and actions in the Soviet Union in the postwar years, especially the years leading up to Stalin's death in 1953.

To return to our story: it is not difficult to list the Jews' motivations to fight, and fight well, beyond the obvious desire to survive. The chief motivation, and the one that recurs constantly in the testimonies, was a burning desire to avenge the murders of other Jews. Jewish partisans killed, without mercy, any and all Belorussian and Polish policemen and peasants whom they knew had been part of the murder machine or had delivered or denounced hidden or fleeing Jews. They killed Ukrainians in the northern parts of Volhynia and Polesie for the same reasons. Many testimonies tell us who was executed, why, and how. Often some or all of the family of the collaborator was executed as well, and sometimes the farmstead was burnt down, too.

When Germans fell into the hands of Jewish partisans, they were killed almost without exception. The very few exceptions were dictated by higher commanders. No quarter was given. When such killings took place, the partisans often yelled, "This is for my mother," "This is for my father," and so on. When Jews fell into the hands of Germans, they were always killed, too, and many testimonies tell us that when Jewish partisans were on the point of falling into German hands—because they were wounded and could not move, or because they were surprised in an ambush—they committed suicide rather than face torture and death at German hands.

The Moscow Command dictated a policy prohibiting national or ethnic units generally; Jewish ones were included under that general prohibition. Partisan units were defined more or less geographically, depending on the Soviet republic in which they were active. Lithuania had become a Soviet republic in 1940, and in the Rudniki forest in eastern Lithuania and western Belorussia, the units were "Lithuanian," although Lithuanians made up only a minority of its members. On that border, in the Rudniki forest, Jewish units established by former underground Jewish fighters from Vilno and Kovno, under the command of Abba Kovner, the second and last head of the Vilno underground, were in the end included in a Lithuanian partisan brigade commanded by a "Lithuanian," Jurgis, who in actual fact was a Jewish communist by the name of Henryk Ziman (Zimanas) who was unsympathetic to the idea of separate Jewish units.

Pro-Soviet Polish partisan units existed as well, and they, too, were allowed to exist as quasi-national groups. More than 2,000 fighters operated in the north-western area of the kresy near Vilno as members of such a group, and another four such groups operated in northern Volhynia. But most of the Polish units belonged to the Armia Krajowa and owed allegiance to the London-based government-in-exile. These troops were mostly very much anti-Soviet and anti-Jewish, although there were exceptions.

Three Jewish units were formed on Belorussian territory: the Zhukov brigade (Brigade 106), the Zorin detachment, and the Bielski partisans. The Jews in the Zhukov unit were dispersed among other units in late 1943, but the two others were Jewish until liberation, against the prevailing Soviet policy. No detailed research has been done on the Zorin detachment, and the little we can add at the moment is to a large extent the result of Cholawsky's summaries: Shalom Zorin was a baker from Minsk; he may have been a party member, but that is not clear. After the first major "action" in Minsk, on November 7, 1941, he fled the city, together with a Soviet officer, Semyon Ganzenko, who had previously been rescued by a Jewish girl from a POW camp. They established a unit named for the Soviet military commander Marshal Semyon Budenny, but later split because

Zorin rescued Jewish children and included them in the subunit in which he was the reconnaissance officer. Ganzenko, who insisted on having only fighters in the unit, threatened to kill him, but in May 1943, a "Zorin Family Camp" was set up. It moved to the Naliboki *pushcha* (jungle-like forest). From an original 100–150 people, the unit grew to 800 in early 1944, including—reportedly—150 children and an armed subunit of 137 men and women. The fighters participated in the usual partisan activities. It is safe to assume that most of the 800 Zorin partisans and families were escapees from the area's shtetlach, and many testimonies at Yad Vashem and the Shoah Foundation in Los Angeles testify to that effect.[17]

The Zhukov brigade was the result of a development that apparently followed the first ghetto rebellion anywhere, the uprising in the shtetl of Nieswiez, in Belorussia (4,600 Jews before the war).[18] When the Germans occupied Nieswiez, they established a Judenrat and placed a Warsaw lawyer by the name of Maghalieff (no first name has been found) at its head. The first months passed with the usual brutal steps of persecution: marking the Jews with special armbands, establishing a ghetto, requiring forced labor of all adults, beating people and occasionally murdering them, all done by the Germans and the local Belorussian police. On October 18, 1941, the general registration of all males was followed by a selection of 200 hostages and the imposition of a "contribution" of half a million rubles and two and a half kilograms of gold. A pro-Jewish local Polish teacher, one Volodka (no other details are available) helped raise the sum. On October 30, an "action" took place in which a German unit of unknown identity murdered about 4,000 Jews with Belorussian help. (I do not know whether the Belorussians actually murdered Jews or "only" provided logistical and other help to the Germans.) The remaining 585 workers and their immediate families remained in a small ghetto, with Maghalieff still at the helm. But now a new element came into play: former members of Zionist youth movements established a committee that demanded of Maghalieff a detailed accounting of what he was up to, and Maghalieff had to yield. While performing forced labor, the committee began collecting arms, but it also engaged in Amidah activities: education for younger people and those children who had survived, mutual aid, and ideological preparation for a future rebellion. They managed to smuggle machine-gun parts into the ghetto, assemble the gun, and place it in the only stone building in the ghetto, the former synagogue.

On July 17, 1942, the conspirators, headed by Cholawsky, Eliyahu Damessek, Syomka Farfel, and others, heard of the liquidation of the shtetl of Horodzei, fourteen kilometers away. Cholawsky made a speech to the ghetto inhabitants, calling upon all of them to resist the coming liquidation with "cold" weapons (knives and such) and the few firearms they had managed to collect—mainly captured Soviet weapons taken from German storage places, where Jews were forced to work—including the machine gun. Fighting broke out when the Germans and the Belorussians surrounded the ghetto on July 21. Jews burned their houses. The machine gun shot a number of rounds until it stopped—the Jews did not know how to repair it. Jews attacked the Belorussian police, who were sent in ahead of the Germans, with scythes, hammers, pitchforks, and anything they could lay their hands on. Those with handguns used them. Then many who were still alive tried to escape into the countryside, aided by the smoke from the burning ghetto. After hiding for a few days, the rest took off, too.

Cholawsky relates how he and a group of survivors made their way, with the help of local Belorussian farmers, to an area in the east (that is, in pre-1939 Soviet Belorussia), where they found a Soviet partisan unit under a Ukrainian communist and former Soviet officer, Philip P. Buchenko (nom de guerre: Kapusta). A Soviet Jew and party member named Lyova Gilchik commanded the subunit that the group from Nieswiez joined. They lacked weapons, despite a successful attack on a small German convoy. In the region of the township of Kopyl, in eastern Belorussia, a farmer told them of a place where Germans had killed and buried Soviet soldiers with their weapons. The Nieswiez group dug up the mass grave and extracted the rotting Soviet rifles and ammunition. The carpenters among them removed the wood and prepared new wooden parts, and the others spent days cleaning the metal, until they had assembled thirty rifles with ammunition, ready for use.[19] Acquiring arms was the crucial element that enabled them to become a real partisan group. They then got hold of a machine gun and rejoined the Kapusta unit.

Jews from another rebellion, in Kleck, and others from Stolpce joined the unit. In Stolpce, the head of the Judenrat, named Wittenberg, cooperated with the underground, and a number of its members—helped by a local Baptist-Mennonite—joined the largely Jewish unit, now named for Marshal Georgy Zhukov.[20] There was plenty of antisemitism among the Russian and Belorussian members of the larger unit, there were murders of Jews and betrayals, but ultimately Kapusta, who was friendly to the Jews, established discipline, and the antisemitic excesses abated, largely because of his leadership. Toward the end of 1943, the Zhukov brigade was disbanded and its members attached, individually, to other units, in pursuance of the Soviet policy of avoiding the establishment of national/ethnic units, mainly Jewish ones.

The Nieswiez case is a central example of a relatively successful rebellion and the subsequent establishment of a partisan unit; however, without those thirty-five rifles extracted from a mass grave it is doubtful whether they would have been as successful as they were. Their being joined by remnants of the Kleck and Stolpce resistance groups was equally important. The help provided by Belo-russian farmers along the way and the presence in the forests of the budding Kapusta detachment played a role, too. The formation of the Zhukov brigade is a typical instance of Soviet partisans, at an early stage, providing essential help to Jews; on the other hand, Cholawsky's account tells in great detail of the anti-semitic behavior of many partisans, even in Soviet units.

The Bielski detachment has been described in Nechama Tec's book *Defiance*, which is based in part on the memoirs of the two surviving commanders, Tuvia and Zus Bielski, and in part on testimonies of survivors from that unit.[21] Her sociological analysis deals mainly with the detachment as it had developed by 1943. My own analysis is based on Tec's, but with some additional elements.

The Bielskis were a family of millers in a tiny Belorussian village called Stan-kiewicze (Bel.: Stankievichi—it no longer exists). There were twelve non-Jewish families in the place, and the Bielskis. The Bielskis had seven children, one of them a girl. The oldest son was Tuvia (Anatoli). He was married to a woman he did not love, and lived for a time in the town of Lida. But what is centrally im-portant for us is that he had grown up on the edge of the forest. He knew his way there, and the six brothers had undergone the harsh education of villagers who had to know how to defend themselves against their neighbors, especially since their being Jews set them apart and was the reason for hostility by some of the village boys. Tuvia served as an NCO in the Polish army, and when the Soviets came, he advanced to a low administrative position in Lida. He was recruited into the Red Army, but his unit fell apart when the Germans invaded, and he made his way home to his parents' mill.[22]

Soon the Germans came and tried to evict the family and transfer them to Nowogrodek, which was not far away. When they arrested two of the brothers (Avreiml and Yakov), the parents tried to free them with the help of bribes. That did not work, and the Germans killed the brothers. The parents were taken soon afterward, and they were killed during the first "action" in Nowogrodek, on December 8, 1941. Three of the brothers, Asael (Alexander), Zus (Sigismund), and Archik (Aaron, who was still a young boy), fled into the forest and hid with friendly peasants. The only sister, Teivl, was married and lived in another shtetl. During the winter of 1941–1942, the brothers lived with Belorussian and Polish friends, moving from one to another: "There were also Polish friends. Without them, we would not have survived the early times."[23]

In early 1942, they acquired their first handgun, and then more arms, and other members of their extended family, including Tuvia, joined them. By March 1942, the group had seventeen people in it; in the summer, twenty-five or thirty, still mostly family members. Tuvia was elected commander, and the group called itself the Zhukov detachment (otriad)—not to be confused with the other, larger detachment by the same name in Kapusta's unit. In July and August the Bielski group grew more, very largely because of the policy adopted by Tuvia and followed consistently until liberation—namely, to accept each and every Jew, man, woman and child, with or without arms. His philosophy was that the main task of his detachment was to rescue as many Jews as possible. Armed action against the Germans and their allies was essential, but rescue was more important. Zorin followed the same policy, as we have seen, with somewhat less success.

Tuvia's success depended largely on the alliances he managed to forge with Soviet partisans. His first weapons he obtained from a Georgian escapee from a POW camp, one Gramov, who had created a small partisan group in the area. Then along came a much larger group, led by Viktor Panchenkov, also a Soviet officer. Panchenkov wanted to annihilate the Bielskis because he believed peasants who claimed that the Jews had robbed them. Tuvia persuaded Panchenkov to put this to a test, and they both confronted the peasant ringleader. It turned out that the peasant had lied to Panchenkov in order to avoid providing him with provisions. Panchenkov wanted to kill the peasant, but Tuvia persuaded him to desist and thereby turn the peasant into an ally. From then on, Tuvia and Panchenko became friends, although Tuvia described Panchenkov's unit as a group of POWs, bandits, and antisemites. In fact, some Jews joined Panchenkov's unit—or another, similar one called Iskra.

Late in 1942, while organizing the partisan detachments in accordance with military principles and discipline, the Soviets sent Platon—General Chernishev—to be the district commander of the Baranowicze-Naliboki area (Baranowicze is only fifty kilometers from Nowogrodek). Platon came to appreciate the contribution made by the Bielskis to the common struggle and defended them against quite a number of antisemitic attacks and intrigues engineered by various commanders in Platon's brigade. In late 1943, the Bielskis were split into two groups—a fighting group named for Sergo Ordzhonikidze (a Georgian Bolshevik in the Soviet Politburo who died in 1937) and commanded by a Russian but in fact led by Asael Bielski and the family camp led by Tuvia. The family camp, which also had a fighting unit, existed from the autumn of 1943 to liberation in July 1944, or about one-third of the time that the Bielski resistance group existed. During that time the camp was located in the Naliboki pushcha, and it developed essential services for the partisans in the area; there were workshops for leather goods and other items, an armory, a bakery, a laundry, health services, and the like. In fact, Tuvia's group re-created a kind of shtetl in the forest, as Nechama Tec has shown in her book. There was even an attempt to create some sort of cultural environment, with music, children's performances, a drama circle, and religious services. The communist commissar sent to the Bielskis by Platon, Ivan V. Shemyatovets, turned out to have a Jewish wife, and he was very friendly (when he was not drunk). This artificial shtetl disintegrated upon liberation—it was a pale ghost of something that had been irretrievably lost. However, it showed the indomitable spirit of the Jews of the shtetl, not in declarations or nostalgic nonsense but in actual throbbing life.

The story of Gedalia Toker shows the kind of relationship that the Bielskis established with antisemitic Soviet units. Toker was a Jewish partisan whose horse and gun had been taken from him by a Soviet unit. Zus Bielski and eight members of his unit surprised the Soviets and forced them to return the stolen items. The Soviets then tried to ambush the Jews, but Zus, realizing the danger, sent a small group of his men behind the Soviets, which threatened them with cross-fire. When they realized that Zus was serious, they gave up their plans, and that enabled the two units to establish reasonably friendly relations.

The Bielskis took bloody revenge on Belorussian collaborators with the Germans. In one case, a Belorussian family betrayed two Jewish girls to the Germans, and the Bielskis killed the whole family—some twelve people.[24] In another case—and there were quite a number of cases—Jews had hid with one Ivan Tzwirkes, whose wife was a converted Jew. Tzwirkes betrayed the Jews to the Germans, whereupon the Bielskis caught him and ordered him to say good-bye to his wife because he was going to be shot. They squeezed additional names of collaborators out of the frightened man and then killed most of the people he had named. He was permitted to return to his family, probably because of his (ex-) Jewish wife.[25]

Partisan fighting was cruel and bitter on both sides, and no quarter was given in most cases. Soviet partisans were merciless not only with Germans and collaborators but also with individuals in their own ranks who did not fulfill their duties as required in accordance with the strict discipline that was introduced in May 1942. Partisans caught sleeping while on guard, partisans who had lost their weapons, and partisans found guilty of similar misdemeanors were executed, usually in front of the whole unit. Jews in the forest had lost their parents, children, wives, husbands, relatives, and all their community. They were in no mood to take pity on whoever had wronged them. There were no courts, no judges, no prosecutors or defenders, no laws except the verdict of the commander of the unit. Life or death.

In the end, the Bielskis kept 1,200 or so Jews alive, and they are, rightly, seen as an extraordinary group of Jews who rescued other Jews on an impressive scale, though faced with tremendous obstacles. Yet when we look at the dry statistics— frightening statistics, I must add—roughly 1.3 million Jews were murdered in the kresy, and the Bielskis, with tremendous courage and taking great risks daily, rescued fewer than 0.1 percent of that number. Saving a life is like saving a whole world, as Jewish tradition has it. They could not save more than 1,200 worlds, that pitiable percentage, and even that was an unequalled, heroic deed.

The crucial period in the Bielski story was perhaps less the final stage, so well analyzed by Nechama Tec, when the Bielskis managed to organize the quasi shtetl in the forest, but the early period. As the Bielskis themselves testified, they could not have survived without help from Polish and Belorussian friends. These friends did not just appear on the horizon at the right time; they were the result of prewar friendships between village Jews and their neighbors, some of whom did not forget the friendships forged then, and risked their necks to hide the brothers. The unusual character of Tuvia Bielski, with his knowledge of the forest and his outstanding diplomatic skills, made the rest possible.

There were other Jewish units, but they had an ephemeral existence, usually not surviving more than a few months at most before they were disbanded and their members were dispersed among other units.

One of these units emerged from the destruction of Glebokie, a shtetl that had 6,000 Jews in 1941. A ghetto was established there in October 1941, and the first mass "action" occurred on June 6, 1942. In its wake, the Germans decreed that there would be no more mass murders, so Jews from a large number of small places around Glebokie went to the ghetto; they did not know whether there were any partisans in the forest, and thought they had no choice—especially families encumbered with children. Nevertheless, quite a number of Jews decided to risk it and fled into the forest. In the meantime, a large partisan unit, the Saburov brigade, had arrived in the vicinity, and one of the commanders, Pyotr A. Chomchenko, agreed to establish a Jewish unit, commanded by David Pintzov. Most of its members were from Glebokie. This was the Kaganovich detachment (otriad).[26] On August 20, 1943, the Germans liquidated the Glebokie ghetto, the Jews rebelled, there was a prolonged firefight, and while some 3,000 Jews were killed, a fairly large number escaped into the forest. Many joined the Kaganovich unit, which had by that time registered a large number of successful armed actions against the enemy. It may have been the fact that so many joined that moved the Soviet command to disband it in the following month and distribute its members among other units.[27]

Another such unit was the *Borba* (Struggle) unit commanded by Hersh Kaplinsky from Zhetl (in Yiddish; Pol.: Zdzieciol; Bel.: Dyatlovo). The Zhetl story is important because of its complicated character. Four thousand Jews lived there in 1941, forming 80 percent of the total population. In February 1942, a ghetto was established. The deputy head of the Judenrat, a lawyer by the name of Alter Dworzecky, decided to organize a rebellion and collected some arms that were hidden outside the ghetto.[28] A number of Russian partisans came into the ghetto and agreed with his plan, but when a larger partisan band appeared in the vicinity in the spring, he changed his plan and decided on an escape into the forest. Then one of the underground members was betrayed to the Germans by a Russian posing as a partisan and was tortured and murdered.[29] Dworzecky decided to leave immediately, with nine trusted friends. On April 30, 1942, there was an "action" in which 1,200 people were murdered, but many were also killed trying to escape. The partisans, whom Dworzecky had joined, refused his pleas to attack the Germans and collaborators during the "action," and in a brief engagement with the Germans he was killed. The partisans left the area, leaving the underground in the decimated community in the lurch.[30]

However, approximately 200 people had fled to the forest, led by Leibl Podlishevsky. They were joined, after the next "action" (August 6) by another 600, including whole families. The rest of the Jews in Zhetl were deported to Nowogrodek. The 800 Zhetl escapees went to the Lipiczansky pushcha, where half of them established a family camp that was under the protection of a Jewish unit named Borba (a name used by a number of partisan units) under Hersh Kaplinsky. The unit itself, which included 180 Zhetl escapees, became part of a Soviet partisan group, the Orliansky brigade; a Soviet commander was nominated (it seems that Jews could not become commanders of larger units), a friendly Russian by the name of Kolya Vekhanin. The other 200 joined various other partisan units. Kaplinsky became a famous fighter, leading his and other units to a number of bitterly fought victories until he was killed in action on December 13, 1942. Non-Jews were introduced into the Borba unit, but Vekhanin saw to it that no overt antisemitism was practiced. In early 1944, Borba was dismantled, and its members were distributed among other units. At the end of the war, there were 370 survivors from Zhetl, and we therefore have a large number of testimonies to compare and use.[31]

Rebellions or at least firefights occurred between armed members of Jewish underground groups and the enemy. On occasion, various forms of physical resistance were combined, as we have seen in Nieswiez, where the Jews burned the ghetto and resisted with firearms and with "cold" weapons. Something similar happened in Lachwa, Dereczin, and Mir.

Lachwa (2,500 Jews in 1941) was a shtetl adjoining the forest. Its Judenrat head was Dov Lopatin, a graduate of the right-wing Zionist Betar. In the shtetl there was a strong presence of former youth movement members, of two right-wing Zionist and one leftist Zionist movements. The underground group comprised some thirty members. A ghetto was established on April 1, 1942. The decision to rebel was taken in the wake of the murder, in late July, of seven young girls who had gone outside the ghetto to beg for food in the neighboring villages. On September 2, 1942, the Germans and Belorussians surrounded the ghetto and declared that they would let thirty people live. Lopatin refused to cooperate. The next day the enemy attacked. The Jews had a few rifles, which they used against the Germans and their helpers, but their main response was the burning of the ghetto, and a mass flight into the forest by about 1,000 people. The Germans and Belorussians killed a large number of the escapees with their machine guns (in one case handled by a local peasant), and only 120 people managed to reach the forest interior. A few dozen survivors emerged after the war. Lopatin was killed.

Each case is different, and it is both impossible and unnecessary to dwell on all of them. However, the case of Dereczin is important because it shows the determination of Jews left alive, after a main "action" by the Germans, to take revenge at any cost. Dereczin had about 3,000 Jews in 1941; the head of the first Judenrat, a man by the name of Feldman, committed suicide when the Germans forced the Jews into a ghetto. Twenty-five hundred Jews were murdered on July 24, 1942, but a mass escape brought 300 others into the forest. Coincidentally, Dr. Yehezkiel Atlas, a Jewish physician from western Poland and former member of Betar who had worked in Rokitno and was transferred by the Germans or Belorussians to a small hamlet called Kozlowczyzna, had fled into the same forest as the people from Dereczin. The majority of the Jews of Kozlowczyzna had been murdered in November 1941, and Atlas fled on July 22, 1942. He organized a Jewish unit, mainly from the Dereczin escapees, with the help of friendly Soviet partisans. Together with the Soviets, he was in charge of an attack on Dereczin, probably in August 1942. The Jews and their allies occupied the place and killed all the Germans and Belorussians they could find. They took bloody revenge on Belorussian collaborators. In November, they attacked Kozlowczyzna as well, and took revenge there, too. Dereczin was left unoccupied by Germans for a whole month. In December, Dr. Atlas fell in battle, and the command over his unit was handed over to a Dereczin Jew (Ilya Lipshowitz). The unit then grew and became part of a larger otriad commanded by a friendly Siberian Russian, Vanka Abramov, who fell in battle in June 1944.[32]

The story of Mir is well known because of the excellent book by Nechama Tec about Oswald Rufeisen, the main character in it.[33] Mir was a shtetl of 2,400 Jews (1941); 1,600 of them were murdered on November 9, 1941, leaving 805. (This very much parallels the development in Nieswiez.) Among those who remained were a group of Hashomer Hatzair youth movement members, led by Shlomo Kharkhas and David Reznik. Some eighty members formed an underground group. Rufeisen had been a member of Akiva, a liberal Zionist youth movement, in his native western Poland and had fled to Vilno at the beginning of the war. He was being sought there, so he made his way to Mir, where he pretended to be a German Pole (*Volksdeutscher*); his command of the two languages was perfect. He was befriended by the Belorussian head of the police, Serafimowicz, and through him made contact with the local German police commander, in effect the leading German officer, Reinhold Hain.[34] Rufeisen became Hain's translator, and a friendly relationship developed between them. Rufeisen tried, as best he could, to protect Belorussian peasants and suspected partisans when Hain organized sorties into the countryside. He also initiated contact with Kharkhas, who recognized him as who he really was—a Jew.

In the meantime, the Jews of Mir were transferred to the local old Polish castle, that of Swiatopluk Mirsky, in May 1942, and it was clear that a final liquidation was just a matter of time. In late July, information came about the uprising in Nieswiez. The Judenrat head, Shulman, knew about the resistance group in his community and did his best to stop their preparations for an escape into the forest; instead, he tried to bribe Hain. When he realized that that was hopeless, he ceased his opposition to a breakout, saying that he would stay with those who would not try to break out. Rufeisen informed the Jews, through Kharkhas, that the liquidation was planned for a date after August 8. He himself organized a false alarm about a supposed partisan presence, which caused the Germans and their helpers to go on a wild-goose chase on August 9–10—Rufeisen wanted to give the Jews a chance to escape to the forest unhindered. Unfortunately, just then two Nieswiez survivors emerged from the forest and told the people in the castle that no one could survive in the forest. As a result, only 300 people, under the leadership of Kharkhas and Reznik, grabbed the opportunity and escaped. The rest stayed and were murdered by the returning Germans and Belorussians.[35]

Hain realized that somebody had misled him, and a Jew (Stanislawsky) denounced Rufeisen to him. Hain still thought Rufeisen was a Pole, but in a confrontation Rufeisen revealed his true identity and was arrested. However, he was guarded only very lightly, perhaps intentionally so, and fled to a local nunnery, where a Polish nun offered him a hiding place.[36] He stayed there for a long time, and through reading and contemplation he decided to convert; he became a Catholic. Finally, at the end of 1943, he left the monastery and joined the partisans. He was almost executed as a German collaborator, but some Mir survivors protected him, and he spent the rest of the war as a partisan, avoiding combat that would lead to killing as much as he could. After the war, he entered holy orders and became a Capuchin monk, Brother Daniel. Like Arcbishop Lustiger in France, he saw himself as a Jew of the Catholic religion; he was placed in a monastery on Mount Carmel, in Haifa, where he spent the rest of his life.

The Mir survivors, in the meantime, joined a Soviet partisan unit, led by a Polish communist, Josef (Juzik) Marchlewsky. Later, some of the escapees joined the Bielski group, and some joined other otriady. Finally, the core of the Mir group, under Kharkhas, joined a unit in Platon's area, called *Za Sovietskayu Belarus* (For a Soviet Belorussia). A violently antisemitic subunit (called *Danila*) killed six Jewish partisans. Platon refused to intervene. Nevertheless, more than half of the original escapees survived the war.

In some shtetlach, resistance came very late, in some it came early, and we have to look at some examples to try to understand why. In Nowogrodek, no organization planned resistance until 1943, when only a few hundred Jews were left alive. However, groups of Jews had been leaving the shtetl's ghetto as early as the spring of 1942, mainly for the Bielskis but also for other units. One testimony even tells us about a young man, Michael Zamkov, who escaped Nowogrodek immediately after the first "action" of December 8, 1941, and hid for a time with a Jewish farmer, who was still in his home, but Zamkov had to return to the ghetto because he could not survive by himself—there were as yet no Soviet partisans in the area. He escaped a second time, probably in June 1942, and joined a partisan group led by a Soviet major. This may be the same group described in the testimony of Eliahu Kowienski, a Jew from Zhetl, who received the highest Soviet decoration, that of a Hero of the Soviet Union. The unit, if it is identical with the one described in the previous testimony, went to the Lipiczansky pushcha, southwest of Nowogrodek, and maintained itself there, later joining a larger Soviet unit, until liberation. Along the way it had to acquire arms, which it did so by taking guns forcibly from reluctant peasants. In addition, they fished abandoned Soviet weapons out of the Szczara River. We have seen this way of acquiring arms in other testimonies about other units.[37]

The second "action" in Nowogrodek took place, as we have seen, on August 7, 1942. Before and especially after that, people began escaping to the Bielski brothers, who by that time had formed a proper partisan unit. The Bielskis sent emissaries to the ghetto to take people out, stopping on the way out with either Bobrowski or Kozlowski before moving on to the forest. The Judenrat opposed the flight to the forest, and its police went so far as to take away the boots of those suspected of planning to escape. The fear there, as elsewhere, was that if the Germans got to know about the plan, they would exact revenge by killing at least all those people who had shared the same dwelling with the escapee. But taking away boots did not work, and people continued to escape. The number of escapees, until the third "action" on February 4, 1943, and especially after that, amounted to hundreds. Some did not go to the Bielskis, who had moved to the Naliboki pushcha, to the north of the shtetl. They went to the Lipiczansky pushcha or to other forests that were even farther away. It was hard going. Quite a number of peasants were hostile, and additional Jewish partisans inevitably meant that villages would be scoured for food by more units. Jews were not welcome in any case. In the forest, Soviet partisans, in many instances, attacked fleeing Jews. As an internal report of the Soviet partisans said: "The population here does not like Jews ... if a Jew calls at a house and asks for food, the peasant says he has been robbed by Jews. When a Russian comes together with a Jew, everything goes smoothly. There are detachments where Jews are not accepted."[38] That last sentence was, of course, an understatement.

The reason, then, why a resistance organization did not emerge in Nowogrodek was probably that it was not necessary; large numbers of people escaped to fight in the forest anyway. In most cases, not just one person or one family fled, but groups of people, and of course they had to meet beforehand to agree on how to proceed. The very fact that the escape took place means that a type of organization was present.

After the third massacre in February, a fourth took place on May 7, 1943, in which 298 people died; and only 237 were left in the courthouse that served as a ghetto. Before May 7, a committee was created, led perhaps by a Dr. Kagan from Baranowicze and perhaps by Berl Josselewicz, both with a prewar background in Labor Zionism and Bundism. At first, the committee made a copy of the key to the gate of the courthouse, intending to arrange a mass escape, but the wife of a doctor who lay wounded in the ghetto and would have been left behind and of course killed, protested and threatened to inform on the conspirators. The plan had to be abandoned. The Germans, who had grown suspicious, tried to penetrate the underground by sending a Jew from Pereseika who had been left alive after the liquidation of the ghetto there to serve as a spy. He aroused the suspicions of the resistance group, and they killed him. They had managed to smuggle in a radio, and they heard news about the Warsaw ghetto rebellion, which made their resolve to act even firmer. They made up their minds to dig a tunnel underneath the courthouse that would lead to a field outside.

The tunnel was built with great care. They had to overcome technical obstacles—where to put the earth that was dug out, how to assure air and lighting in the tunnel, and how to dig so that the Germans would not hear or know. By August they had dug the planned 100 meters. But then the Germans harvested the wheat in the field where the tunnel ended, leaving the field bare. The escapees would not be hidden as they emerged from the tunnel. So the tunnel was extended for another 160 meters; this was just as well, because unbeknownst to the conspirators, the Germans had started a major anti-partisan operation on July 13. Had the Jews tried to escape in August, while the German operation was still going on, they undoubtedly would have all been caught by the very large German forces in the area—25,000 soldiers participated in the German operation—and killed.

Finally, the 260-meter tunnel was completed, but there was opposition to the breakout from within the Jewish group. People were not sure that all of them would be able to crawl through the narrow tunnel, and they did not know what they would do once they emerged—although they all knew about the Bielskis, who were camped somewhere, a few dozen kilometers away. In the end, the matter was put to a vote, and by a majority of 165 against 65 the breakout was decided upon (2 did not vote); it was agreed that everybody who wanted to could participate. Except for five people, everyone did, and the escape took place on a rainy and stormy night, on September 26, 1943. The German searchlight had been put out of action by Jewish electricians—the same electricians who had previously managed to put a line into the tunnel that gave a minimum of light to the escapees. A total of 232 persons crawled through the tunnel and emerged at the other end. Soon, however, the camp police discovered the escape, and the Germans initiated a major search operation with considerable forces. The Jews, disoriented in the pitch darkness and without a compass, split into small groups and tried to find their way to safety. Many of them went around in circles, only to be caught and killed by the Germans. But 170 managed to get away, and the great majority of these found their way to the Bielskis. Others joined other groups, and a few hid in the forest until liberation, which came nine months later. Some were helped along by friendly peasants, some were denounced to the Germans. One peasant refused to help because he said the Jews had been punished by God for not recognizing Jesus as their Savior.[39]

Two stories within the story are worth dwelling on. The commander of the courthouse ghetto was the same Wilhelm Traub, the Gebietskommissar, who had organized and led all the previous "actions" against the Jews of Nowogrodek. In early July 1943, he wanted to liquidate the Jews in the courthouse, but he had to ask the SIPO in Minsk to do it because he did not have enough men to do it himself. The Minsk SIPO commander, one Arthur Wilke, refused, saying that 2,000 of the Jews of Lida—a larger town farther west—were still alive, and if he killed the Jews in the Nowogrodek camp, the Lida Jews, who were much more numerous, would undoubtedly hear about it and rebel. So he had to kill those in Lida before dealing with those under Traub. That saved the Jews still in the courthouse, who had no inkling of these plans. When Traub learned of Wilke's decision, he decided to liquidate the Jews with his own people, leaving just twelve alive. A Russian woman working for Traub heard about this and told two Jewish girls. That speeded up the plans for the escape.[40]

The other story has an almost mystical quality about it. In early 1942, a man who called himself Yakov Groyanovsky had fled from the first death camp that the Germans had started operating in Poland on December 7, 1941, at Chelmno. When he reached Warsaw, he met, among others, heads of the youth movements, who immediately understood that there was an imminent danger of total annihilation. They began preparing themselves and their charges for resistance. Additional information they received of what was happening in Vilno, where mass murders had been going on since September 1941, strengthened their resolve. That was clearly reflected in the underground newspapers they published. In February and March, the head of the Gordonia Zionist youth movement, Eliezer Geller, published articles in which he related the story of a rebellion of Jewish youths in Nowogrodek. He described how the rebels killed a number of Belorussian policemen before they were finally killed in battle by the Germans. After a few days, the papers of the Bund and Hashomer Hatzair published the same story with more details, extolling the bravery of the Nowogrodek youths. From then on, one of the main slogans of the budding resistance movement was "Nowogrodek calls!" (Yid.: *Nowogrodek ruft*). It was used to recruit youths in Warsaw for the uprising that finally took place in Warsaw in April 1943. All that is fine—except that the Nowogrodek rebellion never happened. There was no youth rebellion in Nowogrodek, and no Belorussian policemen were killed, and there was no battle with the Germans. But, as we have seen, in the spring of 1943 the conspirators among the last Jews in the Nowogrodek courthouse obtained a radio, and on it they heard about the Warsaw ghetto rebellion, which had taken place a few weeks before. This information strengthened their resolve to dig the tunnel and break out and join partisan units to fight the Germans.

What happened, then, was a fascinating paradox: a rebellion in Nowogrodek that never happened contributed to the development of a Warsaw uprising that *did* take place, and that uprising then inspired an escape and fight against the Germans by Nowogrodek Jews. It seems that Geller really thought that what he was writing was true. How did he get that (false) information? I checked a number of possibilities: Did something happen in the northern kresy that was brought to his attention by some Polish friends? Was he in contact with the Polish underground, which may have fed him with this information? If so, why would the Poles in Warsaw have given him that information—or did they believe it themselves? The idea that it may have reflected the first rumors about the Bielski detachment is out of the question, because the detachment did not yet exist in February–March 1942. I came up with nothing. I have no solution to this paradox.[41]

Other, quite different ways of organizing and effecting resistance can be seen in a number of other shtetlach. Kurzeniec is a good example. There, almost immediately after the German occupation, the Germans put up a barbed wire enclosure on a market square. During the first few weeks of Operation Barbarossa, hundreds of thousands of Soviets were taken prisoner and marched westward, to more permanent POW camps. Kurzeniec was one of the stations on the way. Thousands of sick, starving, wounded, desperate prisoners, clothed in tatters of uniforms, were brought there, usually for one night, to be marched on the next day. The Germans threw some barrels of bread and water at them (there was no well in the square) and recruited Jewish forced laborers to carry the barrels in and out. There was too little bread for the masses of prisoners, and the Germans outside watched the scenes of wild scrambling for the loaves. The group of eight Zionist young people, members of Hashomer Hatzair who had maintained a sort of underground under the Soviets, volunteered for the job because they wanted to help the prisoners. One of them was the sixteen-year-old Zalman Gurewicz. As he carried a barrel of bread into the enclosure, he was accosted by a wounded, ragged, hungry Soviet captain, a Russian from eastern Ukraine, apparently not a member of the Communist Party. This man, Piotr Mikhailovich Danilochkin, said to Gurewicz, "Get me out of here." Gurewicz went back out with the empty barrel, consulted with his friends, and came back, having put on another set of working clothes, with the obligatory armband identifying the worker as a Jew. He found Danilochkin, who threw off his uniform and put on the second set of working clothes that Gurewicz had brought. For the rest of the night he was one of the Jewish forced laborers. In the morning, all these workers were kicked in their butts and were sent home—there was no ghetto in Kurzeniec. What would a sixteen-year-old boy do with an escaped Soviet POW? He took him to his parents, of course. They put him into a bed in an attic and nursed him back to health, then directed him to the pro-Soviet village of Wolkowczyzna, where Danilochkin set up what was probably the first Soviet partisan detachment in that area of Belorussia, Za Sovietskayu Belarus. All this probably happened in August 1941. The commander, Andrei I. Voliniets, was a local communist, and Danilochkin became the commissar. He did not forget the Jews who had rescued him. Gurewicz and the other young people joined the unit, and when the Jews of Kurzeniec were murdered, in September 1942, some 300 of them managed to escape, most of them to Danilochkin's partisans. Some of them were guided across the lines to unoccupied Soviet territory, others reached an area controlled by the partisans, and most of the young ones joined the fighting units, but of course many died or were killed before the war ended. About half of them survived—the Kurzeniec Jews had a very high rate of survival, close to 10 percent— and we have testimonies from most of them. Here, Jews rescued a non-Jew, during the Holocaust, and that non-Jew was then instrumental in rescuing Jews.[42]

The case of Baranowicze is again quite different. Whereas in Kurzeniec there were a number of young people who were part of a partisan unit that was organized outside the shtetl, in Baranowicze there was an organized, fairly large underground. It consisted of four groups that arose from different Jewish political organizations. The largest one, headed by Eliezer Lidowski, was based on a Labor Zionist membership; another one was formed by members of Hashomer Hatzair, a third was a group of Bundists, and a fourth had a general Zionist character. Although the groups originated in the first months of the German occupation, they did not take practical steps until after the first "action" in March 1942. Then the groups coalesced under Lidowski's leadership and planned an uprising. They managed to collect a fair amount of weaponry—in fact, probably more than the rebels in the Warsaw ghetto had—but the plan misfired because of accidental misunderstandings among the conspirators. That was actually quite lucky, because if they had rebelled, as they had planned, on July 19, 1942, they would have been defeated and killed in the ghetto, because few, if any, partisans were in the area, and the Germans were still very strong. Given that Baranowicze was the headquarters of the HSSPF North, Erich von dem Bach-Zelewski, and had many army detachments posted in and around the town, the chances of escaping to the forest would have been very slim.

Some of the members of the Judenrat—not its chairman—were opposed to resistance because they feared German reprisals, and there were bitter struggles between them and Lidowski and the other resisters. In the end, after the second "action," from September 22 to October 2, 1942, groups of the underground began leaving the ghetto for the forests. Some 250 survived, most of them having fought in Soviet partisan units from late 1942 to liberation in July 1944. It has to be assumed that at least that many people died after fleeing from the town, so that the flight must have included some 500 people, out of 12,000 inmates of the ghetto, or about 4 percent. The cases of Baranowicze and, say, Vilno or Kovno are comparable: there were reasonably well-organized underground movements, failed attempts at a rebellion in the ghetto (though not in Kovno), and then flight to the forests and partisan fighting.[43]

The Baranowicze story highlights another, crucial aspect of Jewish resistance: escapees to the forests usually had to abandon their families in the ghettoes. Sometimes those who fled with members of their family and wanted to join the partisans had to leave their loved ones behind, unprotected, in hideouts. The problem was terrible emotionally and morally. We know of them also in accounts of well-known ghetto rebellions—in Vilno and Bialystok, for example. Abba Kovner, the commander of the Jewish resistance in Vilno, decided to have his whole group leave for the forest, through the sewers, after the attempt to rebel in the ghetto failed. Then his mother came to ask him what she should do, and he had a terrible decision to make. He could not take an older woman with him, crawling through the sewers, and if he had done so, he would have had to agree that all the relatives of the resistance members should join as well. He told her to hide, knowing full well that he was sentencing her to death. Hayka Grossman, the central figure in the later stages of the Bialystok resistance movement, faced the same dilemma with her mother. In the kresy, this was a central issue for practically everyone. They had to leave behind parents, siblings, wives, husbands, and children.

In Baranowicze this was the case with Eliezer Lidowski. Lidowski was a married man, "old" by partisan standards (in his late thirties), with two children. His wife had been a Labor Zionist activist herself, an intelligent and stubborn person. In his postwar contribution to the Memorial Book of Baranowicze, he speaks of the terrible moment when he abandoned his family to go to the forest. Decades later, in a booklet called *In Old Age* (in Hebrew), he wrote something that he obviously had not been able to bring himself to write decades before: he had gone back to the ghetto, from the partisan base, on an assignment that he had volunteered for, and tried to convince his wife to join him. She refused, and although what Lidowski says she said to him cannot be her precise words, there can be no doubt about the general sense of what she said: "I'm staying here in the ghetto. I suggest that you, too, stay in the ghetto after you find some excuse for the days you missed work. I'm afraid that otherwise the Germans will execute the entire family. . . . The lives of our two children are very precious to me. If they stay here—perhaps a miracle will occur and they will survive. But there in the forests, among the antisemitic goyim—and you've already had personal experience of their antisemitism—no miracle will happen there: there is only death." Lidowski left for the forest. He had to live with a feeling of guilt for the rest of his life. Abba Kovner put this in words: he used to ask whether he was a heroic resister or an unworthy son who had abandoned his mother.[44]

If we multiply these cases by thousands, the sheer insurmountable problem that Jewish fighters had to contend with becomes more apparent. The problem was not the same for non-Jews. In most, though not in all, cases, non-Jews left their families in the relative safety of the unoccupied Soviet Union or in the villages and towns of the occupied Soviet territories, where it was difficult for Germans or collaborators to find out where family members who had disappeared had gone. The difference was that Jews were slated for murder—all of them. Everywhere.

There were, as we have seen, some mass flights from shtetlach into the forests, usually during an "action," or just before or after it. Perhaps the most interesting case is that of Rokitno, in northern Volhynia (probably 2,000–2500 Jews in

1941), on the edge of the Polesie forests and swamps. There was no underground movement in Rokitno, although some individuals managed to escape and go to the partisans as early as the spring of 1942. Hundreds of Jews from Rokitno were recruited by the Germans for slave labor—the orders came from the regional headquarters in Sarny—and were executed by the Ukrainian militia and the local Todt organization, which performed construction services for the German army. In August 1942, the Germans decided to liquidate the Jews of Sarny, Rokitno, and a number of other small shtetlach in the vicinity. They prepared for this in Rokitno, as they did in many other shtetlach, by ordering a registration of all inhabitants a few days before the date of the liquidation, then commanded everyone to come to the main square, near the railway station, where a train stood ready to take them to Sarny, where they would be murdered. The date was August 26, 1942. The man in charge was the Polish-German head of the militia, Sokolowsky. Men and teenage boys were separated from women and children. Three sides of the square were guarded by Ukrainians and Germans from the Todt unit, but the fourth side was still open. The square held 1,634 Jews that day (they were counted); no one had tried to hide because the Germans had said it would be another routine registration. In the crowd was a very tall and strong woman, Mindl Eisenberg, who, because of her size, was called "Mindl Cossack." Mindl, being taller than most of the rest, saw a Ukrainian unit in black uniforms marching toward the fourth side of the square and intuitively grasped the situation. She yelled—according to most testimonies—"Yidn, men harget uns" (Jews, they have come to kill us). She might have used slightly different words, but the message was clear. Panic broke out, and masses of people tried to escape through the still-open side of the square. The Germans and the Ukrainians opened fire, and a couple of hundred people were killed on the spot. Of the rest, between 600 and 900 Jews—depending on whose testimony one relies on—managed to flee. Forest lay on both sides of the railroad track and north of the township—it was just 100 meters away. Families were split, of course. Younger people managed to join partisan units in the Polesie forests and swamps, or they fled southwest into the forest adjoining the three Polish villages near Rokitno mentioned in the previous chapter. The survivors' stories are harrowing in the extreme, but there were, at the end of the war, some 150 survivors, possibly more, and most of them testified or wrote memoirs.[45]

Rokitno is an example of a completely unplanned mass escape, and there were a few of these elsewhere as well. As a result of this particular escape, hundreds of women and men joined the partisans. Medvedev's unit was the first to whom the escapees turned, and Medvedev tried to help them and direct them toward the north, where they would find partisans who might accept them. The Jews were disorganized and undisciplined, and some of them fell victim to the pursuing German and Ukrainian units. Some turned toward the northwest, toward the village of Glinna, in the swamps, and found a friendly Soviet unit, Pleskonosov's (no details about Pleskonosov are available).[46] Others went farther afield and joined the otriad of Maxim Missiura, a Ukrainian communist who accepted Jews in his detachments.

In an attempt to pull all these details together, it is of some importance to differentiate, if only in a very general way, between underground groups in the shtetlach, armed rebellions, flight into the forest, family camps, and partisan fighting. It is clear that in most shtetlach, in both the south and the north, there were underground groups, usually small ones. In most cases they were led by former members of prewar Zionist youth movements of all political hues. It was extremely difficult to obtain arms, and the German intelligence service, which employed Jewish informers, was very efficient and managed to liquidate many of the underground groups, especially in the south. (The informers, who had been promised their lives in exchange for information, were all murdered after supplying it.) Hostility on the part of the surrounding populations—again, very much so in the south—prevented any help from that quarter. In the north and in some parts of northern Volhynia, the presence of Soviet partisans meant that the chances of successful rebellions, or of flight and fighting as partisans, were relatively better. Rebellions and armed resistance occurred in a number of shtetlach: Tuczyn in Volhynia; Lachwa, Dereczin, Kleck, Nieswiez, Glebokie, Stolpce, and other places in the north. Members of underground groups often tried to flee into the forests, and so did a number of families. Mass flight into the forests was, in some shtetlach, the result of pure chance—Rokitno is the best example. In some, half-prepared actions by underground members triggered mass escapes, as in Sarny, where more than 1,000 Jews managed to flee from a barbed-wire enclosure on August 27, 1942, after one member of the underground movement there—according to other sources, two members—cut the wire, in the face of fire by Germans and Ukrainians. Individuals and families fled, whether they were former underground members or not, in almost all the shtetlach. The escapees either tried to survive in partisan-protected or even unprotected family camps or tried to find refuge in remote forest villages. Younger people, who were individual survivors in most cases, tried to join partisan groups; many, possibly hundreds or even thousands, were robbed and killed by forest groups posing as partisans or by regular Soviet partisan units, and thousands of others were permitted to join the ranks of the partisans and participated in the fight against the Germans and their supporters. Many were killed, but there still were thousands of survivors—although they were but a tiny percentage of the original inhabitants of the shtetlach.

Cholawsky and others have identified the basic tragedy, and I cannot but re-peat what they have said: The Soviet partisan movement gave Jews their only real chance to survive. But when the Jews of the shtetlach needed the partisans, the partisans were not yet there. When they were a presence in the area, most of the Jews of the shtetlach had already been murdered. In most of the Ukrainian ter-ritories, there were few or no partisans, even in 1943–1944. So most of the shtet-lach Jews had no hope of survival in the face of the unprecedented genocide.

When, for the survivors in the kresy, it was all over, and the Soviets liberated the area, the partisans emerged from the forests into a world of ruins and destruc-tion. Most of the towns and townships in the kresy were bombed out; a majority of the houses were uninhabitable. But the war was still on, and the Red Army recruited the able-bodied men. Some Jews managed to avoid being recruited, but many became soldiers and officers in the advancing Soviet forces. There was still about one year left before the German defeat, and many Jewish partisans fell in battle in the ranks of the Soviet forces. Among the fallen was one of the Bielski brothers, Asael, the deputy commander (and actual leader) of the fighting group that had been separated from the Bielski group. Those who survived had an addi-tional story to tell, of fighting the German army and advancing into Germany.[47]

Those who stayed behind in the shtetlach and towns had different fates. Some joined the Soviet administration and security forces and tried—often success-fully—to take bloody revenge on local collaborators with the Germans. Others, especially women, as well as some of the men, tried at first to find some kind of occupation that would enable them to eat and live in the ruined houses. But very soon they realized that they could not stay. Antisemitism in the shtetlach did not abate, and in the south the Banderovtsy fought against the Soviet army—they even managed to kill a Marshal of the Soviet Union, Nikolai F. Vatutin—and killed any Jew they could find. But, mainly, there was nothing to stay for: the Jewish communities, with all their complicated and well-developed social life, had been destroyed, the families of the survivors had been murdered, and people could not stay in houses where everything reminded them of parents, siblings, children, who now lay in cold graves scattered all over the kresy. People fled, illegally, across the borders into Poland, and after the war ended in May 1945, ar-rangements between the pro-communist new Polish government and the Soviets permitted all who had been Polish citizens, including Jews, to move to Poland legally. As part of the deal, many Poles who had been living in Ukrainian territo-ries were allowed into Poland to escape the mass murder of Poles by Ukrainian nationalists. By 1946, very few Jews were left in the kresy. A history of many hun-dreds of years had reached its bloody end.

Eight

THE DEATH OF THE SHTETL

There are no more shtetlach in eastern Europe; the places where they once existed are now populated by other people, and the memory of the shtetl is kept alive in other countries and on other continents by Jews (and some non-Jews), including many of the descendants of the Jews who lived there a long time ago. It is tempting to ask a question that historians are not supposed to ask, although most of them ask such questions anyway: What might have happened to the shtetlach in the kresy had there been no war? Counterfactual questions can have no clear answers, but here we may venture a guess. In the late thirties, the shtetlach were obviously in deep crisis. Low prices for agricultural produce and high prices for manufactured goods were increasing poverty among both peasants and the Jewish lower middle class—peddlers, small shopkeepers, craft workers—who were the majority of the Jewish population.

Governmental and popular antisemitism were growing along with unemployment and underemployment. Why the growing hostility to the Jews? Part of the answer lies, of course, in the troubled history of these areas, especially the Ukrainian ones. The enmity between the exploited peasants and the Polish or Polonized landowners, with the Jews squeezed in between and hated or despised by both, was exacerbated by the theological animosity of the Christian churches to the people of the Christian Messiah, whom they had rejected. But this explanation is insufficient, because there were relatively long periods of peaceful coexistence, and the enmity was triggered by the events of the interwar period. Undercurrents of animosity became evident as the economic crisis of the thirties plunged larger and larger sections of the population, non-Jewish and Jewish alike, into worse and worse poverty.

A high proportion of the Jews—exact figures cannot be quoted—could not stay where they were, but they had nowhere to go; the world seemed closed to them. As Chaim Weiztmann, head of the Zionist movement, supposedly put it: "The world is divided into countries where the Jews cannot live, and countries into which the Jews cannot enter." The hope in the Zionist shtetlach of the kresy was that somehow, at some point, the gates of Palestine would open and Jews, or many of them, could go there. Indeed, in 1939 they hoped that increased pressure and perhaps a massive illegal attempt to enter Palestine despite British opposition would make emigration to Palestine possible. Those actions were what a number of Zionist leadership groups, both right and left, were seriously considering. The dream of the Bund, to work with the Polish working class to create a socialist Poland, a Poland that would guarantee equality to all and enable the Jews to develop cultural autonomy in the Yiddish language, was not very likely to come true. The Polish working class was in the minority, and peasants, who were mostly no friends of the Jews, were in the majority. Unemployment was rampant in the cities. A social upheaval was not likely to benefit the workers, but rather to establish a much more centralized and dictatorial populist regime than the one in power since the takeover by Pilsudski in 1926, and especially since 1935, when Pilsudski died. Jews would hardly have benefited from that. Pressure to open Palestine could have had some success and eased the situation of the remaining Jews. An autonomous or independent Jewish commonwealth in Palestine of some kind might possibly have been the outcome, but the Holocaust prevented that, and Israel, when it finally arose in 1948, did so despite the Holocaust and not because of it.

There might have been another development: an emergence from the economic crisis and a slow integration of the Jewish population into a gradually modernizing Polish society. A development of that kind was not very likely, but it was marginally possible. It might have been accompanied by a disintegration of the semi-authoritarian regime then in power, either gradually or in an upheaval.

These were possibilities, but what happened in fact was very different, as we know. Modernization came, however slowly and painfully. The Polish intelligentsia had always been under the influence of ideas that came from the West, especially from France. Industries sprang up, universities flourished, a Polish middle class emerged, and with all this came a weakening of traditional customs and usages. Among the Jews, this development was much more radical: it weakened Orthodoxy and strengthened tendencies toward acculturation into Polish society and, on the other hand, the growth of socialist and Zionist movements. In the kresy, the weakening of political orthodoxy was little less than dramatic. Unlike in central and western Poland, Zionism remained strong there, and the socialist Bund was weak. All the shtetlach that I have examined, without exception, including the ones I did not investigate in detail, had Zionist leaders by the end of the thirties. The fact that the Zionists were split into mutually warring factions, including a religious faction, seems to have increased Jews' political awareness. The predominance of nonreligious groups did not mean that customs and ways of life that had their origin in the Jewish religion were abandoned, however—not at all. They were integrated into a developing combination of ethnic and religious streams that were expressed in different ways by different Zionist groups.

What happened was a disaster in two stages: a Soviet-induced stage and a German-induced stage. The Soviet occupation destroyed the shtetl and atomized Jewish society. We have seen that underground resistance to the Soviet regime has been much overrated; in fact, it was limited to a few hundred young people. However, not only terror and totalitarian brutality dissolved Jewish society. So did the prospect of integration and the regime's opposition to antisemitism. By opening educational and employment opportunities unheard of under the Poles, the Soviet regime became popular among the young generation of Jews. The Jews of the kresy were on their way to becoming Soviet Jews, similar to the millions who became part of pre-1939 Soviet society. One might argue that the shtetl would have disintegrated in any case because it was being abandoned as urbanization proceeded and because the traditional closeness of shtetl society was being destroyed as modernization proceeded. However, even if that was true, and if there had been no war, dissolution would have taken a long time. It would have been a natural, slow, and relatively peaceful process. As it was, the Soviet occupation destroyed the shtetl brutally, efficiently, and with great speed.

The Jewish cultural heritage did not constitute a serious obstacle to the destruction of Jewish society by a totalitarian regime that did not endanger the Jews physically. That is a difficult issue, and it has two aspects. First, Jewish (and, arguably, other) traditions are no match for a regime that is determined to destroy, not the carriers of the tradition physically, but the carriers' cultural and social autonomy. Second, and this is a universal issue, the cohesion and culture of a society can be destroyed by a totalitarian regime when it uses not just the stick but also the carrot. A purely terroristic approach might have produced a reaction of resistance. If the Soviet stage had not come to an end, the Jews of the kresy might have had to wait until the implosion of the Soviet Union in the late eighties to awaken from the dream—or the nightmare—of Soviet-style internationalism, antisemitism, and assimilation. As it was, they did not have that chance, because they were murdered by the Germans. In any case, the implosion of the Soviet Union would not have re-created the shtetl in the kresy any more than it did elsewhere in the USSR. The idea that the shtetl tradition is being carried on in North America is a nostalgic notion that has no basis in fact.

Was it the Germans or the German National Socialists, the Nazis, who were responsible for the murder of Jews? Today, German historians rarely speak of Nazis when they discuss the implementation of the genocidal policies, except when they deal with the leadership, the ideology, and the Nazi Party and its various organs. One does not have to be a Daniel Goldhagen to see very clearly that the vast majority of Germans, both in Germany and in the German forces in the USSR, were in agreement with the policies of their government.[1] There were honorable exceptions, and, as this book has shown, the number is greater than is generally appreciated, but it was not "the Nazis" who murdered the Jews. They were the leaders, the propagators of a genocidal ideology, but the murderers were ordinary men: ordinary Germans, helped along by many ordinary Ukrainians, Belorussians, Baltics, and Poles. It is appropriate to talk of Germans as the perpetrators and murderers and to mention Nazis only when talking of the party and the leadership.

The help of the non-Jewish populations in and around the shtetlach was essential for the project of murdering the Jews to succeed. Without that help, what we now know as the Holocaust—a most inappropriate term for the genocide of the Jews—would probably not have happened in the kresy or anywhere else.[2] Again, there were many exceptions, and it would be wrong to stereotype the different ethnicities as universally murderous. But it would be equally wrong to close one's eyes to the fact that the rescuers and helpers made up a small minority; the majority were too scared to help, were indifferent to the fate of an unpopular ethnic group in their midst, or supported the murder, passively or actively. The last seems to have been the most widely applicable attitude.

I have pointed out differences. Ukrainian nationalism moved most Ukrainians to be on the murderous side. Among Belorussians, there was more sympathy for the Jews. The Polish minority apparently differed in attitude depending on where they lived. In the south, many Poles were themselves a minority facing a murderous Ukrainian threat, so they had more of a tendency to make joint cause with the Jews. In the north, on the other hand, the "official" Polish underground, the one connected with the Polish government-in-exile, was motivated both by political considerations and also by violent antisemitism, which expressed itself, especially in 1943–1944, in murderous attacks by Polish guerilla units against Jews. Again, there were exceptions everywhere. Minorities, whether ethnic or religious, tended to be friendlier to Jews than were majorities—we have looked at Baptists-Mennonites, Old Believers, and Czechs.

Given this situation, the rescuers were truly heroic figures. They had to oppose not only the Germans and their helpers but also their own, ordinary neighbors—who may have been motivated not only by antisemitism but by greed and fear.

Once the non-Jewish population had laid hands on Jewish property—whether robbed from the Jews or handed to non-Jews to safeguard—they wanted to keep it. And the Germans and the German-controlled local police were indeed much to be feared. When the Soviets were coming back in 1943–1944, the population also feared that they would be held to account for the murder of the Jews and for collaboration with the enemy; this was in addition to the fear of losing the spoils of their robbery.

When the Germans first came, they did the actual killing, which can be documented for the first half-year of their occupation. By 1942, the killing was increasingly done by both Germans and local militias, and later it was mainly the militias who killed, under German supervision, although German overall initiative and participation always remained crucial. But throughout the whole period of German control, the various local units of collaborators fulfilled centrally important functions in the massacres—preparing the mass graves or chasing the Jews to the railway stations and into the railway cars, encircling the murder sites to prevent escapes, torturing the victims before they were shot, and preventing locals from viewing what was going on—although the locals knew. The motivations of these helpers have been discussed: traditional antisemitism, greed, identification with the Germans in the hope of getting their support for autonomy or independence, fear of the Germans, and, very important, the hope of earning money and gaining status. Young people were unemployed and were in danger of being sent to Germany as forced laborers, and service in a local police unit or in a mobile Schutzmannschaft was likely to protect them from that. The Germans provided uniforms and weapons, but for a price: killing Jews, among other things. That was all right.

The relationship between the Jews and their neighbors in the kresy appeared to be different from minority-majority relationships in other genocidal situations. The Jews were facing not one, but at least two enemy ethnic groups—either Ukrainians and Poles, or Belorussians and Poles. To a considerable extent, these neighbors cooperated with the murderers, at least passively. Very often they joined them in perpetrating the crimes. There was thus little chance for Jews to escape or even offer meaningful resistance. The only comparable case was that of the Roma (Gypsies), and in many ways their dilemma was even worse because they were a much smaller group, with less prior cohesion and without any kind of intellectual leadership. The crucial difference was that every single person defined as a Jew was sentenced to death for the crime of having been born, which was not the case with the Roma. Yet the cases are, in some ways, similar: there was no sympathy for Roma, not among peasants and not even among Soviet partisans.

When we compare the fate of the Jews with that of other victims of other genocides, we have to conclude that the situations are different. In Rwanda, Hutu and Tutsi fought against each other within the same geographical, political, and social frameworks, and the genocide was essentially the outcome of an internal struggle that ended with a civil war—something totally different from the Holocaust. The situation in Darfur only seems similar because of the multiplicity of ethnic groups involved; but in fact, there are only two sides to the horror there—the perpetrators are Arabs, Nilotic Sudanese, or locals who consider themselves to be "white" and who perpetrate genocidal murders or genocide by attrition against people they consider "black," most of whom are (or were) peasants. The fact that these differentiations are to an extent purely ideological or virtual makes little difference. Again, the situation in Darfur is essentially one of a civil war. But another element makes the Holocaust in the kresy different from other genocides: Ukrainians, Belorussians, and Poles were recognized as separate ethnicities or nationalities, and civil strife between them had a character that was different from the character of the genocide of the Jews. Unlike the Rwanda and Darfur examples, the kresy had both collaborators with the Germans and supporters of the Soviets. In a sense, two outside forces that were engaged in a bitter struggle with each other split the local national or ethnic groups. Locally, many Jews had two enemies; the Tutsi and the Fur (the main black ethnicity in Darfur), only one.

The Soviet Union supported its loyalists among Ukrainians and Belorussians. To a limited extent, the Soviets also supported Polish communists in the kresy, and quite a number of Poles saw the Soviets as allies in their struggle against Ukrainian nationalism—which is not something that Poles today like to acknowledge, but the evidence is quite clear. But most Poles supported their government-in-exile in London and thus had what they hoped was a powerful ally outside the local arena. The Jews as a group were, in contrast, ignored by the Soviets, nor did the Western Allies see any reason why Jews should be given more attention than any other group persecuted by the Nazis—in fact, there were reasons why Jews should be ignored as much as possible. After all, the Germans based much of their propaganda on the argument that the Allies were fighting a war for the Jews, and that had some resonance, or might have had some resonance, with Allied soldiers. Overt help for Jews qua Jews could be counterproductive. The result was that the Jews were left in the lurch.

In 1941–1944, the Western Allies could not have helped the Jews, but Allied indifference denied them even moral support. There was no real chance of outside intervention, whereas in other cases of genocide there has been at least a chance that outside factors might influence developments: Tutsis had powerful allies in the largely Tutsi army that was fighting against the Hutu government; Darfuri blacks have weapons with which to fight their enemies; Armenians looked to Tsarist Russia, a powerful enemy of the Ottoman Empire, geographically well positioned to aid the Armenians, and so on. The Jews were totally alone, isolated, and surrounded by a largely hostile population.

The central issue that I addressed was the attitude and the actions of the Jews as they responded to an existential threat that became obvious after a short time. I cannot say that my findings have answered all, or even most, of the main questions. The major question that I posed was whether the Jewish culture that had developed and changed over thousands of years, but remained clearly identifiable, affected Jewish reactions in an extreme crisis. Because Jewish traditions and Jewish society had developed a special character in the shtetlach, the question becomes even more pointed and specific in that connection: Did the shtetl Jews behave any differently from Jews elsewhere? I found no proof that Jewish traditions had any major impact on Jewish reactions to the genocide—either in the shtetlach or anywhere else. When we compare Jews with victims of other genocides, we find pretty much the same reactions: disorientation, despair, individual and group heroism, collaboration with the perpetrators in the hope of surviving, family cohesion—but also occasional abandonment of children or parents—and resistance, chiefly armed resistance.

The only form of reaction that was specific to Jews—and it was very important indeed—was unarmed resistance, unarmed Amidah. It is worth repeating what that was: mutual aid, education, health care, food smuggling, and morale building, chiefly accomplished by maintaining a minimum of cultural life. But unarmed Amidah in the kresy was limited by the impossible external circumstances, although it did exist in some places and was expressed in ways that were specific to the areas discussed here.

But even if we conclude that many forms of reaction were universal, in the sense that variations of them can be found among groups facing genocidal situations, that universality is, paradoxically, specific. Jews behaved (at least partly) like anyone else, and everyone else (at least partly) behaved like Jews, except that the languages were different, and the curses directed against the murderers in the name of religion or human dignity or any other ideology were different, as were the prayers. Many Jews clung to Jewish traditional observances, just as other victims clung to theirs. In the face of death at the shooting pits and on the trains to Belzec, Jews behaved much like victims of other genocides. The differences between the genocide of the Jews and other genocides lie elsewhere, not in the character of the victims' reactions in the face of death. They lie in a combination of two elements: the unprecedented totality and universality of the Nazi policy that targeted every single Jew everywhere on the globe for destruction, and the unarmed Amidah reaction, which, I think, was specific to Jews.

Did the reaction of shtetl Jews differ from the reactions of Jews in other parts of German-occupied Europe? The answer seems to be yes. Let us here concentrate, first of all, on contextual factors. To a not inconsiderable degree the differences were due to geography. Many of the shtetlach in the kresy were located near forests, which offered a chance, however slight, that escape into the forests might make survival possible. This was so especially in western Belorussia and Polesie, much less so in Volhynia and East Galicia. But even the latter regions had forests or woods, and some Jews managed to survive there despite all the seemingly impossible conditions. Such escapes were impossible in central and western Poland, where the land was only lightly forested, if at all, and the population was either indifferent or antisemitic, and in most other Nazi-controlled countries, with the exception of Slovakia, Yugoslavia, Greece, and possibly northern Italy and parts of southern France. But the number of Jews living in these areas was comparatively small.

Another contextual factor that developed, mainly in the northern kresy, was a massive Soviet partisan movement that made it possible for a Jewish remnant to survive, whether as fighters or as family groups protected by fighters. The only parallel elsewhere in Nazi-dominated Europe was in Yugoslavia, and there indeed a proportionately large number of Jews survived as members of Marshal Tito's army, possibly up to 6,000–7,000, a number that corresponds to roughly 8–9 percent of the prewar Jewish population there.

One other main difference for the Jews in the kresy compared with Jews elsewhere was the time factor—the speed with which the Germans proceeded to murder Jews. The Warsaw Jews were under Nazi rule in September 1939. The mass murder occurred in July–September 1942, and a significant armed underground did not appear until the late fall of that year. In other words, it took more than three years for resistance to develop. The Germans took Vilno in June 1941, but for whatever reasons, they permitted a ghetto to exist between September 1941 and September 1943. The time between the establishment of murderous oppression and total annihilation allowed Jewish reactions of the Amidah type to develop there, culminating in an attempt at armed rebellion. In the kresy, on the other hand, the Germans murdered the Jews within one and a half years after their occupation; by the end of 1942 only remnants of the Jewish population were left.

I must also emphasize that Jews in the German-occupied Soviet Union, including the kresy, were the first to experience the German annihilation strategy.

The strategy had no precedent in human history. The total novelty of total annihilation of a whole ethnicity took the Jewish population by surprise and created numbed shock among many. Reaction to it was really not what we today would expect. In a way, we should almost ask the opposite question—not what the Jewish reaction was but how communities and groups within them came to react with what I call Amidah. Why was it that not everyone, everywhere, reacted with stupor and despair? The answer that this may have a connection to Jewish traditions is not very persuasive, for the same traditions were observed by Jews in communities that were totally atomized.

As I have emphasized, the Soviets destroyed the shtetl as a historical-sociological-cultural phenomenon before the Germans annihilated it. I described the scandalous ease with which the Soviet regime managed to do so in some detail because of the implications for Jewish—and general—history. It seems to indicate that cultural structures, even if they are based on centuries-old traditions, are weak and can be destroyed without much trouble. The lesson to learn may well be that it is essential to protect and fortify cultural and societal structures and traditions, especially at times of stress and at times of danger from powerful enemies. The Soviets did not use only terror and compulsion but also persuasion, and they took steps that were positive from an individual's point of view in order to force communities into the fold of a totalitarian, atomized society. Actually, the Soviet inducement went beyond persuasion. It was part of the Soviet project to provide free education and equal opportunities for advancement to all. Antisemitism was frowned upon, and for the first time ever, Jews felt safe from that scourge. Large numbers of young Jews either accepted or identified with the regime for these reasons. Cultural activity, Soviet style, was fostered and developed, and social clubs that broke ethnic barriers were opened everywhere; young people belonged to them, whatever their background. Films, theater performances, dancing, intellectual life—all the things that had been sadly missing under Polish governance were now supplied.

That Polish society imploded under the weight of its own corruption, economic failure, and uselessness is another element that we should take into account, with hindsight, because the period of Soviet rule in the first part of the war was replete with signs of internal contradictions. People were arrested and deported because of trade activities, and every trade activity was illicit. The people most engaged in trade were the rulers themselves—party bureaucrats, managers, municipal clerks, village heads, and officers and NCOs of the Soviet army stationed in the region. What prevailed was the odd combination of a brutal and corrupt dictatorship and remnants of an idealistic, egalitarian approach to governance.

We should therefore beware of a facile comparison between the Nazi and the

Soviet regimes. The Nazi regime was based on an uncompromising enmity to what we inaccurately term Western civilization, to the heritage of the French Revolution, to the concept of human rights (basically a relatively new term), to voluntary participation in society and governance, and to all the political movements that tried to grapple with these issues—liberalism, democratic conservatism, socialism, and so on. The Nazi regime accepted a state-directed form of capitalism, although its control of the German economy was never total or, indeed, very successful. The Soviet regime represented a dictatorial distortion of ideas that were rooted in that very liberal past that the Nazis tried to destroy. Concepts such as participatory democracy and an international, inclusive attitude toward other groups and ethnicities were not entirely foreign to the Soviets, and that created the contradictory attitudes and policies I mentioned, some of which redounded in favor of individuals from among the local Jewish population in the shtetlach. Yet, with all that, the fact remains that the Soviets utterly destroyed the communal structure of the Jewish population and instituted a reign of terror that involved turning many Jews—we do not know how many—into informers, causing great suffering to the rest. The Soviets deported hundreds of thousands of Jews, mainly refugees from German-occupied western Poland, to Soviet Asia, a deportation accompanied by great loss of life and involving tremendous suffering—but most of these people survived, whereas those who evaded deportation were killed.

There were paradoxes: middle-class Jews who were the targets of Soviet nationalization and collectivization programs usually managed much better than many others, because they knew how and where to hide whatever property they retained, and that often formed the basis of (forbidden and illegal) private trading, which in its turn involved Soviet functionaries and officials. The totally corrupt nature of the regime facilitated bribery and private trade. Soviet functionaries profited by it, and some middle-class Jews kept their ordinary lives going. Old people and certain types of intellectuals—lawyers, for instance—had a much harder time. Craft workers survived in artificially formed artels, the government-approved cooperatives. All in all, Jews managed reasonably well, and as the prewar economic situation had been precarious at best, the change was not necessarily for the worse.

Our difficulty lies in our source of information: as far as Jewish testimonies go, we chiefly have those of the survivors of the Nazi murder, and the German occupation tended to obliterate the memory of what preceded it. As far as documentary material goes, it is largely of Soviet provenance and therefore suspect. However, those who wrote about the period, namely Ben-Cion Pinchuk, Dov Levin, and Jan T. Gross, were able to utilize a fair amount of private correspondence and a fair number of memoirs. Even though the deportees to Soviet Asia were witness to only part of the period—until their deportation—their memoirs and testimonies also help to clarify the history of those twenty-one months of Soviet rule. Finally, it must be emphasized that the Soviets did not promulgate any antisemitic policies, at least not at that stage; the whole fury of Soviet terroristic actions was directed, at first, against the Poles and, in the very last stages of Soviet occupation, against Ukrainian nationalists, although purely quantitatively, Jews formed a higher percentage of the deportees than did members of the other ethnicities.

The main findings in this book concern the reactions of the Jews to the murderous German onslaught. Several points emerge. I have already stated that I found no evidence of the impact of Jewish traditions or customs, religious or others, on Jewish behavior during the period of annihilation. Belorussian peasants who were killed by the Germans in the course of the anti-partisan warfare behaved no differently from Jews, and vice versa. When faced with inevitable, violent death, humans react in very much the same fashion everywhere.

But I did not concentrate on the last stage. I asked questions about behavior and reactions before people came face to face with death. There, as we have seen, Jews of the shtetlach behaved in ways that differed practically from shtetl to shtetl. The example of Krzemieniec provides us with one extreme: atomization, disintegration of the community, almost no Amidah (except for the doctors who tried to help and who prevented epidemics from breaking out). There were several reasons for the failure to cohere and help one another: first of all, hunger, which paralyzed all activity except that needed to stay alive; second, a despicable Judenrat leadership that was the epitome of corruption and betrayal; and third, behind the Judenrat, a sadistic, violently antisemitic German civilian governor, Fritz Müller, who did everything in his power to torture the Jews before he ordered them murdered. However, such Germans were in charge in most places: Wilhelm Traub in Nowogrodek, Rudolph Werner and Max Krampe in Baranowicze, and Heinz Krökel in Sarny were hardly any better, nor was Friedrich Wilhelm Rohde in Brest-Litovsk. Hunger existed in other places as well, but arguably not to the extreme extent that it existed in Krzemieniec. As to the Judenrat, it is clear that Müller was looking for people like Bronfeld or Diamant, and he found them. Their predecessors had been different kinds of people, but they were replaced very soon.

The other extreme may be represented by Baranowicze, where the successive Judenräte members were lauded as wonderful human beings and leaders by all the survivors—I have not come across a single dissenting voice so far. The names of Ovsiei (Yehoshua) Isaakson, Genia Menn, Shmuel Jankielewicz, and Mendel

Goldberg stood for attitudes, policies, and actions that were diametrically opposed to those of Bronfeld and Diamant in Krzemieniec. Is it possible that these differences were due to geography? Krzemieniec was in the southern part of Volhynia, where there were no Soviet partisans and where the local population of Ukrainians proved to be particularly murderous, whereas Baranowicze was in the Belorussian north, where Soviet partisans began to appear in the summer of 1942. There may be several answers to that. One is that Isaakson was chosen by the Jews (and approved by the Germans) just slightly before Bronfeld and Diamant were appointed, and while it is true that the local Belorussians in Baranowicze, though hostile, were not as murderous as the Ukrainians in the south, this had little to do with the appointment or otherwise of the Judenräte. The absence of Soviet partisans in the south had no importance until the spring of 1942, when conditions in the ghetto became unbearable, partly because of the Judenrat; in Baranowicze, in contrast, the Judenrat played a heroic role before the partisans appeared in mid-1942. Because the role of the Germans in both places was very similar, none of these explanations is quite convincing.

All the other Judenräte occupied a variety of middle positions between these two extreme cases. The Judenrat in Buczacz (headed by Baruch Kramer), was nearer the negative extreme, as was the Czortkow Judenrat (Dr. Haim Ebner), whereas the Nowogrodek Judenrat (Henryk Ciechanowski) received much more positive ratings from the survivors. The head of the Kurzeniec Judenrat (Schatz) was somewhere in the middle, as were most of the other Judenräte and their heads.

A special position was occupied by the Judenräte that participated in or organized armed resistance, as in Tuczyn, Kleck, Lachwa, and Dereczin, or whose members behaved heroically even when they did not resist by force (Kosow Huculski).

If we conclude that the "objective" circumstances—Germans, accessibility of forests, attitudes of local populations—offer, at most, only partial explanations, we have to look elsewhere. I believe that we have to take recourse to explanations that may sound unusual coming from a professional historian who has been trained to analyze long-term and short-term factors and concentrate on economic, social, and political forces. I think that there are three elements that may explain the differences in behavior under extreme stress: character, chance, and luck. I elucidated these earlier. Character, because who was appointed to head a Judenrat did not depend only on the Germans. In Krzemieniec, to return to that example, the last Judenrat head was a decent fellow, according to the survivors, and the fact that he was unable to avert the final catastrophe is beside this particular point; he had been nominated by the Germans. What if he had been the Judenrat chief, before the final stage, instead of the two other characters? We do not know, of course, but Isaakson was also approved by the Germans, and he made all the difference.

The same can be said about the Judenrat heads in the resistant shtetlach mentioned above and, conversely, about places like Czortkow. Character seems to have mattered a great deal. But the appointment of a Judenrat head was a matter of a decision or approval on the spot by the Germans, whether or not the Jews or the locals suggested someone, and whether or not the Jews themselves elected him. And the German decision was a matter of chance; and that chance was either lucky for the Jews or not. The conclusion here has to be, I think, that that it is impossible to generalize regarding Judenrat behavior in the shtetlach. In situations of tremendous stress, which genocide certainly is, the reactions of the victims may not be determined by tradition or by economic, social, or other factors, but by these three elements, character, chance, and luck, which we rarely take into account when we try to explain historical events.

This conclusion seems to be fortified when we consider not the leaderships and the leadership groups but the community. The community that the Germans destroyed was not the prewar community—that, as we have seen, was destroyed by the Soviets. But when the Germans came, people had to band together simply in order to survive in these new and frightening circumstances; they had to try to maintain some kind of communal existence because they were marked collectively as a community by the conquering enemy, whether they felt they belonged to it or not. The argument famously put forward by Hannah Arendt—namely, that the Jews would have been better off if they had refused to establish institutions under the Germans—is totally unrealistic.[3] The Jews had no choice. They had to somehow manage the community into which they were forced, willy-nilly. The question is whether this community functioned as a kind of collective group, maintaining a minimum of solidarity in the terrible conditions, or whether the communities became random collections of individuals who did not care about each other but tried to survive as individuals and family groups fighting one another for the last pieces of bread. Put differently, the question is: Did the prewar Jewish community resurrect itself under the enormous pressure, or did it disintegrate?

We find the same variety of communal responses that we found with the Judenräte and their heads. In some cases, the community disintegrated completely, or almost so. To take the same examples again, Krzemieniec, an ancient community with a long tradition, was atomized. Almost no attempts at Amidah, no social life or, apparently, even feelings of mutual responsibility could be identified; basic solidarity seems to have withered away as time went on. No doubt this was due in large part to hunger and to the hostility of the surrounding population. But in Nowogrodek, too, there was very little social cohesion; people struck out on their own, although families did stick together. Where people tried to escape, it was often owing to external circumstances. In Nowogrodek, the prospect of escaping to the forests encouraged individual action. People who planned escape had no need for Amidah activities in the starving ghetto. Indeed, when the time came, and the ghetto population had dwindled to a few, determined common action did take place, and resulted in the breakout through the tunnel. In Czortkow, on the other hand, there was no communal action on any level, as far as I can tell, with the exception of attempts at armed resistance, which required some kind of prior organization, though we do not have any record of it. The same applies to a number of other places.

The opposite can be shown to have taken place in Baranowicze—there always seems to be an exception. In Baranowicze there was a well-organized, sustained effort at maintaining the community as such; the details have already been presented. The same applies to shtetlach like Tuczyn and Lachwa. Very small shtetlach, such as Kurzeniec, did not need any organization to maintain basic social cohesion—people knew each other intimately and offered and accepted help of all kinds, even in the difficult circumstances of German genocide.

Just as there can be no generalization about the behavior of the Judenräte, so there can be no generalization about the maintenance of the communities in extremis. There does seem to have been some difference between the Ukrainian and the Belorussian regions, obviously due to a marginally better relationship between Jews and Belorussians than between Jews and Ukrainians. The presence or absence of Amidah depended, clearly, on maintenance of a community morale, just as it depended on the presence or absence of individual and collective initiative. In the end, we have to again resort, not solely but mainly, to the elements of character, chance, and luck.

We found that people in almost every shtetl attempted to organize resistance of sorts. This cannot be said of any other group that was subjected to Nazi terror, although we could argue that since the Jews were threatened more than others— every single one of them was under a sentence of death—attempts at resistance could have been expected. Whether this argument is true or not, there were resistance attempts even in places where there was not the slightest chance that such an attempt would succeed. We found exceptions, to be sure: in Kosow Huculski, in the Carpathian foothills, with vast, beckoning forests no distance away at all. There, as everywhere else, Zionist and other youth movements had been organized prior to the war, but no attempt to form an organized underground under German occupation is recorded. On the other hand, there seems to have been an underground in Krzemieniec, even though any resistance there was doomed to failure.

Many of the attempts to resist ended in nothing because the Germans were too aware of what was going on among the Jewish population, for there always were Jewish informers—mostly desperate people who hoped to earn a piece of bread or be spared when the next "action" occurred. Other efforts developed to the stage of rebellion or escape to the forests, or both. Rebellions were always aimed at mass escape into the forest, and they were relatively few in number.

How many Jews escaped into the forests, and how many of them were murdered by partisan bands, Soviet or other? How many managed to join "real" Soviet partisan units and fought against the Germans? How many fighters survived? How many tried to hide in forest dugouts, and how many of these survived? It is impossible to provide more than guesses. It is possible that some 30,000–35,000 Jews escaped into the forests, the overwhelming majority of them in the north— maybe 23,000. Of the total, possibly 25,000 or more tried to join the partisans, but at least 5,000–7,000 were killed by bandits posing as partisans, as well as by "real"—that is, Soviet—partisans, or by Banderovtsy or Armia Krajowa Poles. Of the Jewish partisans, I would estimate that some 10,000–15,000 survived the war. Of the ones who tried to survive in family camps, including individuals hiding in dugouts, only a small proportion managed to make it, possibly 3,000–4,000— and that may be an overestimate. This number does not include Jews who hid with peasants (very few hid in towns), and the survivors among these did not amount to more than a few thousand individuals at most. The total number of survivors cannot have been much larger than about 25,000, or about 2 percent of the prewar Jewish population of the kresy. However, over the past sixty years or so, most of the survivors have provided us with their testimonies, which explains why I can write a book such as this.[4]

Even though rebellions and mass flights occurred, as in Rokitno and Sarny, the stories told here make it clear that underground organizations in the shtetlach were almost always small and mostly ineffective. Underground organizations and rebellions were led mainly by former Zionist youth movement members and, in a few cases, by young former Bundists. While I did not discern Jewish traditions generally having a major impact on the behavior of Jews, resistance appears to have been connected with prior Jewish (mostly Zionist) youth movement education. Superficially, the Bielskis seem to have been an exception, for they had never been members of any Zionist movement. But any reading of the testimonies of the members of the Bielski unit, as well as of the brothers themselves, makes it clear that their sympathies lay with Palestine-centered activities (they indeed went to Palestine/Israel after the war). In the case of Jewish partisans from Minsk—not included in this study, because it was in prewar Soviet territory—the initiative belonged to Jewish communists. Jewish communists, however small their number, were also prominent among the Jewish partisans in the kresy. As far as resistance was concerned, political ideology seems to have had some importance. Religious ideology, which was at the core of Jewish traditions reaching back thousands of years, played no role. Yes, there were religious Jews among the resisters, and some of them courageously tried to continue their religious observances, but they were not the leaders, and definitely not the majority, of the resisters. On the other hand, many testimonies talk about the maintenance of religious customs in the forest, including by nonreligious Jews. Many viewed fasting on Yom Kippur (Day of Atonement) as a way to maintain a link to the past and identify with fellow Jews generally, as well as a way to remember family members who had been killed.

What were the motivations of the Jewish resisters and partisans? The main motivations were not ideological. Again and again, I read about the burning desire to take revenge for the sake of family and friends brutally murdered by the Germans and their helpers. This appears to have been the main motivation. Another, obvious motivation was the desire to survive. Where there were close family relationships, another main motivation was the hope of keeping family members alive. This was true when the resisters and escapees to the forests were fortunate enough to be with one or more family members. Children and spouses came first, as might be imagined. I have not done any study of the motivations of non-Jewish Soviet partisans, but a comparison would no doubt be of some interest.

A very dark part of the story of the shtetlach in the kresy concerns the murder of probably thousands of Jews by forest groups, many of whom saw themselves as Soviet partisans, and many of whom were indeed later absorbed into the Soviet partisan movement. This, as we have seen, happened primarily in the first year of the German occupation, because after May 1942, the attitude toward Jews in the forest began to change as a result of the introduction of Soviet-style discipline and Communist Party directives—not that there were not serious antisemitic incidents, including many fatalities on the Jewish side, after May 1942. Nevertheless, the Soviet partisan movement, especially in Belorussia, rescued many thousands of Jews and made it possible for them to fight against the Germans. Despite the bitter experiences of Jewish partisans, the Soviet partisan movement must be given almost sole credit for the survival of even some Jews. As I have emphasized again and again, Jews rightly saw the Soviets as their liberators.

Jewish partisans showed absolutely no mercy toward captured Germans or collaborators. They did not deviate from the grim norm of Soviet partisans generally when fighting their war against the murderous enemy.

What about the rescuers? There were too few of them, as Erika Weinzierl has observed for Austria, for instance, and that holds true for all of Europe.[5] Recent apologetic arguments by some Polish historians claim that the Poles were overwhelmingly disposed to rescue Jews—a claim that stands in blatant contradiction to all the evidence we have. In areas where the Poles were a minority, the attitude toward Jews was considerably better than where they were a majority, as we saw in Volhynia, and in some East Galician localities. Somewhat diminished antisemitism was apparent mainly in Polish villages; Polish townspeople were overwhelmingly hostile. In the Belorussian areas, the official Polish underground of the Armia Krajowa murdered Jews, especially in the later stages of the war. This was because the Armia Krajowa's main opponent was the Soviets, and the Jews fought in Soviet units; but the special venom with which Jews were sought out to be killed shows the deep-seated Polish antisemitism in these areas.[6]

Ukrainians, as a group, if I may generalize, were very hostile. However, we do find quite a number of individuals who risked their lives to rescue Jews. I cited some of these cases. When Polish villagers gave shelter to Jews and made common cause with them, that was part of the struggle of the Polish minority against the Ukrainian majority, but when Ukrainian peasants (rarely, Ukrainian townspeople) helped the Jews, it was a conscious act made at great risk to the rescuer, for peasants who were found out would be in dire danger not only from the Germans but from the Banderovtsy and Bulbovtsy as well. As far as can be made out from mainly Jewish testimonies, they were mainly motivated by an empathetic identification with the plight of other human beings—and sometimes by prior acquaintance with the people they were helping.

Jewish attitudes towards Poles, Belorussians and Ukrainians were mixed in return—one might even say mixed up. Testimonies and especially postwar memoirs are full of contradictions. Negative and positive judgments abound, sometimes on the same page, and this seems to reflect reality, because indeed Jewish attitudes differed, naturally enough, since a majority of the neighbors were hostile, while a minority were friendly or at least neutral (that is, they did not deliver Jews to the murderers). Postwar memoirs were influenced by postwar collective memory and may not reflect what the writer thought back when the events happened. Nevertheless, the general conclusions reached in this research, and which I have repeated several times, seem well justified.[7]

That minorities in the Ukrainian regions were friendly to Jews finds expression in many of the testimonies. Baptists-Mennonites, Old Believers, and Czechs stand out in this connection, and the files of the Righteous Among the Nations at Yad Vashem bear evidence of many cases in which they helped Jews. Except with the Czechs, the motivation was apparently religious for the most part and, as with the Ukrainian rescuers, humanitarian.

Individual Germans helped, too. I gave some examples. In fact, their number was surprisingly high—although they were a tiny minority among the millions of Germans who went through the kresy. The Yiddish expression "a guter Daitch" (a good German) appears quite a few times in survivors' testimonies. Germans who helped Jews had to act against the murderous German consensus, which was difficult and dangerous, though not as difficult and dangerous for them as for local rescuers.

Did survivors became more religious as a result of their experiences, or less so? Many commentators have addressed that question. The answer seems to be that on the whole, people kept—or returned to—their prewar religious or nonreligious attitudes; there was no significant movement from religion to the rejection of religion, or the other way round. Occasionally, we can read of exceptions in one direction or another. One of the diaries referred to, that by Berkowicz in Nowogrodek, is consciously and radically atheistic; another, by Klonicki, is not. Some testimonies mention private beliefs, but not enough of them to reach any convincing conclusion.[8] Some local rabbis were very popular and were successful in preserving a vestige of religious observance. One example was Moshe Aharon Feldman in Kurzeniec, whose murder in March 1942 was a real blow to the community. Another was Yosef Aharon Shamess of Rokitno, originally a merchant, though with a rabbinical education, who became the rabbi of the shtetl before the war. He was a real help and loyal adviser to the head of the (popular) Judenrat.

The story of the shtetlach during the Holocaust has to be seen in the context of the Holocaust everywhere. About one-fifth of the total Jewish victims of German policies and actions came from the kresy, and only by looking at the background and history of the Holocaust as a whole can we begin to understand what happened there.

The remnants of the Jewish population were liberated by the Soviet army, which began the reconquest of the area in January 1944—partisans aided by the Red Army liberated Rokitno on January 2, 1944—and completed it by July of that year.

The Red Army liberated the kresy. It came too late. The shtetl was dead.

NOTES

1. I am using the prewar Polish spellings. Ukrainian, Belorussian, and Yiddish spellings are sometimes included in parentheses. In accordance with a convention for books published in English, diacritics in eastern European languages are omitted.
2. Celia S. Heller, *On the Edge of Destruction: Jews of Poland between the Two World Wars* (Columbia University Press, New York, 1977), p. 72.
3. An important exception is the excellent survey by Ban-Cion Pinchuk, "The East European Shtetl and Its Place in Jewish History," *Revue des études juives*, January–June 2005, pp. 187–212. Pinchuk deals with the historical and sociological development of the shtetl in the centuries preceding the Holocaust, and some of my analysis here is based on his study.
4. Shimon Redlich, *Together and Apart in Brzezany: Poles, Jews and Ukrainians, 1919–1945* (Indiana University Press, Bloomington, 2002); Daniel Mendelsohn, *The Lost* (HarperCollins, New York, 2003), and Anatol Reignier, *Damals in Bolechow* (Btb bei Goldmann, Munich, 1997), both of them on the East Galician shtetl of Bolechow; Theo Richmond, *Konin: A Quest* (Vintage, New York, 1996), on Konin in western Poland; Rose Lehman, *Symbiosis and Ambivalence — Poles and Jews in a Small Galician Town* (Berghahn, Oxford, 2001), on Jasliska, in West Galicia; Jack Kagan, *Novogrudok: The History of a Shtetl* (Valentine Mitchell, London, 2006), and Peter Duffy, *The Bielski Brothers* (HarperCollins, New York, 2003), both on Nowogrodek, in western Belorussia. See also Esther Farbstein, *Hidden in Thunder* (Feldheim, New York, 2008).
5. Regina Renz defined a shtetl as a town with more than 2,500 Jews and fewer than 10.000, but that is unconvincing as a defining characteristic, for the most prominent feature of a shtetl was its Jewish calendar and life cycle, expressed in social and cultural terms — hence the importance of determining the percentage of Jews in a township. To emphasize this, I chose to widen the concept and include places with both a smaller and a larger number of Jews. See Regina Renz, "Small Towns in Inter-War Poland," in

Polin: Studies in Polish Jewry, vol. 17, ed. Antony Polonsky (Littman Library, Oxford, 2004), pp. 143–151.

6. Kagan, *Novogrudok*; Duffy, *Bielski Brothers*; Lehman, *Symbiosis and Ambivalence.*

7. Rosa Lehmann, "Jewish Patrons and Polish Clients: Patronage in a Small Galician Town," in *Polin*, vol. 17, pp. 153–169.

8. Yehuda Bauer, "Jewish Baranowicze in the Holocaust," *Yad Vashem Studies* 31 (2003), pp. 92–152; idem, "Buczacz and Krzemieniec," *Yad Vashem Studies* 33 (2005), pp. 245–306; idem, "Kurzeniec, a Jewish Shtetl in the Holocaust," *Yalkut Moreshet* (Tel Aviv; English edition) 1 (2003), pp. 132–157; idem, "Sarny and Rokitno," in *The Shtetl*, ed. Steven T. Katz (Boston University Press, Boston, 2007), pp. 253–289; idem, "Novogrodek, a Shtetl," *Yad Vashem Studies* 35 (2007), pp. 35–70. I also dealt with Kosow Huculski in my book *Rethinking the Holocaust* (Yale University Press, New Haven, 2001), pp. 135–136, 163.

9. Bauer, "Jewish Baranowicze," pp. 92–93.

10. Bauer, *Rethinking*, pp. 149–163.

11. Most of the statistics used here were taken from Ezra Mendelsohn, *The Jews of East Central Europe between the Wars* (Indiana University Press, Bloomington, 1983), mainly pp. 23 ff.

12. I use the term East Galicia, which is disputed, only because it is familiar to most people, including many Polish-American and Polish-Canadian genealogists, to describe the region from which their ancestors came.

13. These were areas that the Tsarist government designated for the Jewish population, and from which it was difficult to move into the other regions of Tsarist Russia.

14. I am grateful to Mrs. Martha Goren of Rechovot, Israel, for permitting me to rely on her manuscript.

15. E.g., by Father Patrick Debois, a French Catholic priest, who is working together with Jewish institutions, such as the French Memorial de la Shoah, Yad Vashem, and others.

16. Bauer, *Rethinking*, pp. 26, 120, 134, 136, 143–163. I prefer to use the term "Amidah" instead of "resistance" because the latter, unless qualified, usually implies armed resistance only, whereas the former includes both unarmed and armed resistance. "Amidah" has a different meaning in Jewish religious life, where it connotes a very important prayer in the synagogue.

17. On East Galicia, see especially Dieter Pohl, *Nationalsozialistische Judenverfolgung in Ostgalizien, 1941–1944* (Institut für Zeitgeschichte, Munich, 1996); and Thomas Sandkühler, *Endlösung in Ostgalizien: Der Judenmord in Ostgalizien und die Rettungsinitiative von Berthold Beitz, 1941–1944* (Dietz, Berlin, 1996). For the Belorussian areas, the main source is Christian Gerlach, *Kalkulierte Morde: Die Deutsche Wirtschafts- und Vernichtungspolitik in Weissrussland, 1941 bis 1944* (Hamburger Edition, Hamburg, 1996). Much of the material I used derives from criminal investigations of German legal authorities, mainly in the nineteen sixties, which can be found in the Zentralstelle der Landesjutizverwaltungen in Ludwigsburg, accessible also at Yad Vashem.

18. Such materials can be found in Belorussian archives. I am grateful to Jack Kagan, who collected some of these.

19. Aryeh Klonicki (Klonymus), *Yoman Avi Adam* (Lohamei Hageta'ot, Tel Aviv, 1970); and Yad Vashem Archive (YVA) M.49.E-5394, and M.49P/192. The name of the Pole who brought the diary to Warsaw was Romuald Pielachowski. I am grateful to Dr. Havi Ben-Sasson for finding the Berkowicz diary and alerting me to its existence. A third diary is that of Joachim Münzer of Buczacz, YVA JM 115 (the diary is in Polish). Münzer wrote in the summer of 1943, after the destruction of the ghetto, about his personal fate. He also records the various "actions" in Buczacz and other places; there is nothing really new in what he writes. As for Eichmann, he said, at his trial in Jerusalem in 1961, that "the gentlemen [at Wannsee] convened their session, and then in very plain terms—not in the language that I had to use in the minutes, but in absolutely blunt terms—they addressed the issue [of how to deal with the Jews]." Quoted in Richard Rhodes, *Masters of Death*, Random House, New York, 2003, p. 236.

20. Binjamin Wilkomirsky, *Fragments* (Schocken, New York, 1996).

21. The document is quoted in Jack Kagan and Dov Cohen, *Surviving the Holocaust with the Russian Jewish Partisans* (Valentine Mitchell, London 1998), pp. 149–150. The source is the archive of Nowogrodek, HB-4625 (I am grateful to Mr. Jack Kagan of London for supplying me with this document). The rabbi's name was Rogatinski. He became a rabbi in Nowogrodek after the war and later emigrated to Israel. The statements in the testimonies are supposed to have been verified by two representatives from the NKVD (Soviet secret police) at the time, one of them a man by the name of Shelyubski. No NKVD personnel could have been in that area in 1941–1942, and Shelyubski was a Bielski partisan in 1944. The documents were dated for 1942 and 1944 and were obviously fabricated in 1944. They were submitted to the German court that tried Johann Artmann, the commander of the German Nowogrodek garrison, in an attempt to "help" in his conviction.

22. Victor Klemperer, *Lingua Tertii Imperii*, English edition (Athlone, London, 2000; the original German edition was published in 1947).

CHAPTER 2. THE THIRTIES

1. The total was 3,310,000, according to a report by the American Jewish Joint Distribution Committee, quoted in Yehuda Bauer, *My Brother's Keeper, a History of the American Jewish Joint Distribution Committee, 1929–1939* (Jewish Publication Society, Philadelphia, 1974), p. 187. The total number of Jews worldwide was about 17 million.

2. Shalom Cholawsky, *The Jews of Bielorussia during World War II* (Harwood, Amsterdam, 1998), pp. xiii, 3; Aharon Weiss, "Haproblematika shel Hahitnagdut Hayehudit Hamezuyenet beUkraina Hama'aravit," *Dapim Leheker Tkufat HaSho'ah* 12 (Haifa University, 1995), p. 191. Weiss puts the figure for the south at 870,000—Volhynia at 250,000, East Galicia at 620,000—and Cholawsky puts it at 825,000, for the two provinces together.

3. Ezra Mendelsohn, *The Jews of East Central Europe between the Wars* (Indiana University Press, Bloomington, 1983), p. 28.

4. According to one source quoted by Mendelsohn in ibid., p. 27 (the source is Janusz Zarnowski, *Spoleczenstwo drugiej rzeczpospolitej*, Warsaw, 1973), the middle class

numbered about 100,000 people (including dependents); the petit bourgeoisie, 2,000,000; the working class, 700,000; professionals and others, 300,000. According to the 1931 Polish census, there were 277,555 "workers," about 200,000 "artisans" (apparently people not employing non-family persons), and 428,965 "traders." If we add nonworking family members, the two sets of figures roughly correspond.

5. An interesting analysis of this group is in Celia S. Heller, *On the Edge of Destruction: Jews of Poland between the Two World Wars* (Columbia University Press, New York, 1977), especially p. 180 ff. She estimates the number of these "assimilationists" at between 5 percent and 11 percent, but the latter figure probably includes many of the acculturated Jews who identified with the Jewish minority. A leader of Jews who wanted to be considered Poles, Zdzislaw Zmigryder-Konopka (1897–1939), was appointed senator by the Polish regime.

6. Emanuel Meltzer, *Ma'avak Medini BeMalkodet; Yehudei Polin, 1935–1939* (Tel Aviv University Press, Tel Aviv, 1982), p. 14.

7. Actually, some of the statistics seemed to indicate an even worse situation. Celia Heller claims that in the nineteen twenties, "about 80% of the total Jewish population lived in what was then considered poverty." Heller, *On the Edge of Destruction*, p. 101. The European director of the American Jewish Joint Distribution Committee, Bernhard Kahn, estimated in 1935 that there were about 1,150,000 Jewish traders, of whom 400,000 were living in "dire poverty." The total number of Jews employed, distressed, or without any income was, he said, over 1,000,000. Bauer, *My Brother's Keeper*, p. 187.

8. Bauer, *My Brother's Keeper*, p. 188. In 1935, some 60 percent of Warsaw's Jews applied for charity at Passover.

9. Joanna B. Michlic, *Poland's Threatening Other: The Image of the Jew from 1880 to the Present* (University of Nebraska Press, Lincoln, 2006).

10. Heller, *On the Edge of Destruction*, p. 64.

11. Bauer, *My Brother's Keeper*, p. 184.

12. Mendelsohn, *Jews of East Central Europe*, p. 39 ff.

13. Heller, *On the Edge of Destruction*, p. 110, quoting from *Przeglad Powszechny* 6 (1936).

14. The SL-Wyzwolenie was founded in 1931; it split later into two main groups.

15. The Allgemener Yiddisher Arbeterbund, or simply Bund, was a Jewish Marxist-Socialist workers' movement founded in Vilno in 1893. It was originally allied to Russian Social Democracy. When that movement split, it allied itself with the Mensheviks, rather than the Bolsheviks. After 1917 it was persecuted in the Soviet Union, and many of its more prominent members joined the Bolsheviks in the twenties. The Polish Bund, on the other hand, developed a radical anticommunist stand. It was anti-Zionist and antireligious, it advocated the use of Yiddish as the Jewish national language, and it worked for Jewish cultural autonomy in a future socialist Poland.

16. Timothy Snyder, *Sketches from a Secret War* (Yale University Press, New Haven, 2005).

17. Heller, *On the Edge of Destruction*, p. 80 ff.

18. In March 1937, the Labor Party declared itself in favor of the "removal of [the] harmful influence of Jewry and Masonry." Heller, *On the Edge of Destruction*, p. 114 ff.

19. Michlic, in *Poland's Threatening Other*, presents an overall synthesis of the political and ideological developments in Poland that provides much of the basis of my analysis.

20. Joanna B. Michlic, *Poland's Threatening Other* (University of Nebraska Press, Lincoln, 2006), pp. 88–89.

21. Quoted in full in Heller, *On the Edge of Destruction*, p. 113. Two of the most prominent lower clergymen who propagandized such views were Stanislaw Trzeciak, who wrote an antisemitic tract called *Talmud o gojach — kwestia zydowska w Polsce* (The Talmud on the goyim [non-Jews] and the Jewish question in Poland), and Maximilian Kolbe, who was later martyred in Auschwitz but who during the thirties was responsible for a violently antisemitic Catholic journal, *Rycerzj Niepokalanej* (Knight of the Immaculate).

22. In 1927, the government recognized Jewish communities as religious communities in a deal with Agudat Israel. This assured the ascendancy of Agudat Israel in the communities. The government reserved for itself the right to veto communal decisions and replace those leadership groups that did not follow imposed governmental or ordinary fiscal rules. Agudat Israel became, in effect, the government's representative among the Jews until 1936, when new laws were proposed and, in principle, accepted, that were intended to curtail *shchite*, or ritual slaughter, one of the mainstays of orthodox Jewish life. This forced Agudat Israel into opposition, much against its will. It even went so far as to support a strike called by its bitter opponent, the Bund, to protest the pogrom instigated by Endeks in the town of Przytyk in 1936.

23. Its full name, Allgemener Yiddisher Arbeterbund, means General Brotherhood (or: Organization) of Jewish Workers.

24. Joseph Marcus, *Social and Political History of the Jews in Poland, 1919–1939* (Mouton, Berlin, 1983), p. 469.

25. Mendelsohn, *Jews of East Central Europe*, p. 83.

26. E.g., in Zborow, East Galicia; see *Sefer Zikaron LeKehillat Zborow* (Zborow Memorial Book), ed. Eliyahu Silberman (Irgun Yotz'ei Zborow, Tel Aviv, 1975), p. 282. Many other sources can be quoted for this development.

27. Bauer, *My Brother's Keeper*, pp. 207–208.

28. Shmuel Spector, *The Holocaust of Volhynian Jews* (Yad Vashem, Jerusalem, 1990), p. 20.

29. In 1933, the results of elections to the eighteenth Zionist Congress were these in "Congress" Poland (the former Russian Poland): General Zionists — 12 percent; Poalei Zion — 40 percent; Revisionists — 30 percent; Mizrachi — 18 percent. These were the results in formerly Austrian Galicia: General Zionists — 40 percent; Poalei Zion — 30 percent; Revisionists — 18 percent; Mizrachi — 11 percent.

30. This Akiva is not to be confused with Bnei Akiva, the religious Zionist youth movement in Palestine.

31. Mendelsohn, *Jews of East Central Europe*, p. 77.

32. The Bund organization taking care of younger children was the Socialist Children's Organization (SKIF — Sotsialistisher Kinder-Farband).

33. Heller, *On the Edge of Destruction*, p. 166.

34. Bauer, *My Brother's Keeper*, p. 300.

CHAPTER 3. THE SOVIET OCCUPATION

Epigraph. Ben-Cion Pinchuk, *Shtetl Jews under Soviet Rule: Eastern Poland on the Eve of the Holocaust* (Basil Blackwell, Oxford, 1990), p. 92.

1. Pinchuk, *Shtetl Jews*, pp. 12, 140.

2. Yehuda Bauer, "Buczacz and Krzemieniec," *Yad Vashem Studies* 33 (2005), p. 260.

3. Leonid Rein, "The Kings and the Pawns" (unpublished manuscript, Yad Vashem), p. 82, quoting Yad Vashem Archive (YVA) 033/296, p. 225. I am grateful to Dr. Rein for letting me use his manuscript. For more on the number of Jews, see Chapter 2.

4. *Sefer Zikaron LeKehillat Zborow* (Zborow Memorial Book), ed. Eliyahu Silberman (Irgun Yotz'ei Zborow Vehasviva, Tel Aviv, 1975), testimony of Hannale (Helena) Broida, pp. 107–110.

5. *Dereczin Memorial Book*, ed. Yehezkiel Raba (Jacob S. Berger, Mahwah, NJ, 2000; Hebrew original, 1966), p. 196.

6. Pinchuk, *Shtetl Jews*, p. 12. The numbers are disputed, and this is a very major issue. Shalom Cholawsky, in *The Jews of Bielorussia during World War II* (Harwood, Amsterdam, 1998), pp. 16, 28, argues that there were about 500,000, excluding those who returned to German-occupied Poland, but this seems to be an exaggeration.

7. The first Jews came to Birobidjan in 1928, and official immigration started in 1929. In 1934, Birobidjan was designated an autonomous Jewish Soviet Republic, although the Jews were never more than a minority in the region.

8. Jan T. Gross, *Revolution from Abroad: The Soviet Conquest of Western Ukraine and Western Belorussia* (Princeton University Press, Princeton, NJ, 2002), p. 29.

9. Ibid., pp. 19–26, 261 ff. "In Rowne, the county prefect came out personally with a retinue of local officials to greet the spearhead of the Soviet columns . . . in Kopyczynce . . . Red Army commanders embraced Polish officers and Polish soldiers threw flowers into the Soviet tanks." Ibid., p. 23. See also Shalom Cholawski [Cholawsky], *Soldiers from the Ghetto* (Herzl Press, New York, 1980), p. 14. Referring to the Poles in the shtetl of Nieswiez in Belorussia, the author writes that Polish "osadniks" (colonists), "including demobilized officers . . . threw flowers to the marching [Soviet] columns. Someone cheered: 'They are going to help the Poles beat the bloody *Schwaab* [Germans].'"

10. Yehuda Bauer, "Nowogrodek—The Story of a Shtetl," *Yad Vashem Studies* 35 (2007), p. 41 n. 15: "Some aristocrats [*pritzim*] hid with the Jews."

11. Bielaruskaja Sielanska-Rabotnickaja Hramada is the full name of the party in Belorussian. Gross, *Revolution*, p. 6.

12. Ibid., p. 262.

13. Ibid. p. 32.

14. Dov Levin, *The Lesser of Two Evils: Eastern European Jewry under Soviet Rule, 1939–1941* (Jewish Publication Society, Philadelphia, 1995), pp. 32–33.

15. Gross, *Revolution*, p. 31. Gross says that some 30,000 Ukrainians had fled to the Germans by late 1939 and that 10,000 more went later.

16. Pinchuk, *Shtetl Jews*, p. 21.

17. In Czortkow, "nobody believed them." Martha Goren, "Kolot min Haya'ar Hashachor" (unpublished manuscript, 2007), chap. 1, p. 15. Jews heard accounts by the refugees,

"but refused to believe them." Jack Kagan and Dov Cohen, *Surviving the Holocaust with the Russian Partisans* (Valentine Mitchell, London, 1998), p. 36.

18. Bogdan Musial is a defender of this position. See his *Konterrevolutionäre Elemente sind zu erschiessen* (Propyläen, Munich, 2000), quoted in Rein, "Kings and the Pawns," p. 140.

19. Gross, *Revolution*, p. 273.

20. Levin, *Lesser of Two Evils*, p. 34.

21. Cholawsky, *Jews of Bielorussia*, p. 7, quoting a testimony from Wiszniewo, Belorussia.

22. Levin, *Lesser of Two Evils*, p. 35.

23. Gross, *Revolution*, p. 206.

24. Cholawsky, *Jews of Bielorussia*, p. 7, quoting a testimony from Dobszyce, Belorussia.

25. Levin, *Lesser of Two Evils*, p. 33.

26. Ibid., p. 34.

27. As in Czortkow (Galicia); see Pinchuk, *Shtetl Jews*, p. 24.

28. Gross, *Revolution*, p. 270.

29. In Czortkow, "most of the Jewish community were proletarians, and adjusted to the new cultural system. A major part of the youth accepted the socialist ideology." Goren, "Kolot," chap. 2, pp. 13–14.

30. Levin, *Lesser of Two Evils*, pp. 190–191. There appears to have been a demonstration in Minsk by Jews who were being prevented from returning from the Soviet interior. Cholawsky, *Jews of Bielorussia*, p. 16.

31. Pinchuk, *Shtetl Jews*, p. 46.

32. Actually, in most places very small numbers indeed were Jewish communists. In the town of David-Horodok, for instance, the communist rank and file was composed of six to seven Jews and three to four Poles. Cholawsky, *Jews of Bielorussia*, p. 5.

33. Levin, *Lesser of Two Evils*, pp. 73–74.

34. Ibid., p. 44.

35. Bauer, "Buczacz and Krzemieniec," p. 260. But the local militia remained under the control of a Jew.

36. E.g., in Sarny (Ukraine), where the Jews were a majority, a Ukrainian became mayor. Pinchuk, *Shtetl Jews*, p. 49.

37. Cholawsky, in *Jews of Bielorussia*, p. 5, tells the possibly apocryphal story of Shmuel Yossel, a poor Jew from the shtetl of Michaliszki, who, wearing the militia's hat and holding a rifle, knocked at the window of a wealthy storekeeper who had exploited his sisters under the Poles. When asked, "Who's there?" he answered: "Shmuel Yossel the government" (in Yiddish: "Shmuel-Yossel di Macht [the Power]").

38. Levin, *Lesser of Two Evils*, p. 44.

39. Pinchuk, *Shtetl Jews*, p. 31. The first two quotations are from a testimony from the shtetl of Byten; the third comes from Pinsk. See also *Sefer Zikaron LeKehillat Zborow*, pp. 162–164: "All communal life crumbled as though it had never existed before" (my translation).

40. In Sarny there was an instruction to the former kehilla secretary to transfer the property of the community to the municipality. *Kehillat Sarny, Sefer Yizkor*, ed. Yossef Karib (Yad Vashem, Jerusalem, 1961), p. 266.

41. Ibid., p. 32.

42. "Informers fared best of all. If you didn't like someone, you informed on them." Bauer, "Nowogrodek," p. 43, quoting Kagan and Cohen, *Surviving the Holocaust*, pp. 136–137.

43. One testimony recounts the story of a Jewish trader who hid with a group of Roma ("Gypsies") and thus escaped deportation. Goren, "Kolot," chap. 2, p. 5. Others were denounced by Jewish communists and deported.

44. Levin, *Lesser of Two Evils*, p. 50.

45. Ibid., p. 48; Yosef Segal, in *Rokitna Vehasviva, Sefer Yizkor*, ed. Eliezer Leoni (Irgun Yotz'ei Rokitna Vehasviva [Rokitno Survivors Organization], Tel Aviv, 1967), p. 254; Yehuda Bauer, "Sarny and Rokitno," in *The Shtetl*, ed. Steven T. Katz (Boston University Press, Boston, 2007), p. 260. Schuster's daughter survived and emigrated to the United States.

46. Levin, *Lesser of Two Evils*, p. 91.

47. Ibid., p. 94; Cholawsky, *Jews of Bielorussia*, p. 18.

48. Levin, *Lesser of Two Evils*, pp. 106, 109. "Down with the rotten Hebrew language," said the former Hebrew teacher Mordechai Gendelman in Rokitno, after he had emerged from a Soviet jail. *Rokitna Vehasviva*, p. 107. (An English translation by Lora M. Hull can be found at www.jewishgen.org/Yiskor/rokitnoye.hmtl.)

49. Goren, "Kolot," chap. 2, p. 8.

50. Levin, *Lesser of Two Evils*, p. 107.

51. At one of the great yeshivot (Talmudic academies), in the shtetl of Mir (Belorussia), a library of 6,000 volumes was shredded. Levin, *Lesser of Two Evils*, p. 157.

52. Levin *Lesser of Two Evils*, p. 158. Often, at first at least, marriages were held in synagogues, although that, too, seems to have tapered off by early 1940.

53. But synagogues did not close everywhere. In Kurzeniec, for instance, one synagogue was closed, but some others, apparently smaller ones, continued to be open. Yehuda Bauer, "Kurzeniec, a Jewish Shtetl in the Holocaust," *Yalkut Moreshet* (Tel Aviv; English edition) 1 (2003), p. 137.

54. In some places, however, especially outlying ones, there was less pressure to close the synagogues—e.g., in Rokitno, where two synagogues were left open. *Rokitna Vehasviva*, p. 239. On the other hand, the synagogues closed in Nieswiez; one became a bicycle workshop, one a furniture warehouse, and one a clubhouse "with a young Jew as its director." See Cholawski, *Soldiers from the Ghetto*, p. 17.

55. Thus, in Zalesczyki (East Galicia), local inhabitants who were preparing a pogrom against the local Jews in October 1939 were arrested by the Soviets and severely punished. Goren, "Kolot," chap. 2, p. 11.

56. Levin, *Lesser of Two Evils*, p. 62.

57. Zev Katz, *From the Gestapo to the Gulags: One Jewish Life* (Valentine Mitchell, London, 2004).

58. For Rokitno, for instance, we have the testimony of a Zionist who had to become the principal of a local Ukrainian school and whose special assignment was to teach the Stalin Constitution. See Eliezer Leoni, in *Rokitna Vehasviva*, p. 239.

59. Katz, *From the Gestapo to the Gulags*, especially pp. 72–82.

60. Gross, *Revolution*, passim.

61. Ibid., especially pp. 114–122 but also elsewhere.
62. In Czortkow, there was a Polish attempt at rebellion against the Soviets, on January 20, 1940, by a group of 150–200 men after the deposition of a popular Polish mayor, Stanislaw Michalowski. The rebellion was put down with great brutality, and the survivors were arrested and deported. See Goren, "Kolot," chap. 2, p. 9.
63. Gross, *Revolution*, p. 224.
64. E.g., in Nieswiez, Cholawski, *Soldiers from the Ghetto*, p. 29 ff.
65. Bauer, "Nowogrodek," p. 42 n. 17. Bogdan Musial, in his "Jewish Resistance in Poland's Eastern Borderlands during the Second World War, 1939–1941," *Patterns of Prejudice* 38, no. 4 (2004), pp. 371–382, argues that in the kresy, Zionist youth movements established an underground of considerable strength. He relies on Soviet materials, which are mostly false denunciations: "the most active among them, according to an evaluation by the Soviet security apparatus, was the youth organization . . . of Betar." Ibid., p. 376. In fact, right-wing Zionist activity by the Betar movement was practically nonexistent, but it is true that Zionist youths were sought and many were arrested and sentenced to the Gulag (see, for instance, the testimony of Stern Klorfein of Rokitno, who says that the local Betar chapter tried to maintain an underground existence, but the members were denounced and arrested; *Rokitna Vehasviva*, p. 83). Musial also overestimates the activities of the left-wing Zionist youth movements (Hashomer Hatzair and Dror). However, these small cells were not discovered everywhere. Thus, in Kurzeniec, a Hashomer Hatzair group of eight members continued to meet throughout the Soviet occupation. Bauer, "Kurzeniec," pp. 137–138. In any case, all these tremendously courageous efforts were made by no more than a few hundred young people at most. Musial shows little understanding of these youth movements and their inner workings and errs in a number of places with names, memberships, etc. See also Cholawsky, *Jews of Bielorussia*, pp. 22–25.
66. Bauer, "Buczacz and Krzemieniec," p. 261: "There was no problem making a living." Shoah Foundation Testimonies (SF)—45180, Moshe Schwartz.
67. Shopkeepers stashed away some of their goods before their shops were closed and then sold these stocks to supplement their insufficient earnings, despite the constant threat of severe punishment if caught. See Bauer, "Nowogrodek," pp. 42–43.
68. *Sefer Zikaron LeKehillat Zborow*, pp. 111–122.
69. Goren, "Kolot," chap. 2, p. 8: "Many of the youth movement members changed their ideology and joined the Komsomol."
70. Gross, *Revolution*, p. 267.
71. For Czortkow, see Goren, "Kolot," chap. 2, p. 12.
72. E.g., Shoah Foundation Testimonies (SF)—9757, Josephine Fiksel: "we did not believe their stories"; "You don't believe what you don't want to believe."
73. The Lithuanians understood very well what was behind this Soviet gesture: a future Soviet Lithuania would include the Vilnius (Vilno) region. Among Lithuanians a saying spread: "Vilnius musu, Lietuva rusu" (Vilnius will be ours, and Lithuania will be Russian).
74. Yehuda Bauer, "Jewish Baranowicze in the Holocaust," *Yad Vashem Studies* 31 (2003), p. 104.

75. Gross, *Revolution*, pp. 198–199.

76. Cholawsky, *Jews of Bielorussia*, pp. 27–28, has a detailed table of deportations, culled from a variety of sources. Cholawsky gives a total of 880,000 deportees: 120,000 on February 8, 1940 (Poles), 320,000 in April 1940 (mixed), 240,000 in June–July 1940 (mostly Jews), and 200,000 in June 1941 (mixed). He estimates the total number of Jews deported by the Soviets at 264,000. His figures are similar to Gross's (see text) but not the same.

77. According to Andrzej Zbikowski, "Why Did Jews Welcome the Soviet Army?" in *Polin: Studies in Polish Jewry*, vol. 13, ed. Antony Polonsky (Basil Blackwell, Oxford, 2000), pp. 62–72, in the June 1940 deportations, out of 78,000–79,000 deportees, 82–84 percent were Jews, as Soviet sources said.

78. Gross, *Revolution*, pp. xxiii, 269. The figures are disputed; see Leonid Rein, "Local Collaboration in the Execution of the 'Final Solution' in Nazi-Occupied Belorussia," *Holocaust and Genocide Studies* 20, no. 3 (2006), p. 386. However, it is clear that proportionately more Jews were deported than Poles. The document detailing the official Polish figures is dated April 25, 1943. Gross, *Revolution*, p. 199. Alexander Gurjanov puts the total as low as 315,000–320,000, but his arguments are not convincing. Alexander Gurjanov, "Überblick über die Deportationen der Bevölkerung in der UdSSR in den Jahren 1930–1950," in *Vertreibung europäisch erinnern?* ed. Dieter Bingen, Wlodzimierz Borodziej, and Stefan Troebst (Harrasowitz, Wiesbaden, 2003), quoted in Rein, "Local Collaboration," p. 385.

79. Pinchuk, *Shtetl Jews*, pp. 7–12.

80. Sarny can serve as an example. According to a probably reliable testimony, 2,000 refugees from the west had to be received by about 5,000 local Jews. Most of the refugees were deported. See *Kehillat Sarny*, p. 271, testimony of Yitzhak Geller.

CHAPTER 4. THE HOLOCAUST IN THE KRESY

1. Christian Gerlach, *Kalkulierte Morde: Die Deutsche Wirtschafts- und Vernichtungspolitik in Weissrussland, 1941 bis 1944* (Hamburger Edition, Hamburg, 1999).

2. This is not the place to examine the reasons for the very quick German advance, nor for the lack of preparedness of the Soviets. But I would argue for the interpretation that says that Stalin's policy seems to have been based on the recognition of the fact that the Soviet armies were no match for the German armies. As a result, in 1941 Stalin was desperately trying to avoid war; he knew it was ultimately inevitable, but he hoped to gain time to make the Red Army ready. He was very suspicious of the British, and he feared they would make a deal with Hitler to free the Germans to attack the USSR, perhaps with British help. So he tried to avoid what in his eyes could be interpreted by the Germans as provocation; the result was orders to the Soviet military that prevented any real preparations for the German onslaught. Even on June 22, he still thought that the invasion was at the initiative of German military commanders and against Hitler's wishes. He thought this despite detailed information that he had received from Soviet intelligence, which was actually even more detailed than the famous intelligence reports that were sent to the Kremlin by Britain, the United States, and Soviet spies in

Japan and elsewhere. However, knowing Stalin's preconceived notions, the Soviet intelligence chiefs feared for their own lives if they insisted too much on reports that did not fit Stalin's concepts. See Gabriel Gorodetsky, *Grand Delusion: Stalin and the German Invasion of Russia* (Yale University Press, New Haven, 1999); and below in the text.

3. On June 26, the Soviet government established an Evacuation Council that organized the evacuation of factories and equipment in order to relocate them in the Soviet interior.

4. Thus, one testimony says that a Soviet officer offered to take Jews on his truck, because if they stayed, the Germans would slaughter them. Shoah Foundation Testimonies (SF)—37869, Edmund Dickman of Bukaszowce in East Galicia.

5. In Tuczyn (Volhynia), seventy Jews were killed in a pogrom; in Ludvipol (also in Volhynia), peasants "stormed into each Jewish house they took a liking to." In Miedlyrzecz (Ukr.: Mezhirichi; in Volhynia) the "peasants, satchels in hand, appeared in the townlet together with the Germans . . . they broke Jewish stores and the Soviet cooperative stores open." Shmuel Spector, *The Holocaust of Volhynian Jews* (Yad Vashem, Jerusalem, 1990), p. 65. Similar events can be documented from all over the kresy.

6. Yehuda Bauer, "Kurzeniec, a Jewish Shtetl in the Holocaust," *Yalkut Moreshet* (Tel Aviv; English edition) 1 (2003), p. 139. The villagers nevertheless tried to loot and rob, and in this case the Jews put up resistance, with the help of some of their neighbors.

7. Spector, *Holocaust*, p. 69. This was done after quite a number of German soldiers had participated in the looting—e.g., in Tuczyn and Stepan (Volhynia).

8. Yehuda Bauer, "Sarny and Rokitno," in *The Shtetl*, ed. Steven T. Katz (Boston University Press, Boston, 2007), p. 263.

9. Spector, *Holocaust*, p. 55.

10. One wrenching story is recorded in ibid., p. 50: Two brothers decided to board a Soviet evacuation train. "Mother chased after the rolling train, tearing hair out of her head, screaming after me to stay. But my brother gripped my hand strongly and didn't let go until the train moved away from the station."

11. Spector calculates that about 15,000 Jews were killed in Volhynia in thirty-seven localities in July–August 1941, or 6 percent of all the Jews—the victims being the Jewish leadership groups and young men. The perpetrators included, apart from the EG units, the 213th Defense Division, a rear army unit of the regular Wehrmacht, and ORPO battalions. Spector, *Holocaust*, p. 79.

12. Yehuda Bauer, *Rethinking the Holocaust* (Yale University Press, New Haven, 2001), pp. 153–154.

13. Bauer, "Kurzeniec," p. 140.

14. Ibid., p. 139: One of the first places where women and children were murdered was Vilejka, a few miles north of Kurzeniec, where at least 400 people fell victim to a subunit (*Einsatzkommando* 9) of EG "B."

15. Spector, *Holocaust*, pp. 106–107.

16. Spector, *Holocaust*, pp. 107–109.

17. There are a number of survivor testimonies relating experiences in these hellholes— e.g. SF—37869, Edmund Dickman.

18. Martha Goren, "Kolot min Haya'ar Hashachor" (unpublished manuscript, 2007), chap. 8, pp. 18 ff. Goren gives the commander's name as Epner. Another army commander, by the name of Patti (the name is not quite clear), in Tluste, also protected Jews. This person seems to be identical with a man called Vathie by Mojzesz Szpigiel (U.S. Holocaust Museum Archive, Reel 37, 301/3492). Goren also says that when the Wehrmacht retreated from the area, their attitude toward the surviving Jews was friendly.

19. Gerlach, *Kalkulierte Morde*, passim.

20. For rape by Lithuanians in Stolpce (Belorussia), see U.S. Holocaust Memorial Museum (USHMM), Reel 7, 564 ff., testimony of Berko Berkowicz. For Zaloszce (East Galicia), see Sarah Kataiksher, Yad Vashem Archive (YVA) 033/477 ("most of the women were raped, and then murdered" [hot men aich di gresste teil fun froien geshendet un nachher sei geschossen]). Similar testimonies exist for Baranowicze and Krzemieniec. In Stolin, a Ukrainian was executed after Jews proved to the Germans that he had raped Jewish girls. *Sefer Zikaron liKehillat Stolin Vehasviva*, ed. A. Avatichi and Y. Ben Zakai (Irgun Yotz'ei Stolin, Tel Aviv, 1952), p. 220.

21. See, e.g., *Nationalsozialistische Vernichtungspolitik 1939–1945*, ed. Ulrich Herbert (Fischer, Tübingen, 1998).

22. Michael Wildt, *Generation des Unbedingten* (Hamburger Edition, Hamburg, 2003).

23. David Bankier, *The Germans and the Final Solution* (Basil Blackwell, Oxford, 1993); Bernward Dörner, *Die Deutschen und der Holocaust* (Propyläen, Munich, 2007).

CHAPTER 5. THE SHTETL COMMUNITY AND ITS LEADERSHIP, 1941–1943

1. See my articles cited in Chapter 1, note 1.

2. See Israel Gutman, *The Jews of Warsaw, 1939–1943* (Indiana University Press, Bloomington, 1982).

3. Yehuda Bauer, "Buczacz and Krzemieniec," *Yad Vashem Studies* 33 (2005), pp. 262–263.

4. Ibid., passim and especially p. 268.

5. Ibid., p. 275.

6. Omer Bartov has different figures. From the census of 1931, which counted 4,439 Jews in a total population of 7,517, he moves to 1939 and says there were 10,000 Jews among the 17,000 inhabitants in the town. This does not sound persuasive, even if one adds the refugees who arrived from German-occupied Poland. The figure of 7,500 is repeated in a number of testimonies and seems more realistic. See Omer Bartov, "From the Holocaust in Galicia to Contemporary Genocide: Common Ground—Historical Differences," Meyerhoff Lecture, U.S. Holocaust Memorial Museum, Washington, DC, 2002.

7. The mayor, Ivan Bobyk, is reported to have been well disposed toward Jews. Ibid., p. 386.

8. Cf. Aharon Weiss, "Ledarkam shel Hayudenratim Bidrom-Mizrach Polin," *Yalkut Moreshet* 15 (1972), pp. 59–122.

9. Martha Goren, "Kolot min Haya'ar Hashachor" (unpublished manuscript, 2007), chap. 8, pp. 7, 11 (quoting the witness Baruch Milch).

10. Bauer, "Buczacz and Krzemieniec," pp. 295–298.

11. No first name is available for Kruh.

12. Goren, "Kolot," chap. 8, pp. 2–16 (quotation); Abraham Belgoraj, Yad Vashem Archive (YVA) 04/3584; and *Sefer Yizkor Lehantsachat Kdoshei Kehillat Czortkow*, ed. Yeshayahu Ostri-Dunn (Published by the Czortkow Survivors, Tel Aviv, 1967), pp. 69–71, 313.

13. That is the view of a majority of survivors. But there are dissenting voices: "The Jewish Council was a tool in German hands." *Kehillat Sarny* (Sarny Memorial Book), ed. Yossef Kariv (Yad Vashem, Jerusalem, 1961), p. 274, testimony of Yitzhak Geller. But, literally on the next page, Geller says, "One has to note with appreciation the people who fulfilled various functions in the Jewish Council. Especially the late Mr. Gershonok, the Chairman, a man of noble spirit, stood out."

14. Yehuda Bauer, "Sarny and Rokitno," in *The Shtetl*, ed. Steven T. Katz (Boston University Press, Boston, 2007), passim.

15. Bauer, "Kurzeniec," p. 152.

16. Ibid., passim.

17. Bauer, "Sarny and Rokitno," passim.

18. Yehuda Bauer, "Jewish Baranowicze in the Holocaust," *Yad Vashem Studies* 31 (2003), pp. 107, 110–112.

19. Thus, for instance, in Kosow Huculski (East Galicia), there was some attempt to take care of orphans, and the Judenrat collected money to support Jews from Kosow who were deported to the larger ghetto of Kolomya. There were several other similar instances.

20. Shmuel Spector, *The Holocaust of Volhynian Jews* (Yad Vashem, Jerusalem, 1990), p. 140.

21. Ibid., pp. 144–145. False messianism made its appearance, for instance, in Vladimirets, Stepan, and Varkovichi in Volhynia, spreading the hope that the Messiah would appear and the murder would be stopped.

22. Ibid., p. 159.

23. Weiss, "Ledarkam," p. 67.

24. This took place, for instance, in Wysock and Rafalowka (Volhynia-Polesie). Ibid., pp. 72–73.

25. Ibid., pp. 69–70. The head of the Judenrat in Bursztyn was Minne Tobias.

26. Ibid., pp. 62–63. This happened in Bursztyn, Busk, and Hoszcza, for instance.

27. See Yakov Soltzman, YVA 03/1546, for one of many positive opinions about the Judenrat in Rokitno.

28. Ida Berger wrote on April 18, 1943: "Until now he fulfills his task excellently." *Sefer Zikaron LeKehillat Zborow* (Zborow Memorial Book), ed. Eliyahu Silberman (Irgun Yotz'ei Zborow, Tel Aviv, 1975), p. 80. However, Sima Zeiger says (ibid., p. 97) that "the Judenrat was a tool in Nazi hands."

29. This is supported, for example, by the testimony of Armand Dickman, Shoah Foundation Testimonies (SF)—37689, who praised the "loyal work of the Judenrat," reported

that they brought bread to the camps, and said that "they worked well to save as much as possible." There are more testimonies like that.

30. Spector, *Holocaust*, pp. 152–153.

31. Isaiah Trunk, *Judenrat* (Collier-Macmillan, London, 1972); Aharon Weiss, "Jewish Leadership in Occupied Poland—Postures and Attitudes," *Yad Vashem Studies* 12 (1977), pp. 335–365.

32. Aharon Weiss, "Leha'arachatam shel Hayudenratim," *Yalkut Moreshet* 11 (1969), pp. 108–112.

33. At Rafalowka in Volhynia and Horodenka in East Galicia. Ibid., p. 62.

34. Weiss, "Ledarkam," p. 79.

35. Spector, *Holocaust*, p. 167.

36. Weiss, in "Ledarkam," p. 63 (and elsewhere), mentions the case of Abraham Schwetz of Miedlyrzecz (Volhynia), who committed suicide more or less publicly as a protest against the German policies after he refused to send 120 young Jews "to Kiev," as the Germans said—obviously to their deaths.

37. Thus, in Ratno, the head of the Judenrat, a rabbi—Rabbi David Aharon Shapira— refused a German demand to select seven Jews to be hostages, to be executed if German demands were not met. The Germans then caught seven people themselves. In the end, Shapira managed, by a bribe, to get the seven released.

38. Weiss, "Leha'arachatam," pp. 110–111.

39. For an example of the latter, see, for instance, a statement about the head of the Judenrat of Rawa Ruska (East Galicia), who was killed by the Germans: "The wonderful and compassionate and devoted Jew, Dr. Josef Mandel [der herrlecher un hartziger ibergegebener Yid Dr. Josef Mandel]." Weiss, "Ledarkam," p. 63.

40. Weiss, "Ledarkam," p. 107, quoting the Ostra'a Memorial Book ("keiner fun di lebensgeblibene dermant nisht kein einem fun die Judenrat forshteier mit kein shlecht wort"). The Judenrat chairman in Wlodzimierz (Yid.: Ludmir), a lawyer named Weiler, committed suicide after he declared, according to testimony, "I am not God, and will not judge [people] to decide who should live and who should not" (Ja nie jestem Bogiem i nie bede sadzit kto ma zyc, a kto nie).

41. Bauer, "Buczacz and Krzemieniec," pp. 269–270. I could not find out the first names of Schumann and Mendel.

42. While survivors overwhelmingly accuse Kramer of traitorous behavior, there is at least one dissenting voice: "These men [Kramer and another Judenrat member, Benjamin Engelberg] were highly respected and displayed great integrity." Etunia Bauer Katz, *Our Tomorrows Never Came* (Fordham University Press, New York, 2000), p. 35.

43. Krökel, officially the "Stabsleiter des Gebietskommissars," took his orders from the SIPO command in Rowne.

44. Bauer, "Sarny and Rokitno," pp. 266–268.

45. Here is one negative testimony, by Rafael Shaffer, YVA M-49.E 866): "he helped the Germans [er hot migeholfn di Daitshn]").

46. Yehuda Bauer, "Nowogrodek—The Story of a Shtetl," *Yad Vashem Studies* 35 (2007), passim.

47. The Hasidic "dynasty" of the Slonimer Rebbes was well known and well connected.

Between the world wars the Slonimer Rebbe set up his "court" in Baranowicze. Shlomo David Weinberg was a young man with a charismatic personality. After the second "action," on September 22, 1942, he helped to hide arms for the underground and supported Amidah activities. He was deported to the concentration camp at Koldyczewo, where other Baranowicze Jews tried to protect him, but he died there.

48. SF—50670, Noah Roitman; *Baranowicze Memorial Book*, ed. A. S. Stein (Irgun Yotz'ei Baranowitz, Tel Aviv, 1953), pp. 483–484.

49. Hersh Smolar, *Soviet Jews behind the Ghetto Barrier* (Tel Aviv University, Tel Aviv, 1984), pp. 120–123; Yitzhak Arad, *Ghetto in Flames: The Destruction of the Jews of Vilna in the Holocaust* (Holocaust Library, New York, 1982), pp. 387–395.

50. Bauer, "Jewish Baranowicze," passim.

51. The name of the head of the Judenrat was Feldman; I could not find his first name.

52. Spector, *Holocaust*, p. 207.

53. Marcus Lecker, *I Remember*, Memoirs of Holocaust Survivors, vol. 5 (Canadian Jewish Studies, Concordia University, Montreal, 1999), p. 43.

CHAPTER 6. THE NEIGHBORS

1. Yehuda Bauer, "Buczacz and Krzemieniec," *Yad Vashem Studies* 33 (2005), pp. 286–294.

2. Alicia Appleman-Jurman, *Alicia: My Story* (Bantam, Toronto, 1988), passim. The author specifically mentions the Polish village of Wojciechowka as one that forged an alliance with Jews. Etunia Bauer Katz, in *Our Tomorrows Never Came* (Fordham University Press, New York, 2000), pp. 98–99, mentions the village of Matuszowka. Both were in the general area of Buczacz, in East Galicia. Katz adds explicitly that Poles were trying to rescue their "colony" (which would indicate that they were probably Polish settlers from the interwar period) from the Banderovtsy and that therefore they saved Jews.

3. Bauer, "Buczacz and Krzemieniec," pp. 298–299; Shoah Foundation Testimonies (SF)—33516, Herman Blumenfeld. Omer Bartov puts the number of Buczacz Jews who were found by the Soviets in March 1944 at 800. See Omer Bartov, "From the Holocaust in Galicia to Contemporary Genocide: Common Ground—Historical Differences," Meyerhoff Lecture, U.S. Holocaust Memorial Museum, Washington, DC, 2002.

4. Bauer, "Buczacz and Krzemieniec," pp. 266, 272–274.

5. It is worth mentioning the case of Jula Werbiczka, a Polish woman from the hamlet of Tustoglowy, near Zborow, who rescued twenty-five Jews when the Ukrainians held a pogrom after the Soviets left. She then hid a Jewish woman, Faye Shapira. Jula died of typhoid contracted either in the ghetto, where she helped people with food, or from one of the people she was hiding. After a series of adventures, Faye Shapira, with "Aryan" papers provided by a priest (no name available, but probably Jan Pawlicky), was hidden by another Polish woman (Kasia Rozumkiewicz). The case shows that most of the survivors had to be rescued not once but a number of times—here, by a number of Polish people. Testimony of Faye Shapira, Yad Vashem Archive (YVA) 03/3485.

6. A number of testimonies document rescues by elderly, lonely individuals, mostly women, but sometimes men as well (e.g., the "Uncle" in the story of Alicia Appleman-Jurman, *Alicia*, pp. 129 ff.). A particularly touching case is that of Olina Horyhorishin, an unmarried woman, a Ukrainian of some sixty-five years of age, sister of a violent man who despised her. A twelve-year-old Jewish girl, Dunia Rosen, from Kosow Huculski, approached the brother, who, very briefly, gave her shelter, but then he told her to leave. Olina embraced the girl and stuck by her, rescuing her on a number of occasions in the unfriendly Ukrainian village (Mikitinice). Finally, when police were about to search the house for an unrelated purpose, she took the girl up into the wilderness of the Carpathian Mountains and built a temporary shelter for her, bringing her food every day or two. The girl survived thus for many months. Then she ventured down into the village again, and was again hidden by Olina. In the end, Dunia was caught by the police, but she escaped and fled beyond the Bug River, the eastern side of which was already in Soviet hands. After Dunia grew up in Israel, she looked for Olina but could not find her. Clearly, the woman's loneliness and her craving for a child to care for was the deciding motivation, and the same would apply, to some extent at least, in other cases. See Dunia Rosen, *Yedidi, Haya'ar* (The Forest, My Friend) (Yad Vashem, Jerusalem, 2005).

7. A peculiar sidelight on motivations is provided by the story of Yitzhak Geller of Sarny, who was persuaded by a Ukrainian peasant, Andrea Zacharko, not to commit suicide but to try and save himself. Zacharko told him that he had to persuade Geller to stay alive in order to atone for the sin of having himself killed a Jew. *Rokitna Vehasviva, Sefer Yizkor*, ed. Eliezer Leoni (Irgun Yotz'ei Rokitna Vehasviva [Rokitno Survivors Organization], Tel Aviv, 1967), p. 281.

8. YVA, Righteous, M.31/6325. "A peasant said to Petro [after the war]: 'All my admiration to you, my friend. You had enough strength to persist until the end. I did not: I killed my Jews.'" Anatol Reignier, *Kikar ha'ir reika* (Yad Vashem, Jerusalem, 2001; the original German edition was titled *Damals in Bolechow*), passim, p. 23.

9. Shalom Cholawsky, *Meri VeLochama Partizanit* (Resistance and Partisan Struggle) (Yad Vashem, Jerusalem, 2001), p. 341 (quotation); also, YVA 03/3402.

10. SF — 21873, Yitzhak Goren. The following story is based on Goren's testimony. I find no reason to doubt its general accuracy.

11. This is the reason that I emphasized recognition by Yad Vashem in each case where I used such a testimony.

12. See the translation of the Hebrew-Yiddish Yizkor (Memorial) at Rokitno (Rokitnoye, Ukraine), available at JewishGen: The Home of Jewish Genealogy, www.jewishgen.org, in the Yizkor Book Project, under Translations.

13. YVA M/E 1907.

14. YVA M/E 1907.

15. *Sefer Zikaron LeKehillat Zborow* (Zborow Memorial Book), ed. Eliyahu Silberman (Irgun Yotz'ei Zborow, Tel Aviv, 1975), pp. 100–104.

16. SF — 04160 and 00964.

17. YVA 03/1366.

18. *Sefer Yizkor LeKehillat Sarny* (Sarny Memorial Book), ed. Yosef Kariv (Sarny Survivors

Association, Tel Aviv, 1961), testimony of Feige Schwartz. Rüdiger testified, and his testimony, translated into Yiddish, is also published here, pp. 322–329.

19. *Sefer Yizkor LeKehillat Sarny*, p. 317.

20. As one might expect, some rescue stories, improbable as they may sound, are nevertheless fairly well documented. Perhaps one of the most outlandish is the story of Haim Ben-Zvi, of Rokitno. He was a tailor, recruited into the Red Army before Operation Barbarossa. Taken prisoner near Vitebsk, he escaped three times and settled, as a Polish non-Jew named Stefan Koniewski, in the village of Vidreja, in eastern Belorussia. He married there, but someone denounced him as a Jew. However, the German commander of the "Stützpunkt" (apparently the local SS and police post), who had made friends with him, pronounced him a non-Jew. He was recruited as a local collaborator to guard a railway line, but then he persuaded the Germans that he actually was of German stock (a *Volksdeutscher*), because he spoke very good German. He became a German soldier and, as a trained tailor, found employment in an army craftsmen's unit (*Handwerkerstelle*). A German army paper that he had, which provides proof of an important part of the story, said that the NCO Stefan Koniewski was entitled to wear German army insignia ("ist berechtigt deutsche Dienstgradabzeichen zu tragen"). In late 1944, when he got "leave," he went to a village near Stuttgart. After he returned to the east, he became a Soviet spy who delivered Germans into Soviet hands, or so he claimed. He ended his life in Israel. YVA 03/3288.

21. YVA, Righteous, M.31/3254.

22. SF—22720, Abraham Wolonski; and YVA 0.3/7741, Haya Bar-Yohai.

23. Tadeusz Piotrowski, *Genocide and Rescue in Wolyn* (McFarland, Jefferson, NC, 2000), p. 7.

24. YVA 03/1594, Yakov Soltzman; and Bronislaw Janik, *Bylo Ich Trzy* (Kciazka i Wiedza, Warsaw, 1970).

25. Such as the villages of Karpilowka, Malinsk, and Maloszki.

26. Yehuda Bauer, "Sarny and Rokitno," in *The Shtetl*, ed. Steven T. Katz (Boston University Press, Boston, 2007), p. 273.

27. YVA, Righteous, M.31/4712.

28. Appleman-Jurman, *Alicia*, passim.

29. Etunia Bauer Katz, *Our Tomorrows Never Came*, p. 70f., mentions a Polish woman aristocrat, "Pani [Madame] Blawudowa," who hid her in the same area.

30. There are many stories about individual Poles who rescued Jews in East Galicia. One example is that of Josephine Fiksel (SF—9757), who was kept for twenty-two months in a hole in the ground by a Polish woman, Maria Bartoszewicz, and her son, Mironko, of Tustoglowy, near Zborow.

31. Here is another story from Zborow. David Mauerstein reports that a Pole by the name of Miller gave him food, another Polish villager nursed his brother back to health, and then, when he was caught and put with some Polish arrestees, his fellow arrestees helped and protected him, too. *Sefer Zikaron LeKehillat Zborow* (Zborow Memorial Book), ed. Eliyahu Silberman (Irgun Yotz'ei Zborow, Tel Aviv, 1975), pp. 71–73.

32. Bauer, "Buczacz and Krzemieniec," p. 296.

33. *Sefer Zikaron LeKehillat Zborow*, testimony of Rozia Altmann, p. 408.

34. Sabina Schweid, *Milchama, milchama, Gveret Nehedara* (War, O War, What a Lady Art Thou) (Yad Vashem, Jerusalem, 2004). Sabina Schweid is the wife of Eliezer Schweid, the author of authoritative work on Jewish ultra-orthodox thinkers during the Holocaust. Her memoir, which is of great literary merit, is not only fascinating but supported by the testimonies in *Sefer Zikaron LeKehillat Zborow*.

35. Schweid, *Milchama*, pp. 151–192. Schweid received falsified documents that enabled her to survive from the Catholic priest Jan Pawlicky.

36. *Sefer Zikaron LeKehillat Zborow*, testimony of Leib Kronish, pp. 111–122.

37. SF—48362, Miriam Kunofsky.

38. SF—5641. See also Schweid, *Milchama*, pp. 145, 155–156.

39. Josephine Fiksler, SF—9757, tells the story of a priest from the village of Friszna, not far from Zborow, who helped her and her family and even told them when Yom Kippur occurred so they could fast.

40. According to Shmuel Spector, in *The Holocaust of Volhynian Jews* (Yad Vashem, Jerusalem, 1990), pp. 96–97, in Vladimirets the local Polish (Catholic) priest offered the church jewels to the Jews so they could pay the German tax.

41. Bauer, "Buczacz and Krzemieniec," p. 299.

42. YVA M.1.E/2309.

43. SF—7350, Sarah Kirshenbaum.

44. Bauer, "Buczacz and Krzemieniec," p. 293.

45. Bauer, "Sarny and Rokitno," p. 272.

46. YVA 03/3477; *Sefer Yizkor LeKehillat Sarny*, pp. 347–349; SF—515303–13; also, Moshe Trossman and Issaschar Trossman, interview by the author, YVA, 2005 (no number assigned yet, but accessible upon request).

47. Jan T. Gross, *Neighbors* (Princeton University Press, Princeton, NJ, 2001).

48. YVA, Righteous, M.31/7599.

49. YVA, Righteous M.31/13.

50. Yehuda Bauer, "Kurzeniec, a Jewish Shtetl in the Holocaust," *Yalkut Moreshet* (Tel Aviv; English edition) 1 (2003), passim.

51. *Megillat Kurzeniec*, ed. Aharon Meirovitz (Published by Kurzeniec Survivors, Tel Aviv, 1956), p. 247, testimony of Rivka Dudik. Shalom Yoran, a refugee from central Poland (Raciaz), who later became a partisan, and in that sense an outsider, testified that "we found the relations between the Jews, the Belorussians, and the Poles in Kurzeniec to be friendly." Shalom Yoran, *Hakore Tigar* (Lohamei Hageta'ot and Moreshet, Tel Aviv, 1998), p. 60.

52. Shalom Cholawsky, "Machteret Upartizanim Migetto Kurzeniec," *Yalkut Moreshet* 59 (1995), pp. 63–73.

53. YVA, Righteous, M.31/5927 and 6457.

54. Yehuda Bauer, "Jewish Baranowicze in the Holocaust," *Yad Vashem Studies* 31 (2003), p. 109.

55. Ibid., p. 123.

56. YVA 0.3/1053.

57. Yossi Halpern, *Ne'urim Be'azikim* (Moreshet, Tel Aviv, 2002), passim.

58. Saul Friedlander, *The Ambiguity of Good* (Knopf, New York, 1969).

59. Christian Gerlach, *Kalkulierte Morde: Die Deutsche Wirtschafts- und Vernichtungs-politik in Weissrussland, 1941 bis 1944* (Hamburger Edition, Hamburg, 1996).

60. Moshe Smolar, *Ne'evakti al Chayay* (Moreshet, Tel Aviv, 1978), passim; *Sefer Zikaron LeKehillat Zborow*, testimony of Benedikt Friedman, pp. 131–132.

61. Gross, *Neighbors*.

CHAPTER 7. REBELS AND PARTISANS

1. Yehuda Bauer, "Buczacz and Krzemieniec," *Yad Vashem Studies* 33 (2005), pp. 295–299.

2. Aharon Weiss, "Haproblematika shel Hahitnagdut Hayehudit Hamezuyenet beU-kraina Hama'aravit," *Dapim Leheker Tkufat HaSho'ah* 12 (Haifa University, 1995), pp. 195–196.

3. Ibid., pp. 199–203.

4. Ibid., pp. 206–208.

5. Shmuel Spector, *The Holocaust of Volhynian Jews*, (Yad Vashem, Jerusalem, 1990), pp. 212–216; Shalom Cholawsky, "Tuczyn" (Hebrew), *Yalkut Moreshet* 2 (1964), pp. 81–95; Yad Vashem Archive (YVA) M49E-364, Jozef Elber, Abraham German, and Sender Gornstein; and M49E-1679, Melech Bakelczuk.

6. There were at least two more rebellions, combined with flight to the forests, in central Volhynia: at Mizoch and in a labor camp near Lutsk. Spector, *Holocaust*, pp. 218–219.

7. Spector, *Holocaust*, p. 272. After liberation, Polishuk was executed as an anti-Soviet partisan by the Soviets.

8. The names of the friendly commanders were Maxim Missiura; Nikola ("Kruk") Koni-shchuk; Terentyi Novak; Jozef ("Max") Sobiesak, a Pole who hailed from Lublin; and some others. Most of these units joined the Rowne brigade of Anton Brinski, which was sent south from Belorussia to establish a Soviet presence in Volhynia, beginning in late 1942. Brinski even removed an antisemitic commander (Nasychkin) who had killed Jews.

9. Spector, *Holocaust*, pp. 287 ff.

10. Ibid., p. 332.

11. Ibid., pp. 356–358.

12. Shalom Cholawsky, *Meri VeLochama Partizanit* (Resistance and Partisan Struggle) (Yad Vashem, Jerusalem, 2001), passim. In this discussion I have excluded the parti-san units near the Lithuanian border, such as the large unit commanded by Fyodor Markov, because most of the Jews there did not come from the shtetlach of the kresy but from the large Lithuanian ghettoes of Vilno (Vilnius) and Kovno (Kaunas), or from Lithuanian border townships such as Swienciany (Yid.: Swencian; Lithuanian: Svien-conis) and Eisiskes (Yid: Eishishok).

13. Ibid. Much of what follows is based on Cholawsky's detailed study, which is not likely to be translated into English, because it is not so much an analysis as a very comprehen-sive accumulation of factual material.

14. Christian Gerlach, *Kalkulierte Morde: Die Deutsche Wirtschafts- und Vernichtungs-politik in Weissrussland, 1941 bis 1944* (Hamburger Edition, Hamburg, 1996), pp. 859–1054.

15. E.g., the unit with a commander by the name of Pleskonosov, in the swamp area of Glinna, north of Sarny. Moshe Trossman and Issaschar Trossman, interview by the author, YVA, 2005.

16. One of many testimonies telling us about the antisemitism of the partisans is that of Yitzhak Geller, in *Kehillat Sarny, Sefer Yizkor,* ed. Yossef Karib (Yad Vashem, Jerusalem, 1961), p. 283: "Many of the Jewish partisans were killed by the bullets of Russians, their brothers-in-arms."

17. Cholawsky, *Meri VeLochama Partizanit*, pp. 457–465.

18. Shalom Cholawski [Cholawsky], *Soldiers from the Ghetto* (Harwood, Amsterdam, 1998), passim.

19. There were other somewhat similar cases. Thus, Eliyahu Kowienski, who received the highest Soviet decoration—Hero of the Soviet Union—and who was part of a group of partisans from Zhetl (Zdzieciol), relates that they recovered "many weapons" from the Szczara River, in Belorussia. YVA 03.2088.

20. Cholawsky, *Meri VeLochama Partizanit*, pp. 265–274. Kleck had 6,000 Jewish inhabitants in 1941; two-thirds, 4,000, were murdered in the first "action," on October 31, 1941. The Judenrat chairman, Czerkowicz, told the young people who wanted to rebel to do as they saw fit. They collected some arms, and on July 22, 1942, when the Germans and Belorussians surrounded the ghetto, they opened fire; a mass flight to the forest followed. At the war's end, there seem to have been no more than sixteen survivors. In Stolpce, there were 3,000 Jews. The underground there acquired thirteen rifles, and in May 1942 a group of youngsters fled to the forest. Five hundred Jews were taken to a forced labor camp, from which some escaped. In September 1942, under Hersh Possessorski, an organized group managed to flee from Stolpce into the forest, during an "action" in which most of the remaining Jews in the shtetl were murdered.

21. Nechama Tec, *Defiance: The Bielski Partisans* (Oxford University Press, New York, 1993). See also Peter Duffy, *The Bielski Brothers: The True Story of Three Men Who Defied the Nazis, Saved 1200 Jews, and Built a Village in the Forest* (HarperCollins, New York, 2003)—a journalistic account that does not add much to our knowledge. An important memoir is that of Baruch Levin, *Bi'yearot Nakam* (In the Forests of Revenge) (Lohamei Getaot, 1968).

22. What follows here is essentially what I wrote in my article on Nowogrodek: "Novogrodek, a Shtetl," *Yad Vashem Studies* 35 (2007), passim.

23. Tuvia Bielski and Zusia Bielski, *Yehudei Haya'ar* (Am Oved, Tel Aviv, 1946), p. 44.

24. YVA 0.3/4156.

25. Bauer, "Nowogrodek," p. 57.

26. Lazar M. Kaganovich, Stalin's brother-in-law, an economic expert, was a Jew. He was the person chiefly responsible, in the nineteen thirties, for organizing the artificial starvation in Ukraine that killed millions of people.

27. Cholawsky, *Meri VeLochama Partizanit*, pp. 76–79.

28. He had been a moderate left-Zionist activist before the war.

29. The underground member who was betrayed was Shalom Fiolin.
30. The partisans were commanded by a man named Gromov.
31. Cholawsky, *Meri VeLochama Partizanit*, pp. 169–185.
32. Ibid., pp. 185–195.
33. Nechama Tec, *In the Lion's Den: The Life of Oswald Rufeisen* (Oxford University Press, New York, 1990).
34. I could not find the first name of Serafimowicz.
35. Sometimes Jews refused to go into the forest even when they could. Thus, Jewish partisans occupied Miadziol (Yid.: Miadel, with 800 Jews in 1941) on November 9, 1942, and liberated the Jews in the ghetto there. But the Jews refused to go with them and had to be forced to do so—the partisans threatened to burn their houses if they did not. See Cholawsky, *Meri VeLochama Partizanit*, pp. 95–96.
36. I could not find the first name of Stanislawsky. The nun was Eusebia Bartakowiak, from Poznan.
37. Michael Zamkov, SF—23383; and Kowienski, YVA 0.3/2088; also Mordechai Meirowicz, YVA 0.3/2106.
38. National Archive of Belarus (NARB), fond 3500, inv. 4, fond 241/1, p. 98, quoted in Jack Kagan, *Novogrudok: The History of a Shtetl* (Valentine Mitchell, London, 2006), pp. 183–184.
39. Bauer, "Nowogrodek," p. 63 n. 108.
40. Ibid., p. 63.
41. The underground newspaper of Gordonia was *Slowo Mlodych*, and the articles were published there in issues 9 and 10, February–March 1942. See Bauer, "Nowogrodek," p. 59.
42. "Kurzeniec, a Jewish Shtetl in the Holocaust," *Yalkut Moreshet* (Tel Aviv; English edition) 1 (2003), p. 42. Testimonies of Gurewicz and another member of the group, Nahum Alperowicz (the others did not survive), were confirmed by Danilochkin himself, in the Belorussian youth journal *Znemia Iunosti*, of December 18, 1957. Danilochkin had no idea that Gurewicz had survived, and Gurewicz was unaware of Danilochkin's whereabouts—in fact, Danilochkin had become an employee of a Belorussian municipality.
43. Yehuda Bauer, "Jewish Baranowicze in the Holocaust," *Yad Vashem Studies* 31 (2003), pp. 130–138.
44. He said it to me, in so many words, in 1963, in a discussion about the then newly founded journal on the Holocaust, *Yalkut Moreshet*.
45. Yehuda Bauer, "Sarny and Rokitno," in *The Shtetl*, ed. Steven T. Katz (Boston University Press, Boston, 2007), passim; YVA 03/3477, Issaschar Trossman; YVA 03/1546, Yakov Soltzman.
46. YVA 03/3477, Issaschar Trossman.
47. One of many testimonies that touch this issue is that of Shmuel Levin (YVA M.I.E-141), from Rokitno. On August 26, 1942, when Jews tried to escape from the market square into the surrounding forest, he and his brother went in the opposite direction and hid in the house from which Germans with the Todt organization were shooting at the Jews. The Germans, busy with shooting, did not notice them, and they managed

to exit through a back door and join a group of escapees in the forest, who, however, were caught by the Germans and brought to Sarny to be killed with the Rokitno Jews who had not managed to flee. The brothers fled again, from the shooting pit at Sarny, hid in a truck carrying the clothes of the murdered people back to Sarny, and fled from the truck into the local cemetery and from there into the countryside. The locals refused to help them. Desperate, they wanted to go back to Rokitno to surrender to the Germans, but at the last minute they decided otherwise. They killed two Ukrainians who wanted to hand them over to the Germans, and joined the partisans, with whom they fought until liberation. Shmuel Levin then became a Soviet soldier; he advanced to the rank of officer and commanded a unit that fought in the Battle for Berlin. After the war, he made his way to Palestine/Israel. See also my interview with the Trossman brothers, YVA 2005. Issaschar Trossman became an NKVD man in order, together with his father, to exact revenge on Ukrainian collaborators. His father was killed by the Banderovtsy. Exacting revenge was the motivation for many others, such as Israel Pinchuk. YVA M.49.E-214.

CHAPTER 8. THE DEATH OF THE SHTETL

1. Daniel J. Goldhagen, *Hitler's Willing Executioners: Ordinary Germans and the Holocaust* (Knopf, New York, 1996).
2. The word "Holocaust" originally comes from a Greek term meaning "whole burnt offering," which is definitely not what the Holocaust was. Before 1943–1944 there was no term for mass annihilation of groups; only after that did the term "genocide" come into use. In the same way, there is no satisfactory term for the unprecedented genocide of the Jews. The increasingly accepted Hebrew term *Shoah* means "catastrophe," but the original, biblical use was for a natural disaster, which makes it unsatisfactory as well. The Yiddish term *Churbn*, derived from the Hebrew *Churban*, means "destruction." I am no fan of semantic arguments, so I use the (wrong) terms: *Holocaust* and *Shoah*.
3. Hannah Arendt, *Eichmann in Jerusalem* (Viking Press, New York, 1964).
4. The exact number of victims of the German annihilation policy is hard to establish. It is not certain that German figures are reliable, and they are very incomplete in any case. Thus, according to German sources, there were roughly 500,000 Jews in East Galicia, and of these, according to the SS HSSPF Friedrich Katzmann, 434,329 Jews had been "resettled," i.e., murdered, by June 27, 1943. It is reasonable to estimate that by the end of the German occupation in the spring of 1944, the figure had risen to 490,000. No parallel figures are available for Volhynia and the north, only vague estimates. YVA TR/10/518.
5. Erika Weinzierl, *Zu wenig Gerechte* (Styria Verlag, Graz, 1997).
6. These were areas where radical antisemitic movements, supported by the local clergy (from Lomza, for instance), had gained a great deal of support before the war. See, e.g., Jan T. Gross, *Neighbors* (Princeton University Press, Princeton, NJ, 2001), passim.
7. A very clear case of internal contradiction is the memoir of David Farfel, a Nieswiez survivor. The peasants in the Mir area were friendly, he says. He and his wife and father were repeatedly rescued by Belorussian and Polish peasants and threatened and

pursued by others. His general judgment varies between total condemnation of all Poles and Belorussians and great appreciation of the essential help that was extended to him and his family. As I said, both judgments can be documented in other testimonies, too, and both are, to an extent, historically accurate. David Farfel, *Begetto Nieswiez Uveya'arot Naliboki* (Self-published, Ramat Gan, 1995).

8. Shoah Foundation Testimonies (SF)—37869, Edmund Dickman. The witness was raised in a religious atmosphere, and he devotes considerable space in his testimony to argue for a nonreligious or antireligious stance.

WORKS CITED

Appleman-Jurman, Alicia, *Alicia: My Story*, Bantam, Toronto, 1988.

Arad, Yitzhak, *Ghetto in Flames: The Destruction of the Jews of Vilna in the Holocaust*, Holocaust Library, New York, 1982.

Arendt, Hannah, *Eichmann in Jerusalem*, Viking Press, New York, 1964.

Avatichi, A., and Y. Ben Zakai, eds., *Sefer Zikaron liKehillat Stolin Vehasviva*, Irgun Yotz'ei Stolin, Tel Aviv, 1952.

Bankier, David, *The Germans and the Final Solution*, Basil Blackwell, Oxford, 1993.

Bartov, Omer, "From the Holocaust in Galicia to Contemporary Genocide: Common Ground—Historical Differences," Meyerhoff Lecture, US Holocaust Memorial Museum, Washington, DC, 2002.

Bauer, Yehuda, "Buczacz and Krzemieniec," *Yad Vashem Studies* 33 (2005).

———, "Jewish Baranowicze in the Holocaust," *Yad Vashem Studies* 31 (2003).

———, "Kurzeniec, a Jewish Shtetl in the Holocaust," *Yalkut Moreshet* (Tel Aviv; English edition) 1 (2003).

———, *My Brother's Keeper, a History of the American Jewish Joint Distribution Committee, 1929–1939*, Jewish Publication Society, Philadelphia, 1974.

———, "Novogrodek, a Shtetl," *Yad Vashem Studies* 35 (2007).

———, *Rethinking the Holocaust*, Yale University Press, New Haven, 2001.

———, "Sarny and Rokitno," in Steven T. Katz, ed., *The Shtetl*, Boston University Press, Boston, 2007.

Bielski, Tuvia, and Zusia Bielski, *Yehudei Haya'ar*, Am Oved, Tel Aviv, 1946.

Bingen, Dieter, Wlodzimierz Borodziej, and Stefan Troebst, eds., *Vertreibung europäisch erinnern?* Harrasowitz, Wiesbaden, 2003.

Cholawski [Chowlawsky], Shalom, *Soldiers from the Ghetto*, Harwood, Amsterdam, 1998.

Cholawsky [Cholawski], Shalom, *The Jews of Bielorussia during World War II*, Harwood, Amsterdam, 1998.

———, *Meri VeLochama Partizanit*, Yad Vashem, Jerusalem, 2001.

———, "Tuczyn" (Hebrew), *Yalkut Moreshet* 2 (1964).

————, *see also* Cholawski, Shalom.

Dörner, Bernward, *Die Deutschen und der Holocaust*, Propyläen, Munich, 2007.

Duffy, Peter, *The Bielski Brothers*, HarperCollins, New York, 2003.

Farbstein, Esther, *Hidden in Thunder*, Feldheim, New York, 2008.

Farfel, David, *Begetto Nieswiez Uveya'arot Naliboki*, Self-published, Ramat Gan, 1995.

Friedlander, Saul, *The Ambiguity of Good*, Knopf, New York, 1969.

Gerlach, Christian, *Kalkulierte Morde: Die Deutsche Wirtschafts- und Vernichtungspolitik in Weissrussland, 1941 bis 1944*, Hamburger Edition, Hamburg, 1996.

Goldhagen, Daniel J., *Hitler's Willing Executioners: Ordinary Germans and the Holocaust*, Knopf, New York, 1996.

Gorodetsky, Gabriel, *Grand Delusion: Stalin and the German Invasion of Russia*, Yale University Press, New Haven, 1999.

Gross, Jan T., *Neighbors*, Princeton University Press, Princeton, NJ, 2001.

————, *Revolution from Abroad: The Soviet Conquest of Western Ukraine and Western Belorussia*, Princeton University Press, Princeton, NJ, 2002.

Gurjanov, Alexander, "Überblick über die Deportationen der Bevölkerung in der UdSSR in den Jahren 1930–1950," in Dietrich Bingen, ed., *Vertreibung europäisch erinnern?* Harrasowitz, Wiesbaden, 2003.

Gutman, Israel, *The Jews of Warsaw, 1939–1943*, University of Indiana Press, Bloomington, 1982.

Halpern, Yossi, *Ne'urim Be'azikim*, Moreshet, Tel Aviv, 1978.

Heller, Celia S., *On the Edge of Destruction: Jews of Poland between the Two World Wars*, Columbia University Press, New York, 1977.

Janik, Bronislaw, *Bylo Ich Trzy*, Wydawactwo Panstwowe, Warsaw, 1970.

Kagan, Jack, *Novogrudok: The History of a Shtetl*, Valentine Mitchell, London, 2006.

Kagan, Jack, and Dov Cohen, *Surviving the Holocaust with the Russian Jewish Partisans*, Valentine Mitchell, London, 1998.

Karib, Yossef, ed., *Kehillat Sarny, Sefer Yizkor*, Yad Vashem, Jerusalem, 1961.

Katz, Etunia Bauer, *Our Tomorrows Never Came*, Fordham University Press, New York, 2000.

Katz, Zev, *From the Gestapo to the Gulags: One Jewish Life*, Valentine Mitchell, London, 2004.

Klemperer, Victor, *Lingua Tertii Imperii*, English edition, Athlone, London, 2000.

Klonicki [Klonymus], Aryeh, *Yoman Avi Adam*, Lohamei Hageta'ot, Tel Aviv, 1970.

Lecker, Marcus, *I Remember*, Memoirs of Jewish Survivors, vol. 5, Canadian Jewish Studies, Concordia University, Montreal, 1999.

Lehman, Rosa, "Jewish Patrons and Polish Clients: Patronage in a Small Galician Town," in Antony Polonsky, ed., *Polin: Studies in Polish Jewry*, vol. 17, Littman Library, Oxford, 2004.

————, *Symbiosis and Ambivalence—Poles and Jews in a Small Galician Town*, Berghahn, Oxford, 2001.

Leoni, Eliezer, ed., *Rokitna Vehasviva, Sefer Yizkor*, Irgun Yotz'ei Rokitna Vehasviva, Tel Aviv, 1967.

Levin, Baruch, *Be'ya'arot Nakam*, Lohamei Geta'ot, Tel Aviv, 1968.

Levin, Dov, *The Lesser of Two Evils: Eastern European Jewry under Soviet Rule, 1939–1941*, Jewish Publication Society, Philadelphia, 1995.

Marcus, Joseph, *Social and Political History of the Jews of Poland, 1919–1939*, Mouton, Berlin, 1983.

Meirovitz, Aharon, ed., *Megillat Kurzeniec*, Published by Kurzeniec Survivors, Tel Aviv, 1956.

Meltzer, Emanuel, *Ma'avak Medini BeMalkodet; Yehudei Polin, 1935–1939*, Tel Aviv University Press, Tel Aviv, 1982.

Mendelsohn, Daniel, *The Lost*, HarperCollins, New York, 2003.

Mendelsohn, Ezra, *The Jews of East Central Europe between the Wars*, Indiana University Press, Bloomington, 1983.

Michlic, Joanna B., *Poland's Threatening Other: The Image of the Jew from 1880 to the Present*, University of Nebraska Press, Lincoln, 2006.

Musial, Bogdan, "Jewish Resistance in Poland's Eastern Borderlands during the Second World War, 1939–1941," *Patterns of Prejudice* 38, no. 4 (2004).

———, *Konterrevolutionäre Elemente sind zu erschiessen*, Propyläen, Munich, 2000.

Ostri-Dunn, Yeshayahu, ed., *Sefer Yizkor Lehantsachat Kdoshei Kehillat Czortkow*, Published by the Czortkow Survivors, Tel Aviv, 1967.

Pinchuk, Ben-Cion, "The East European Shtetl and Its Place in Jewish History," *Revue des études juives*, January–June, 2005.

———, *Shtetl Jews under Soviet Rule: Eastern Poland on the Eve of the Holocaust*, Basil Blackwell, Oxford, 1990.

Piotrowski, Tadeusz, *Genocide and Rescue in Wolyn*, McFarland, Jefferson, NC, 2000.

Pohl, Dieter, *Nationalsozialistische Judenverfolgung in Ostgalizien, 1941–1944*, Institut für Zeitgeschichte, Munich, 1996.

Raba, Yehezkiel, ed., *Dereczin Memorial Book*, Jacob S. Berger, Mahwah, NJ, 2000.

Redlich, Shimon, *Together and Apart in Brzezany: Jews and Ukrainians, 1919–1945*, Indiana University Press, Bloomington, 2002.

Reignier, Anatol, *Damals in Bolechow*, Btb bei Goldmann, Munich, 1997.

Rein, Leonid, "The Kings and the Pawns," unpublished manuscript, Yad Vashem, Jerusalem.

———, "Local Collaboration in the Execution of the 'Final Solution'" *Holocaust and Genocide Studies* 20, no. 3 (2006).

Renz, Regina, "Small Towns in Inter-War Poland," in Antony Polonsky, ed., *Polin: Studies in Polish Jewry*, vol. 17, Littman Library, Oxford, 2004.

Richmond, Theo, *Konin: A Quest*, Vintage, New York, 1996.

Rosen, Dunia, *Yedidi, Haya'ar*, Yad Vashem, Jerusalem, 2005.

Sandkühler, Thomas, *Endlösung in Ostgalizien: Der Judenmord in Ostgalizien und die Rettungsinitiative von Berthold Beitz, 1941–1944*, Dietz, Berlin, 1996.

Schweid, Sabina, *Milchama, Milchama, Gveret Nehedara*, Yad Vashem, Jerusalem, 2004.

Silberman, Eliyahu, ed., *Sefer Zikaron LeKehillat Zborow*, Irgun Yotz'ei Zborow, Tel Aviv, 1975.

Smolar, Hersh, *Soviet Jews behind the Ghetto Barrier*, Tel Aviv University, Tel Aviv, 1984.

Smolar, Moshe, *Ne'evakti al Chayay*, Moreshet, Tel Aviv, 1978.

Snyder, Timothy, *Sketches from a Secret War,* Yale University Press, New Haven, 2005.

Spector, Shmuel, *The Holocaust of Volhynian Jews,* Yad Vashem, Jerusalem, 1990.

Stein, A. S., ed., *Baranowicze Memorial Book,* Irgun Yotz'ei Baranowitz, Tel Aviv, 1953.

Tec, Nechama, *Defiance: The Bielski Partisans,* Oxford University Press, New York, 1993.

———, *In the Lion's Den: The Life of Oswald Rufeisen,* Oxford University Press, New York, 1990.

Trunk, Isaiah, *Judenrat,* Collier-Macmillan, London, 1972.

Weinzierl, Erika, *Zu Wenig Gerechte,* Styria Verlag, Graz, 1997.

Weiss, Aharon, "Haproblematika shel Hahitnagdut Hayehudit Hamezuyenet beUkraina Hama'aravit," *Dapim Leheker Tkufat haSho'ah* 12 (1995).

———, "Jewish Leadership in Occupied Poland—Postures and Attitudes," *Yad Vashem Studies* 12 (1977).

———, "Ledarkam shel Hayudenratim Bidrom-Mizrach Polin," *Yalkut Moreshet* 15 (1972).

———, "Leha'arachatam shel Hayudenratim," *Yalkut Moreshet* 11 (1969).

Wildt, Michael, *Generation des Unbedingten,* Hamburger Edition, Hamburg, 2003.

Wilkomirsky, Binjamin, *Fragments,* Schocken, New York, 1996.

Zarnowski, Janusz, *Spoleczenstwo Drugiej Rzeczpospolitej,* Wydawactwo Panstwowe, Warsaw, 1973.

Zbikowski, Andrzej, "Why Did Jews Welcome the Soviet Army?" in Antony Polonsky, ed., *Polin: Studies in Polish Jewry,* vol. 13, Basil Blackwell, Oxford, 2000.

INDEX